Developing a Mixed Methods Proposal

Mixed Methods Research Series

**Vicki L. Plano Clark and Nataliya V. Ivankova,
Series Editors**

Developing a Mixed Methods Proposal

A Practical Guide for Beginning Researchers

Jessica T. DeCuir-Gunby
NC State University

Paul A. Schutz
University of Texas at San Antonio

Los Angeles | London | New Delhi
Singapore | Washington DC | Melbourne

FOR INFORMATION:

SAGE Publications, Inc.
2455 Teller Road
Thousand Oaks, California 91320
E-mail: order@sagepub.com

SAGE Publications Ltd.
1 Oliver's Yard
55 City Road
London, EC1Y 1SP
United Kingdom

SAGE Publications India Pvt. Ltd.
B 1/I 1 Mohan Cooperative Industrial Area
Mathura Road, New Delhi 110 044
India

SAGE Publications Asia-Pacific Pte. Ltd.
3 Church Street
#10-04 Samsung Hub
Singapore 049483

Printed in the United States of America

Names: Decuir-Gunby, Jessica T., author. | Schutz, Paul A., author.

Title: Developing a mixed methods proposal : a practical guide for beginning researchers / Jessica T. DeCuir-Gunby, North Carolina State University, Paul Schutz, The University of Texas at San Antonio.

Description: First Edition. | Thousand Oaks : SAGE Publications, Inc., 2017. | Series: Mixed methods research series | Includes bibliographical references and index.

Identifiers: LCCN 2016006983 | ISBN 978-1-4833-6578-7 (pbk. : alk. paper)

Subjects: LCSH: Mixed methods research.

Classification: LCC H62 .D355 2017 | DDC 001.4/4—dc23
LC record available at https://lccn.loc.gov/2016006983

This book is printed on acid-free paper.

Acquisitions Editor: Helen Salmon
Editorial Assistant: Yvonne McDuffee
eLearning Editor: Katie Ancheta
Production Editor: Kelly DeRosa
Copy Editor: Cate Huisman
Typesetter: Hurix Systems Pvt. Ltd.
Proofreader: Theresa Kay
Indexer: Maria Sosnowski
Cover Designer: Michael Dubowe
Marketing Manager: Susannah Goldes

16 17 18 19 20 10 9 8 7 6 5 4 3 2 1

Brief Contents

Detailed Contents

List of Elements

Box

Editors' Introduction

The interest in using mixed methods research has been growing steadily across the educational, social, behavioral, and health sciences since the 1990s. Nowhere is the evidence of this growth greater than among beginning researchers such as doctoral and master's students. One needs only conduct a search of the *ProQuest Dissertation and Theses* database to see the consistent increase in the number of theses and dissertations that contain the term *mixed methods* in the title or abstract. Emerging scholars' interest in and use of mixed methods research is particularly important for the development of the field of mixed methods because today's beginning researchers will become tomorrow's leaders in conducting mixed methods research and contributing to the growth of the field.

Beginning researchers bring considerable enthusiasm and effort to their use of mixed methods research, but they also face many challenges when applying this approach. In our own conceptualization of the field, we note that researchers using mixed methods must plan a rigorous research process that is both informed by key mixed methods methodological considerations and influenced by researchers' personal, interpersonal, and social contexts. Navigating this dynamic and complex process can be a significant challenge for beginning researchers who may have little prior experience with planning a research study, who are still learning about mixed methods research, and who are just starting to become aware of the importance of the socio-ecological perspective for research and the role and influence of multiple contexts on the research process. In the midst of navigating this complexity, beginning researchers are typically expected to prepare a high-quality research proposal for a dissertation project or a funded study. This critically important step in the process is challenging for all mixed methods researchers, but can also be quite mysterious for those beginning researchers who are developing their first formal research proposal.

As editors of the Mixed Methods Research Series, we are therefore pleased to introduce this book, *Developing a Mixed Methods Proposal: A Practical Guide for Beginning Researchers*, by Jessica T. DeCuir-Gunby and Paul A. Schutz. We initiated the series to provide researchers, reviewers, and consumers of mixed methods research with practice-focused books that address issues of current interest to the field of mixed methods in an applied and practical way. The authors of this book fulfill this goal by presenting a practical guide that takes the mystery out of developing a mixed methods research proposal for a dissertation-quality study. Recognizing that beginning researchers need to understand both the reasoning behind the content of research proposals as well as how to adapt that content to a mixed methods approach, they provide step-by-step guidance and practical advice well suited for graduate students and other beginning researchers. Several features of the book—the Guided Questions, Practice Sessions, Sample Sessions, and fully developed example proposal—will help readers think through the important decisions required for developing their own mixed methods research proposals or for mentoring the proposal process of their advisees. This book is an important addition to the series and to the field of mixed methods research as a practical resource aimed at preparing the next generation of mixed methods researchers!

Vicki L. Plano Clark and Nataliya V. Ivankova

Editors, *Mixed Methods Research Series*

Preface

The idea for creating this book originated in our respective doctoral-level mixed methods research classes, where we often have students who struggle to create research proposals. Specifically, we tend to encounter two major problems. First, in most cases, our students are aware of the many seminal methodological pieces in their respective fields. However, they often find those resources to be challenging to understand. They want and need resources that are written to match their level of expertise and feature simple guidelines. Second, our students have little experience at writing research proposals. They tend to not understand the basic components of a research proposal. In many cases, they do not know where or how to begin. This book is our attempt to address the needs of our students and the many other beginning researchers that are struggling with the development of a mixed methods research proposal.

We crafted this book as a practical guide to assist beginning researchers in the development of mixed methods proposals. Most research proposal books that are currently on the market provide general guidelines for research proposal development or focus strictly on either quantitative or qualitative approaches. This book differs in that it provides novice researchers, from a variety of disciplinary backgrounds, with practical steps to develop their own mixed methods research proposals. Many fields are moving toward the use of mixed methods approaches rather than singular quantitative or qualitative approaches (Creswell, 2010). Mixed methods approaches are needed because of the complexity of understanding and solving social and behavioral problems (Ivankova & Kawamura, 2010). Similarly, major funding agencies such as the National Science Foundation and the National Institute of Health are encouraging researchers to use mixed methods research strategies rather than singular methodological approaches (Plano Clark, 2010).

● PURPOSE OF THE BOOK

This book is for researchers from a variety of disciplines that are new to mixed methods research and are interested in developing mixed methods research proposals for their dissertations, grants, and general research studies. This book will not address all of the major issues in mixed methods research and is not intended to be a stand-alone mixed methods research textbook. Instead, this book should be used in conjunction with other mixed methods resources (e.g., Creswell & Plano Clark, 2011; Teddlie & Tashakkori, 2009). As such, this book is designed to be a hands-on guide for the creation of a mixed methods research proposal. In order to assist you in the development of your methods research proposal, the book is composed of nine chapters and organized around the major components of a research proposal: introduction, literature review, and methods sections.

Why a Guide for Developing Mixed Methods Proposals?

In the first chapter of the book, we provide a general introduction to mixed methods research. Specifically, we discuss basic definitions of mixed methods research as well as the advantages of engaging in mixed methods research. We also challenge you to critically reflect upon your abilities to engage in mixed methods research. We end the chapter by describing the function of research proposals.

The Role of Theory in Mixed Methods Research

In Chapter 2, we address one of the key components of a mixed methods research proposal—the role of theory. Specifically, we address *inquiry worldviews, subjectivity statements,* and *substantive content theories,* which transact to create your *theoretical framework.* The theoretical framework helps to inform all aspects of your research study. The process of understanding how you view the world, how your experiences have influenced your research interests, and how theories in your field can be applied to your problem of interest is essential to developing a successful mixed methods research proposal. Therefore, in this chapter we guide you through the process of understanding how you situate yourself as a researcher by articulating how you experience the world.

Asking Appropriate Mixed Methods Research Questions

From our perspective, the research questions (Chapter 3) you develop are key to creating a successful mixed methods research proposal. Your research questions guide the direction of the study in that they help to organize and give direction to the development of your literature review. In addition, they also help you to determine what research methods you will employ. In order to assist you in creating useful research questions, we guide you through an iterative process of developing mixed methods research questions. In addition, we provide you with guidelines for the characteristics of what we consider to be appropriate and useful research questions for a mixed methods study.

The Mixed Methods Proposal Introduction

In Chapter 4, we discuss the function and development of the *introduction*. The introduction serves as a primer of your research proposal to the reader. It includes a discussion of the research problem, your subjectivity statement, and the purpose of the research. This section is also where you provide a context for your study, including your definition of mixed methods, your rationale for using a mixed methods approach, your intended audience, and the significance of your work. In this chapter we guide you through the process of developing an introduction that will make the case for the importance of your research problem(s) and how you will be addressing those problems (using mixed methods).

The Literature Review: Situating
Your Mixed Methods Study in the Larger Context

The *literature review,* discussed in Chapter 5, is a synthesis and extension of the current literature that leads the reader through your thinking about what the problem is, how others have looked at this problem, and where you think the research should go related to the problem(s). Most important, the literature review funnels the reader to the research questions that will be addressed in your research methods section. In this chapter we guide you through the process of synthesizing and extending the research literature in your research area as the groundwork for a mixed methods study.

Mixed Methods Designs: Frameworks
for Organizing Your Research Methods

In Chapter 6 we discuss the variety of ways that mixed methods have been and could be used to collect and analyze the data that you will use to answer your research questions. The focus of this chapter is on providing you with preliminary understandings of the types of mixed methods designs and how those designs help to organize your research methods. We provide examples for some of the most common mixed methods designs. Also, we demonstrate how to create diagrams to best illustrate mixed methods designs.

The Heart of the Mixed Methods Research Plan: Discussing Your Methods Section

In Chapter 7, we describe the many elements that are needed to develop a successful research *methods* section. In other words, this section of the mixed methods research proposal tells the reader exactly how you are going to go about answering your research questions. Thus, in this chapter we guide you through the process of writing about, among other things, identifying your sample, data collection procedures, data analysis procedures including data integration, and validity/trustworthiness and reliability/credibility. The key to a successful methods section is to be able to make connections between your research questions, data collection, and data analysis. Your goal is to have the reader come away from that section with a clear idea of how the mixed methods research will be done.

A Little *Lagniappe* . . . A Little Something Extra

In Chapter 8 we provide some general suggestions regarding the final proposal and the writing process, including the reference section and the appendices. We also discuss general issues such as creating a budget and a timeline. For example, we provide some suggestions for issues such as securing committee members who are receptive to mixed methods research, and we provide ideas related to getting your research proposal approved. The goal of this chapter is to provide you with some suggestions that will give your proposal that extra quality that will move you along in the research process.

An Example of Real-World Mixed Methods Research: The Racial Microaggressions Study Proposal

The last chapter of the book, Chapter 9, is where we showcase our sample mixed methods research proposal. We begin the chapter by reviewing the components of a mixed methods research proposal. Then we provide guiding questions for reviewing mixed methods proposals and the methods snapshots that appear in the appendices. We end the chapter with the example proposal on racial microaggressions.

FEATURES OF THE BOOK

In discussing the various components of a mixed methods research proposal, this book has several important pedagogical features. First, each chapter begins with a list of learning objectives that give you a general summary of the issues to be discussed in the chapter. Second, in order to help ensure accessibility and practicality, each chapter features a section called "Practice Session." Each Practice Session consists of *guided questions*, *exercises*, and *extra resources*. The *guided questions* are intended to help you think more deeply about the research chapter topic in relation to your research topic. The *exercises* are specific activities that assist in the creation of a specific component of the research proposal. These components are discussed in a logical manner that follows the proposal creation structure. If you engage in the exercises that are provided throughout the practice session sections within each chapter of the book, by the end of the book, you will have an individualized, detailed template for a mixed methods research proposal. The *extra resources* component includes a list of relevant readings and web resources. In addition, following each Practice Session is a "Sample Session" that demonstrates how to complete each exercise using a real-world research example that focuses on students' experiences with racial microaggressions in the college context. Specifically, we demonstrate how to use the aforementioned activities to develop the various components of a mixed methods research proposal. The book features the entire racial microaggressions research proposal, in Chapter 9, in order for you to observe the mixed methods proposal development in its entirety. Last, the book gives research methods snapshots featuring examples of various mixed methods designs in the appendices in order to demonstrate the variability in mixed methods research.

Acknowledgments

We would like to take this opportunity to show appreciation to everyone who helped this book come to fruition. We truly appreciate every gesture, both big and small.

First, we would like to thank our students. Writing this book was truly a labor of love that stemmed from our enjoyment of engaging in mixed methods research, teaching research methods, and working with graduate students. This book exists because of our students. We would like to thank our students for reading various chapter drafts of the book, including the students enrolled in ED/EDP 750 Mixed Methods Research in Education during fall 2014, spring 2015, and fall 2015 at NC State University, and those enrolled in EDU 7043 Educational Research Statistics at the University of Texas at San Antonio in spring 2015 and fall 2015.

Next we would like to thank our colleagues and friends who read drafts, provided professional consultations, or gave us encouragement when we needed it. Their assistance proved to be invaluable. These individuals include Lisa Bass, Kakali Bhattacharya, Tuere Bowles, Tiffany Davis, Cameron Denson, Joy Gayles, DeLeon Gray, Norris Gunby Jr., Matthew Lammi, Sonja Lanehart, Demetrius Richmond, and Linda Robinson.

Finally, we would like to thank the SAGE publication team. The project was first presented to acquisitions editor Helen Salmon, who recognized its potential and recommended that the book be included in the Mixed Methods Research Series. She forwarded our book proposal to Vicki Knight, another acquisitions editor, who helped the book to officially become a part of the series. As we completed the project, Vicki retired, and the project was given back to Helen. As such, we would like to thank *both* Vicki and Helen for their hard work and dedication to the project. Similarly, we are grateful to Vicki Plano Clark and Nataliya Ivankova, series editors, for including our book. We truly appreciate all of your guidance and the opportunity to participate in such a groundbreaking series. In addition, we are thankful for the constructive feedback that we received from the SAGE external reviewers:

Billy Bai, University of Nevada Las Vegas

Kakali Bhattacharya, Kansas State University

Dennis Cavitt, Abilene Christian University

Regina Conway-Phillips, Loyola University Chicago

Jacqueline S. Craven, Delta State University

Tabitha Dell'Angelo, The College of New Jersey

Catharine Dishke Hondzel, Western University

Anne J. Hacker, Walden University

Lu Liu, University of La Verne

Hisako Matsuo, Saint Louis University

Cheryl Poth, University of Alberta

Suzanne R. Sicchia, University of Toronto

Shanon S. Taylor, University of Nevada

Holly Thomas, Carleton University

Wenfan Yan, University of Massachusetts Boston

We know that we were able to craft a better book because of their insightful suggestions and recommendations.

About the Authors

Jessica T. DeCuir-Gunby, PhD, is an associate professor of educational psychology and University Scholar in the Department of Teacher Education and Learning Sciences at NC State University. She serves as a faculty mentor with the multidisciplinary and interinstitutional Center for Developmental Science at the University of North Carolina, Chapel Hill. She is also an associate editor for the *American Educational Research Journal*. DeCuir-Gunby's research interests include race and racial identity development, critical race theory, mixed methods research, and emotions in education. She recently served as co–principal investigator on two National Science Foundation funded grants, totaling over $4.3 million: Nurturing Mathematics Dream-keepers (DRK-12 Grant) and Peer Mentoring Summits for Women Engineering Faculty of Color (ADVANCE Leadership Award Grant). Both grants funded studies that used mixed methods approaches, were multidisciplinary, and explored important issues in diversity and STEM. Her work has been featured in top-tier journals such as *Educational Psychologist, Educational Researcher*, and *Review of Educational Research*, among others.

Paul A. Schutz, PhD, is currently a professor in the Department of Educational Psychology at the University of Texas at San Antonio. His research interests include the nature of emotion, the influence of emotional experiences on teachers' identity development, research methods, and issues related to race and social justice. He has several publications related to the use of mixed methods and has taught a variety of different research methods course, including qualitative, quantitative, and mixed methods research courses. He is a past president for Division 15: Educational Psychology of the American Psychological Association and a former coeditor of the *Educational Researcher: Research News and Comment,* a lead journal for the American Educational Research Association.

We dedicate this book to our sources of inspiration, our families, Norris Gunby Jr., Norris Gunby III, Sonja Lanehart Schutz, and Isaac Schutz.

SAGE was founded in 1965 by Sara Miller McCune to support the dissemination of usable knowledge by publishing innovative and high-quality research and teaching content. Today, we publish over 900 journals, including those of more than 400 learned societies, more than 800 new books per year, and a growing range of library products including archives, data, case studies, reports, and video. SAGE remains majority-owned by our founder, and after Sara's lifetime will become owned by a charitable trust that secures our continued independence.

Los Angeles | London | New Delhi | Singapore | Washington DC | Melbourne

1

Why a Guide for Developing Mixed Methods Proposals?

Objectives

1. To be able to define mixed methods research.

2. To develop an understanding of the advantages of mixed methods research.

3. To describe the resources needed to engage in a mixed methods study.

4. To be able to judge whether mixed methods is the appropriate approach for your research.

5. To be able to discuss the components of a mixed methods research proposal.

So, you want to conduct a mixed methods research study? Are you ready to learn about how to develop a mixed methods research proposal? If so, recognize that you are part of a growing trend and that this will be a complex undertaking. However, before you get started, there are some important issues for you to take into consideration. First, you have to understand what is meant by the term *mixed methods*. Second, you need to know the advantages for using a mixed methods approach. Third, you need to be reflective and honest about your abilities to successfully conduct a mixed method study. Last, you need to understand the components of a mixed methods research proposal.

● WHAT IS MIXED METHODS RESEARCH?

In the past, social science and behavioral researchers have been categorized into two traditions, quantitative (using numerical representations, such as statistics, to understand phenomena) and qualitative (using non-numerical representations, such as interviews, to understand phenomena), with many viewing the two as polar opposites. However, many researchers feel that quantitative and qualitative traditions can be better viewed as a continuum rather than a dichotomy (Ercikan & Roth, 2006). It is from this perspective that mixed methods research, a third research tradition, emerged during the last few decades (Teddlie & Tashakkori, 2009). Mixed methods research can be defined as "research in which the investigator collects and analyzes data, integrates the findings, and draws inferences using both qualitative and quantitative approaches or methods in a single study or program of inquiry" (Tashakkori & Creswell, 2007, p. 4). Over the years, the definition has been expanded to include multiple ways of viewing the social world (Greene, 2007) and philosophical orientations (Creswell & Plano Clark, 2011). (For a detailed discussion on the definitions of mixed methods, see Johnson, Onwuegbuzie, & Turner, 2007.)

● WHAT ARE THE ADVANTAGES OF MIXED METHODS RESEARCH?

Mixed methods approaches have been widely used in a variety of research disciplines, including the health sciences, nursing, business, sociology, psychology, and education (Creswell & Plano Clark, 2011). Their popularity continues to increase, as indicated by the prevalence of mixed methods studies in mainstream research journals as well as the creation of the *Journal of Mixed Methods Research* and the *International Journal of Multiple Research Approaches*. In addition, mixed methods courses are becoming fixtures at many universities around the world (Tashakkori & Teddlie, 2010). This increased interest in mixed methods research has occurred because of the advantages associated with conducting mixed method research, such as the following:

- Mixed methods research allows for the examination of complex problems within a single study by providing evidence to triangulate or corroborate findings with multiple sources of evidence. For example, you can use qualitative interview data to add to or challenge the evidence from your quantitative survey data.

- Mixed methods approaches allow you the opportunity to maximize the strengths of both quantitative approaches (e.g., generalizability) and qualitative approaches (e.g., in-depth analysis of a small number of cases) while minimizing the weaknesses of both quantitative approaches (e.g., lack of participant voice) and qualitative approaches (e.g., lack of generalizability). For example, you can use qualitative data as a case study of a particular group(s) of participants that were identified from quantitative data analysis.

- Another advantage is that mixed methods research allows for the use of multiple tools. When using a mixed methods approach, researchers can use a variety of quantitative and qualitative methods as well as multiple worldviews/paradigms. Simply stated, many of the social science problems we face are complex, and therefore they require multiple perspectives and methods to help solve. A mixed methods perspective encourages the use of multiple methods and theoretical approaches.

- A practical advantage of mixed methods research is that you may increase the possibility of finding results that you can write up and publish. On the other hand, using a singular method may result in nonsignificant or unpublishable findings. For example, you may have results from the quantitative data that were not statistically significant; however, the collection of qualitative data may provide new insights as to why the results may not have been significant, thereby suggesting new approaches for both theory and future research.

WHAT SHOULD YOU CONSIDER WHEN ENGAGING IN MIXED METHODS RESEARCH?

As just discussed, using mixed methods research approaches provide a variety of advantages over engaging in single method approaches.

Using such an approach is very tempting to beginning researchers. However, there are a variety of issues to consider before taking on a mixed methods study. For example, you want to specifically consider your own research methods skills, time, resources, and the necessity of using a mixed methods design (see Table 1.1). Use Table 1.1 to help you to consider whether you have the appropriate resources needed to engage in a mixed methods study.

Table 1.1 What to Consider When Conducting a Mixed Methods Study

	Something to Think About	Advice
Personal Experiences and Skills		
	How well do you understand quantitative and qualitative research methods?	If you do not have an adequate background in either quantitative or qualitative research, you should consider taking additional research courses or attending research workshops.
	Do you feel confident enough in your abilities to use either a quantitative or a qualitative approach?	Before embarking upon a mixed methods study, you need to be confident in your abilities to conduct both quantitative and qualitative research studies. If you are not confident, take more courses/workshops, or get more hands-on experiences conducting quantitative or qualitative research.
Time		
	How much time do you realistically have to conduct your study?	Create a realistic timeline to help guide your study.
Resources		
	Will you need finances to pay for transcription services or to provide financial incentives for participation?	Create a budget to help determine if you can afford such services. If you can't, you will need to consider adjusting your timeline for transcribing and/or recruiting participants.

	Something to Think About	Advice
	Do you have access to the appropriate quantitative and qualitative software?	Investigate whether your organization has access to specific software packages. If you need to purchase additional software, make sure to add this to the budget. If you do not have access to the software or have funds to purchase the software, you will need to consider an alternative software package. This may require adjusting your timeline in order to account for learning a new software package.
	Do you have access to the population of interest?	Make connections and develop relationships with your population of interest while preparing your research proposal. This will help you to gain faster access to participants once you are ready to conduct your study.
Mixed Methods Design		
	Do I really need to use a mixed methods design?	Use a mixed methods design only if your research questions are best answered by this approach, and you have the abilities, the time, and the resources for such a study.
	Can I answer my research questions using a different approach?	You should answer your research questions using the simplest approach possible.

First, when choosing mixed methods research, you want to make sure that you take your personal experiences and skills into account. What is your background in both quantitative and qualitative research methods? How well do you understand these perspectives? How comfortable are you conducting quantitative and qualitative studies separately? Do you feel confident enough in your abilities that you can take either approach? If you cannot conduct quantitative research and speak to the quantitative field as well as conduct qualitative research and speak to the qualitative field, then it will be challenging to combine the approaches. Moreover, engaging in mixed methods research requires learning a new language and methodological approach. Thus, it is necessary to consider your skill level.

Another consideration is that of time. Mixed methods research may be more time consuming than either qualitative or quantitative research alone. There may be substantial time needed for data collection, data analysis (e.g., transcribing interviews, coding qualitative data, conducting statistical analyses, data transformation), and writing (e.g., putting the quantitative and qualitative components together in a coherent fashion). You have to ask yourself: How much time do I realistically have to conduct my study? As you plan your study, you should also consider creating a timeline that includes all of the major components of the research process. This will help you to determine if you truly have the time to take on a mixed methods study. The construction of the timeline tends to be a challenging task for anyone, but sometimes it is even more difficult for the beginning researcher. In fact, a common rule of thumb on the timeline is to figure out how long you think the study will take, and then double that time. The research process almost always takes longer than planned. For this reason, it is useful to begin the process of gaining research approval from your institutional review board (IRB), the research governing board, early in the research process. (See Chapter 8 for specific IRB suggestions.)

A third consideration is resources. Before embarking upon a mixed methods study, you have to determine if you have all of the necessary resources. It is important for you to determine the financial cost of your study. Creating a budget will be helpful in guiding you through this process. Will you need to pay for transcription services? It is important to remember that transcription services can be expensive and that transcribing on your own is very time consuming. On the other hand, many researchers prefer to do their own transcribing. Yes, transcribing on your own will add time to the process, but you can also begin the process of data analysis while transcribing. So even if you are having someone else transcribe your data, it would be useful for you to do some of the transcriptions yourself. Similarly, if you use a transcriptionist, you should always double check the quality of the transcriptions by listening to the interviews while following along on the transcripts, making any needed changes. In short, transcription is a lengthy process regardless of the approach you utilize.

Other questions you should ask yourself include these: Do you need to provide financial incentives for participation? It is important for you to consider resources in terms of access. Do you have access to the appropriate quantitative and qualitative software? If not, you may need to make software purchases. Do you have access to the population of interest? Do you have access to other researchers with skills in these research methods? It is important to consider access to all of these resources, and if you do not have access, how will you get access?

The last consideration is the need to use a mixed methods design. You have to ask yourself: Do I really need to use a mixed methods design? Can I answer my research questions using a different approach? A rule of thumb in quantitative research is that your research designs/models should be as parsimonious as possible. This suggests that you should try to answer your research questions with the simplest model possible. This same rule may apply to your decision to use a mixed methods approach. If your research questions are better answered using a single research method, you may not need to embark upon a mixed methods study.

Is a Mixed Methods Design Right for You?

When determining whether a mixed methods design should be used, it is essential to examine the purpose of the study, your explanation as to why the research is being conducted (Newman, Ridenour, Newman, & DeMarco, 2003). Understanding the purpose is necessary because it assists you in making decisions about your research methods and in developing research questions, which also play an important role in helping to determine the appropriate research methods. According to Newman et al. (2003), research studies (quantitative, qualitative, or mixed methods) are generally conducted to predict, add to knowledge, measure change, understand phenomena, test new ideas, generate new ideas, inform constituencies, and examine the past. For students, in particular, the most common reason for engaging in research is to *add to the knowledge* in a specific content area. This is the case because most dissertations are conducted with the goal of researching a novel idea within a discipline.

In addition, when engaging in a mixed methods study, a secondary purpose will be methods oriented, in that the very use of both quantitative and qualitative methods to explore a phenomenon becomes a goal. It is important to remember that mixed methods approaches have not commonly been used to explore a variety of topics in some fields. However, Greene, Caracelli, and Graham (1989) suggest that there are five additional and specific purposes for conducting mixed methods research: triangulation (using quantitative and qualitative methods to demonstrate convergence or explain a lack of convergence), complementarity (using qualitative and quantitative methods to examine overlapping but different aspects), development (using quantitative and qualitative methods sequentially with one method informing the other method), initiation (using one method to discover or explore contradictory findings that resulted from the other method), and expansion (using one method to extend a study).

In order to help determine whether a mixed methods design is the right approach for your study, there are a series of questions you should ask yourself (see Table 1.2). The first set of questions concerns the purpose of study: Why am I conducting this study? What is the

Table 1.2   When Is a Mixed Methods Study Appropriate for You?

	Questions to Consider	Answers	Suggestions
Study Purpose			
	Will I use data to attempt to triangulate, complement, develop, initiate, or expand findings?	Yes	Mixed methods is the option for you.
		No	Consider using a quantitative or qualitative approach.
Research Methods			
	Is a mixed methods approach necessary to answer my research questions?	Yes	Mixed methods is the option for you.
		No	Consider using a quantitative or qualitative approach.
	Can I more effectively conduct this study using a singular method?	Yes	Consider using a quantitative or qualitative approach.
		No	Mixed methods is the option for you.
Ability			
	Do I have the skills, abilities, and resources needed to effectively conduct a mixed methods study?	Yes	Consider using a mixed methods approach.
		No	Consider using a quantitative or qualitative approach; become more proficient in quantitative and/or qualitative approaches.

goal of my study? What is the purpose of using a mixed methods approach to my study? Will I use data to attempt to triangulate, complement, develop, initiate, or expand findings? The second set of questions involves research methods: What methods are most appropriate to answer my research questions? Is a mixed methods approach needed? Can I more effectively conduct this study using a singular method? The last question concerns your ability to carry out a mixed methods study. You should be very honest when considering the following question: Do I have the skills, abilities, and resources needed to effectively conduct a mixed methods study? If you have reflected on the goals of your study, examined the research methods needed to carry out your study, evaluated your research skills, and determined that a mixed methods research design is an appropriate approach for your study, this book will serve as an essential guide to helping develop your mixed methods research proposal.

WHAT DOES A MIXED METHODS RESEARCH PROPOSAL LOOK LIKE? ●

Now that we have a shared understanding of what taking on a mixed methods study entails, it is essential that we discuss the components of a research proposal. A research proposal is a tentative plan for the implementation of your study. The research proposal consists of three major areas (introduction, literature review, and research methods) and two minor areas (references and appendices). The primary goal of the research proposal is to communicate to readers your plan for your research study. In the proposal, you make the case for your study by discussing the history, relevance, and the significance of your topic; this is considered the *introduction* section. Then you provide context for your study by connecting your topic to the current research; this is the *literature review* section. Last, you provide the detailed steps for how the study is to be conducted and the methods you will use throughout the study; this is the *research methods* section. It is also important to properly document all of your sources and citations in the *references*. In the *appendices*, you include any other relevant information that you could not discuss in the previous sections (e.g., consent forms, interview protocols, survey instruments).

In addition, the research proposal is a flexible contract between you and your stakeholders (e.g., dissertation committee, granting agency). As such, research proposals are often augmented once the research study begins. However, it is important to note that the component or parts of a thesis, dissertation, or grant proposal are based on the local norms, rules, and accepted procedures of the particular organization involved (e.g., the mission of your department, college, or granting agency). Thus if you are writing a dissertation proposal, it is important to work with your dissertation chair, ask for advice from fellow students who have recently gone through the process, and use any guidelines that are provided. For example, most graduate programs have a thesis or dissertation guideline document or even templates that explain what the final document should contain. Make sure you acquire a copy of those guidelines early in the process and keep them handy throughout the development of your proposal. We have organized this book to match the key elements required for various research proposals (see Table 1.3).

Table 1.3   The Mixed Methods Research Proposal

Chapters or Sections of the Proposal	Chapter(s) in This Book Where the Topic Is Discussed
Title Page	8
Abstract	8
Introduction	4
Background of the Study	4
Theoretical Framework	2 & 4
Purpose Statement	4
Significance of the Study	4
Literature Review	5
Specific Research Questions	3 & 5
Methods	6 & 7
Mixed Methods Design/Definition	6 & 7
Participants	7
Data Collection	7
Data Analysis	7
Data Integration	7
Validity/Trustworthiness	7
Reliability/Credibility	7
References	8
Appendices	8

You have now considered your need to take a mixed methods approach to your study and your ability to conduct a mixed methods study. In addition, you have become aware of the major components of a research proposal. Are you ready to begin crafting a mixed methods research proposal? If so, this book will assist you on your journey. We are ready to guide you through the process and provide examples from our own research, just in case you get lost along the way. Good luck and have fun!

PRACTICE SESSION

Guided Questions

As you begin to reflect upon your mixed methods study, think about the following questions:

1. What is your experience with quantitative and qualitative research? Do you feel comfortable conducting both quantitative and qualitative research?
2. Are you familiar with mixed methods designs? Do you feel confident engaging in a mixed methods study?
3. What is your timeline for implementing your research study? Can you effectively conduct a mixed methods study within that time frame?
4. Is a mixed methods design necessary for your study? Are there other approaches you can take for your study?

Self-Assessment Activity: Are You Ready For a Mixed Methods Proposal?

This activity will give you a basic assessment of your readiness to begin developing a mixed methods proposal. In addition, the activity will help you to begin thinking about all of the resources you may need to complete a mixed methods study. It will be important for you to use this assessment when you talk with your dissertation chair (or other guiding authority) about making decisions regarding where you need more training and if mixed methods is the best path for you.

It is important to note that these issues will need to be revisited once the proposal has been developed, because your initial responses may evolve as a result of your actual mixed methods proposal development. Specifically, the issues of budgeting and time will be revisited in Chapter 8.

Assessment Areas	Questions to Consider	Responses
Skills		
	What quantitative data collection and analyses are you proficient in?	
	What qualitative data collection and analyses are you proficient in?	
	What is your experience with mixed methods research?	
	What research skills do you need to acquire before attempting a mixed methods research study?	
	What software packages are you proficient with?	
Resources		
	Do you have access to relevant software packages? If so, which software packages? If not, what would you like to have access to?	
	Do you have access to relevant populations of interest?	
	Do you have assistance for data collection and analysis (if applicable)?	
Potential Budget Needs		
	Do you envision compensating participants for their participation in your study?	
	Do you need to purchase software?	
	Do you envision paying for transcription services?	
	Do you need to pay assistants for data collection and analysis (if applicable)?	
Tentative Timeline		
	How long will it take to get your study approved?	
	How much time do you have to conduct your study?	
Overall Assessment	Do you feel adequately prepared to begin developing a mixed methods research proposal? If not, what do you need to do in order to become prepared? When will you be prepared?	

Additional Readings on Mixed Methods Research and Proposals

For more readings on mixed methods research and research proposals, see the following:

Creswell, J. W., & Plano Clark, V. L. (2011). *Designing and conducting mixed methods research* (2nd ed.). Thousand Oaks, CA: Sage.

Locke, L. F., Spirduso, W. W., & Silverman, S. J. (2013). *Proposals that work: A guide for planning dissertations and grant proposals* (6th ed.). Thousand Oaks, CA: Sage.

Morgan, D. L. (2014). *Integrating qualitative and quantitative methods: A pragmatic approach.* Thousand Oaks, CA: Sage.

Ogden, T. E., & Goldberg, I. A. (2002). *Research proposals: A guide to success* (3rd ed.). Salt Lake City, UT: Academic Press.

Punch, K. F. (2006). *Developing effective research proposals* (2nd ed.). Thousand Oaks, CA: Sage.

Tashakkori, A., & Teddlie, C. (2010). *Handbook of mixed methods in social and behavioral research* (2nd ed.). Thousand Oaks, CA: Sage.

Teddlie, C., & Tashakkori, A. (2009). *Foundations of mixed methods research: Integrating quantitative and qualitative approaches in the social and behavioral sciences.* Thousand Oaks, CA: Sage.

Sample Session

We are interested in conducting a study of African American college students' experiences with racial microaggressions (conscious or unconscious negative gestures and/or statements that convey hurtful messages regarding racial minority group membership) within the college context. (For more information on racial microaggressions, see Sue, Capodilupo, Torino, Bucceri, Holder, Nadal, & Esquilin, 2007.) Below is the self-assessment we used to determine if we are ready to develop a mixed methods proposal. Because we are a team on this particular research project, we have combined our information on this table. What is listed below is what we both bring to the table for this project.

Assessment Areas	Questions to Consider	Responses
Skills		
	What quantitative data collection and analyses are you proficient in?	ANOVA; multiple regression; EFA/CFA; SEM
	What qualitative data collection and analyses are you proficient in?	Thematic content analysis; narrative analysis; counterstorytelling

(Continued)

(Continued)

Assessment Areas	Questions to Consider	Responses
	What is your experience with mixed methods research?	Years of experience teaching mixed methods research; published writings regarding mixed methods research; conducted several mixed methods research studies
	What research skills do you need to acquire before attempting a mixed methods research study?	None
	What software packages are you proficient with?	Quantitative software: SPSS; SAS; LISREL; AMOS Qualitative software: Atlas.ti
Resources		
	Do you have access to relevant software packages? If so, which software packages? If not, what would you like to have access to?	Yes—SPSS; SAS; AMOS; Atlas.ti
	Do you have access to relevant populations of interest?	Yes—college students
	Do you have assistance for data collection and analysis (if applicable)?	Yes—graduate students
Potential Budget Needs		
	Do you envision compensating participants for their participation in your study?	Maybe
	Do you need to purchase software?	No
	Do you envision paying for transcription services?	Maybe
	Do you need to pay assistants for data collection and analysis (if applicable)?	Maybe

Assessment Areas	Questions to Consider	Responses
Tentative Timeline		
	How long will it take to get your study approved?	4–6 weeks
	How much time do you have to conduct your study?	6–12 months
Overall Assessment	Do you feel adequately prepared to begin developing a mixed methods research proposal? If no, what do you need to do in order to become prepared? When will you be prepared?	YES!

2

The Role of Theory in Mixed Methods Research

Objectives

1. To develop an understanding of the *inquiry worldview, subjectivity statement,* and *substantive content theory* and how they transact to become the *theoretical framework* for mixed methods inquiries.

2. To develop and construct your own *inquiry worldview* for developing a mixed methods research proposal.

WHAT ROLE DOES THEORY PLAY IN A MIXED METHODS RESEARCH PROPOSAL?

Once you begin telling others that you are thinking about doing a mixed methods study, inevitably people will begin to ask you, "How are you theoretically approaching your study?" In order to answer that question, it is essential for you to continue to develop your thoughts or theories about research. As a beginning researcher, this can be a daunting task because you may not have thought about your worldview (or even heard of the concept). In fact, some of you may be just beginning to understand the content theories in your field of study.

17

Thus, making sense of these theories and explaining how they work together to inform your mixed methods research proposal can be both confusing and frustrating.

Therefore, when you embark upon developing a mixed methods research proposal, it is useful to take into consideration the role theories play in shaping your investigation. To help this effort we will elaborate on three aspects of theory: *inquiry worldview, subjectivity statement*, and *substantive content theory*. Our focus in this chapter is to help you develop clarity about these concepts and to help you identify and construct your own theories about research. To do so, we will begin by discussing inquiry worldviews.

Before we continue, it must be noted that the terms *worldview, substantive theory, subjectivity statement,* and *theoretical framework* are not necessary agreed-upon terms within the larger social science research community (e.g., see Crotty, 1998). For instance, instead of *worldview,* some fields use the terms *paradigm, metatheory,* or *theoretical perspective.* Also, many of the terms are used interchangeably (e.g., conceptual framework and theoretical framework). Thus, it is important for you to identify the common terminology for your respective field.

Inquiry Worldviews

As you think about your research proposal, it will be useful to examine your beliefs and understandings about the nature of research. For simplicity, we use the term *inquiry worldview* to describe your current overarching beliefs regarding how you see, understand, and interpret how research investigations works. These beliefs about research involve both ontological (i.e., what is the nature of reality?) as well as epistemological (i.e., what is the nature of knowledge and knowing?) assumptions about the world. Thus, understanding your beliefs is essential because your worldview overtly or covertly informs every aspect of your research study. Yet, examining your inquiry worldview is often a challenging process for you as a beginning researcher, because you may have never been asked to think about how you view the world or how you think about knowledge, knowing, and science. Therefore, this process requires considerable reading and reflecting. Before we begin our discussion of the most common worldviews, we would like you to begin thinking about how you see the world and the nature of inquiry. Use Table 2.1 to help you organize your thinking and to attempt to align yourself with a particular inquiry worldview.

Table 2.1   Making Sense of Your Worldview

	Questions to Consider	Possible Worldview
1	Do you tend to think in absolutes?	Positivist/Postpositivist
2	Do you believe in one truth?	Positivist/Postpositivist
3	Do you believe that context influences your interpretations?	Constructivist/Interpretivist
4	Do you believe in multiple interpretations of a situation?	Constructivist/Interpretivist Critical Transformative/Participatory
5	Do you like to question authority?	Critical
6	Do you often critique power structures?	Critical
7	Do you like to be engaged with the community?	Transformative/Participatory
8	Are you flexible in terms of the approaches you take to solve a problem?	Pragmatist/Pluralist
9	Do you like to create change?	Critical Transformative/Participatory

Now that you have started thinking about how you experience the world, it is important for you to get a better understanding of the common worldviews. Fortunately, other scholars have laid the groundwork, and Table 2.2 shows some brief descriptions of five common worldviews. While reading these summaries, it is important to keep in mind that we are providing only brief descriptions of some potential worldviews to help your thinking about these issues. Throughout the discussion we provide references where you can find more in-depth readings on these topics.

We focus on five families of inquiry worldviews that guide much of the current research practice in the social sciences: positivism-postpositivism, interpretivism-constructivism, critical perspective, transformative-participatory perspective, and pragmatism-pluralism (Koro-Ljungberg, Yendol-Hoppey, Smith, & Hayes, 2009; Lincoln & Guba, 2000; Mertens, 2003). Each worldview has its own philosophical underpinnings and differs from the others in its ontology (beliefs about the nature of reality), epistemology (beliefs about the nature of

Table 2.2 Common Worldviews

	Positivist-Postpositivist	Constructivist-Interpretivist	Critical	Transformative-Participatory	Pragmatist-Pluralist
What is the nature of reality? (ontology)	Singular reality/truth	Multiple realities	Multiple realities	Multiple realities	Singular truth/reality Multiple realities
What is the nature of knowledge and knowing? (epistemology)	Tend to be absolutist—truths and human processes are universal and knowable	Tend to be relativist—"truths" and human processes are contextual and can be understood only from particular contexts	Tend to be universalist—there may be some basic "truths"; however, those truths and human process are influenced by particular contexts	Tend to be universalist—there may be some basic "truths"; however, those truths and human process are influenced by particular contexts	Tend to be universalist—there may be some basic "truths"; however, those truths and human process are influenced by particular contexts and used for problem solving within those contexts

What is the nature of inquiry? (relationship between researcher and participants)	Distant	Close	Close Collaborative	Collaborative	Distant Close Collaborative
What is the nature of inquiry? (research process and types of data collected)	Experimental Quasi-experimental Mostly quantitative	Mostly qualitative	Mostly qualitative	Quantitative Qualitative Involves participants in all stages of the research process	Quantitative Qualitative Mixed methods
What types of mixed methods designs are most common? (mixed methods designs)	Quantitative-dominant mixed methods designs	Qualitative-dominant mixed methods designs	Quantitative- or qualitative-dominant mixed methods designs	Quantitative- or qualitative-dominant mixed methods designs	Quantitative- or qualitative-dominant methods designs

knowledge and knowing), and research methods (the process used to discover or examine a phenomenon) (Guba & Lincoln, 1994; Lincoln & Guba, 2000). We also provide a discussion on an emerging inquiry worldview within mixed methods—dialectic approaches.

Positivism-Postpositivism

Those researchers who approach inquiry from this worldview tend to believe there are absolute truths. In believing there are absolute truths, researchers from this perspective adhere to the belief that if research methods are used properly, researchers can gain access to these truths (Phillips, 1990; Popper, 1972). Researchers with a postpositivistic worldview also tend to believe there are truths. However, because our research methods are somewhat imperfect, researchers will have challenges accessing these truths; thus researchers may be able only to obtain close approximations of these truths. In addition, from this perspective, there is a tendency for researchers to see those truths and therefore human processes and activities from an absolutist perspective, which suggests that human behaviors are universal and culture free (Berry, Poortinga, Segall, & Dasen, 2002; Zusho & Clayton, 2011). This suggests, for example, that human motivational processes for high school students in the United States would be the same as those for students in other cultures, and therefore the assumption would be that research findings could be generalized outside of the original research context. As such, a positivist-postpositivist mixed methods study tends to be quantitatively dominant, in that the attempt would be to focus on making generalizations from the sample back to the population. To do this, the tendency would be to focus on the use of inferential statistics, which requires quantitative data.

Constructivism-Interpretivism

Individuals who embrace this worldview tend to believe there are multiple truths and realities. For these researchers, people's interpretations are based upon their own lived experiences, which lead to multiple truths (Angen, 2000; Glasersfeld, 1995). As such, individuals, and the cultures in which they live, construct their own context-based realities. Thus, there is a tendency for these researchers to approach inquiry from more of a relativist perspective, which means that human processes are situational and therefore best investigated at the local level (Berry, Poortinga, Segall, & Dasen, 2002; Zusho & Clayton, 2011). This belief tends to imply that inquiry should be situated within local contexts, and that attempts should not be made to generalize research findings outside of the local context. Thus, from this perspective, the idea of being able to generalize from a sample to a population would be questioned, because the importance of the local context would limit your ability to make useful generalizations. So for the inquiry worldview, the tendency would be toward a qualitative-dominant mixed methods design.

Critical Perspective

Individuals with a critical worldview also tend to view the world from the perspective of multiple realities. However, researchers with a critical perspective focus on critiquing the current power structures with the ultimate goal of changing and transforming those structures (Giroux, 1988; Habermas, 1971). Thus, there is a tendency for these researchers to approach inquiry from a universalist perspective, which suggests there may be some basic "truths"; however, those truths and related human processes tend to be influenced by particular contexts (Berry, Poortinga, Segall, & Dasen, 2002; Zusho & Clayton, 2011). For example, one of the basic tenets of critical race theory (CRT) is racial realism, or the permanence of racism (DeCuir & Dixson, 2004); however, how racism manifests itself depends on the local contexts. Theories such as feminism, CRT, and queer theory are considered examples of critical theories. For an inquiry from a critical worldview (e.g., CRT, critical feminism, queer theory, or postcolonialism), the goal is to trouble and critique existing power structures. This means that whatever types of data that would help bring attention to power disparities would be fair game, suggesting that a mixed methods study that emerged from this worldview could be qualitative-dominant, quantitative-dominant, or make a more balanced use of both approaches.

Transformative-Participatory Perspective

Researchers with this worldview also adhere to the belief of multiple truths. Researchers with this perspective attempt to understand phenomena within context, similar to those with a constructivist-interpretivist perspective. Yet, these researchers also attempt to actively involve the community that is being served with the goal of change, and this makes them similar to those with a critical perspective (Mertens, 2007). The goal of transformative-participatory research is to understand and transform the situation based upon the needs of the participants involved in the research. As such, the participants are actively involved in various stages of the research. Thus, there is a tendency for these researchers to approach inquiry from a universalist perspective, which suggests there may be some basic "truths"; however, those truths and related human processes tend to be influenced by the particular contexts (Berry, Poortinga, Segall, & Dasen, 2002; Zusho & Clayton, 2011). Transformative/participatory studies rely upon the needs of the participants. As such, using such an approach requires you to be open to using a variety of methods. A mixed methods study derived from this inquiry worldview could be qualitative- or quantitative-dominant, or it could make a more balanced use of both approaches.

Pragmatism-Pluralism

Pragmatists/pluralists tend to see inquiry as an approach to solving problems. A researcher with this perspective would tend to take the middle ground, often choosing practical problem-solving research methods (Dewey, 1910; James, 1907). As such, these researchers would be receptive to blending worldviews and research methods in order to solve a problem (Schutz, 2014; Schutz, Chambless, & DeCuir, 2004; Schutz, Nichols, & Rodgers, 2009). Many mixed methods researchers tend to be pragmatists/pluralists in that they are willing to use multiple approaches in order to solve problems. Thus, there is a tendency for these researchers to approach inquiry from a universalist perspective, which suggests there may be some basic "truths"; however, those truths and related human processes tend to be influenced by the particular contexts (Berry, Poortinga, Segall, & Dasen, 2002; Zusho & Clayton, 2011). Taking a pragmatic approach to a mixed methods study implies that you are open to using whatever methods best address your problem. This approach could result in a qualitative- or quantitative-dominant mixed methods study or a more balanced use of both approaches.

Emerging Inquiry Worldview

Although this is not considered to be a commonly used worldview, it is important for us to discuss some of the emerging inquiry worldviews within the field of mixed methods, particularly dialectics (Greene, 2007; Greene & Hall, 2010). *Dialectics* involves the blending of paradigms, methodologies, and methods, while engaging their interactions throughout the research process. Specifically, dialectics recognizes the legitimacy of multiple paradigmatic traditions, views the primary goal of mixed methods inquiry as better understanding, and encourages a multiplicity of thought based upon culture (Greene & Hall, 2010). Dialectics can be viewed as an extension of pragmatism or a real integration of quantitative and qualitative approaches.

After reading about these five families of worldviews (and the emerging inquiry worldview), it is important for us to remind you that we have provided only some beginning thoughts to help you identify your own beliefs about these issues. (See the reading list at the end of the chapter for more in-depth writings on these issues.) It is also important to remember there are other worldviews that are continually being developed and that may influence approaches to research in the future. In addition, as you have already surmised, there are some overlaps among these five families and other potential worldviews, so you may find that you do not fit nicely into one of those families. Thus, it is necessary to keep in mind that what is important is the process of developing your beliefs and ideas about inquiry and making those beliefs explicit—not fitting neatly in a particular category.

Subjectivity Statement

In addition to understanding how you view the world, it is also important for you to ascertain how your personal experiences impact your research. A *subjectivity statement* is basically an explanation of your relationship with the research topic or area you would like to study. How did you become interested in this topic, what is your personal relationship with the topic? For example, it is not uncommon for someone who has a personal experience with addiction (e.g., being an addict or have a family member who is an addict) to develop an interest in researching issues related to addiction. In qualitative research, the subjectivity statement has basically become standard procedure for researchers. As indicated by Preissle (2008), this statement has two basic purposes:

(1) to help researchers identify how their personal features, experiences, beliefs, feelings, cultural standpoints, and professional predispositions may affect their research; and (2) to convey this material to other scholars for their consideration of the study's credibility, authenticity, and overall quality or validity. (p. 846)

In the research proposal, the subjectivity statement tends to be a part of the introduction. Thus, we will return to this topic in Chapter 4, The Mixed Methods Proposal Introduction.

Substantive Content Theory

In addition to explicating one's worldview and subjectivity statement, it is also important to understand the specific substantive theories or specific theories you will use to guide your inquiry. A *substantive content theory* describes your particular area of research (Maxwell, 1996; Punch, 2006). Every discipline has a number of substantive theories. For example, in psychology, there are several different learning and motivation theories, while in sociology there are anomie and strain theories. Most mixed methods research studies are guided by multiple substantive theories. Sometimes researchers use substantive theories that originate from a variety of disciplines. For instance, a researcher can use physics' chaos theory and theories in organizational behavior to examine a particular phenomenon in management.

These substantive content theories provide the content for the literature review section of your research proposal. It may be useful to think about this process as like trying to join a conversation that has been going on for a time before you got there. In order to contribute to the conversation, you need to understand what has been discussed, who the key players in the discussion are, and where the discussion is headed. It is important to keep in mind that there are no easy roads to developing your substantive content theories. The process involves a lot of reading, thinking, and writing about your area of interest. We will talk more about this process in Chapter 4, The Literature Review.

Theoretical Framework

As you are developing your inquiry worldview, subjectivity statement, and substantive content theories, it is important to consider the relationships among them. We will call that combination your *theoretical framework*. The inquiry worldview serves as the umbrella theory to help describe your general thinking and views about inquiry. The subjectivity statement explicates your relationship with your research topic, and the substantive theories provide context for how you think the phenomena can be explored within your research discipline. It is your theoretical framework that focuses on the relationships among these three dimensions (see Figure 2.1). Again remember this is an iterative process, where thinking about your subjectivity statement may result in a refocusing of your substantive content theories, which may in turn call for adjustments in your inquiry worldview.

Figure 2.1   Components of the Theoretical Framework

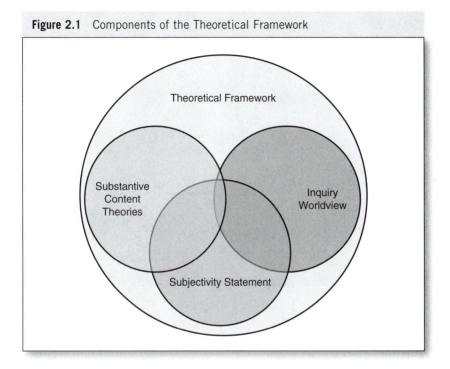

As a researcher, it is important to use your theoretical framework to guide the components of your mixed methods research proposal, particularly your methods. Thus, your theoretical framework helps to inform your research questions, data collection, data analysis, and the implications you can draw from your findings (see Figure 2.2). We designed this figure to represent the transactions among the different components of your mixed methods proposal. In Figure 2.2 you will see that the *Theoretical Framework* is made up of the *inquiry worldview*, your *subjectivity statement* (Chapter 4), and your *substantive content theo*ry (Chapter 5). Those components represent the theoretical foundation for your proposal. The *Proposal Framework* represents your focus on the particular study you will discuss in your proposal; it includes your *problem statement* and *research questions,* as well as your *substantive content theory.* You will notice that the connection between the *Theoretical Framework* and the *Proposal Framework* is your *substantive content theory,* thus providing the key link between your theoretical foundation and the particular problem area and the research questions that emerged for your proposal. Finally, you also see that the connection between the *Proposal Framework* and the *Proposal Research Methods* is the set of *research questions.* These questions, as we will suggest in

Figure 2.2   Mixed Methods Research Proposal Framework

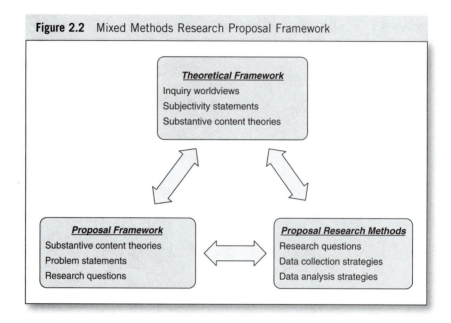

Chapter 3, are the key to the selection of useful *data collection* and *data analysis* strategies you will discuss in your research methods section (Chapters 6 and 7). In addition, we will discuss the development of your theoretical framework more when we return to your *problem statement*, your *subjectivity statement* (Chapter 4), and your *substantive content theory* (Chapter 5).

PRACTICE SESSION

Guided Questions

As you begin to reflect upon your mixed methods study, think about the following questions:

- What inquiry worldview most closely aligns with how you understand the world? Why?
- Think about the seminal articles in your content area. What inquiry worldviews do the authors suggest? Do the authors of those seminal articles differ from each other on their inquiry worldviews?
- What inquiry worldviews does your major professor (or do your research collaborators) seem to have? What about other professors/collaborators you have worked with?

Activity for Developing Your Inquiry Worldview

To continue the process of developing your theoretical framework, in this practice session we focus on explicating your own inquiry worldview. To do so, answer the following questions:

- What is the nature of reality? (For example, is there an external reality? Is there a single reality, or are there multiple realities?)
- What is the nature of the knower and knowledge? (For example, are there ultimate truths? How do we come to know things?)
- What is the nature of inquiry? (For example, what purpose[s] does science have? How should we choose what to study, and how should we study it?)

Additional Readings on Theory and Mixed Methods Proposals

For more readings on theory, worldviews, and mixed methods research, see the following:

Anafara, V. A., & Mertz, N. T. (2006). *Theoretical frameworks in qualitative research.* Thousand Oaks, CA: Sage.

Biesta, G. (2010). Pragmatism and the philosophical foundations of mixed methods research. In A. Tashakkori & C. Teddlie (Eds.), *SAGE handbook of mixed methods in social and behavioral research* (2nd ed., pp. 95–118). Thousand Oaks, CA: Sage.

Crotty, M. (1998). *The foundations of social research: Meaning and perspective in the research process.* Thousand Oaks, CA: Sage.

Hesse-Biber, S. (2012). Feminist approaches to triangulation: Uncovering subjugated knowledge and fostering social change in mixed methods research. *Journal of Mixed Methods Research, 6*(2), 137–146.

Johnson, B., & Gray, R. (2010). A history of philosophical and theoretical issues for mixed methods research. In A. Tashakkori & C. Teddlie (Eds.), *SAGE handbook of mixed methods in social and behavioral research* (2nd ed., pp. 69–94). Thousand Oaks, CA: Sage.

Koro-Ljungberg, M., Yendol-Hoppey, D., Smith, J. J., & Hayes, S. B. (2009). (E)pistemological awareness, instantiation of methods, and uniformed methodological ambiguity in qualitative research projects. *Educational Researcher, 38*(9), 687–699.

Lather, P. (1991). *Getting smart.* New York, NY: Routledge.

Lincoln, Y., & Guba, E. (2000). Paradigmatic controversies, contradictions, and emerging confluences. In N. Denzin & Y. Lincoln (Eds.), *Handbook of qualitative research* (2nd ed., pp. 163–188). Thousand Oaks, CA: Sage.

Mertens, D. M. (2007). Transformative paradigm: Mixed methods and social justice. *Journal of Mixed Methods Research, 1*(3), 212–225.

Schutz, P. A. (2014). Inquiry on teachers' emotion. *Educational Psychologist, 49*(1), 1–12.

Schutz, P. A., Chambless, C. B., & DeCuir, J. T. (2004). Multimethods research. In K. B. deMarrais & S. D. Lapan (Eds.), *Research methods in the social sciences: Frameworks for knowing and doing* (pp. 267–281). Hillsdale, NJ: Erlbaum.

Schutz, P. A., Nichols, S. L., & Rodgers, K. (2009). Using multimethod approaches. In S. D. Lapan & M. T. Quartaroli (Eds.), *Research essentials: An introduction to design and practices* (pp. 243–258). San Francisco, CA: Jossey-Bass.

Sample Session—Inquiry Worldview

As indicated in Chapter 1, our sample session will focus on a study we are interested in conducting on African American college students' experiences with racial microaggressions within the college context. Below is our current answer to the inquiry worldview questions. Our answers will help to inform how we will proceed in the development of our mixed methods proposal. For this joint project, we are approaching the project from the same inquiry worldview and therefore will present a joint worldview.

- What is the nature of reality? (For example, is there an external reality? Is there a single reality, or are there multiple realities?)

For us there are external realities; however, the boundaries between internal and external realities vary and are socially constructed and reconstructed. Take for example issues of race and the microaggressions experienced by African American students within college contexts. An example of the potentially changing psychological boundaries is exhibited in an article by Krosch and Amodio (2014). In that article, the authors, using an experiment, demonstrate that perceived economic resource scarcity resulted in participants judging pictures of African Americans as being "Blacker" and less similar to Whites than when there was no perceived scarcity. In addition, this visual distortion tendency resulted in inequalities when participants were asked to allocate resources to racial groups. This suggests that the realities of African American college students and the racial microaggressions they experience will be tied to the social historical contexts in which they are located.

- What is the nature of the knower and knowledge? (For example, are there ultimate truths? How do we come to know things?)

We tend to view inquiry from a universalist perspective. We think that there are probably some basic "truths" that tend to be influenced by particular social historical contexts. For example, we are informed by tenets of CRT, a theory that is used to critique and transform race, racism, and power within all aspects of society (Bell, 1993; Delgado & Stefancic, 2012).

A major tenet of CRT is that racism is endemic and a permanent component of society. However, we believe the manner in which racism manifests itself (e.g., different aspects of microaggressions) depends on the local social historical contexts in which the microaggresions emerge.

- What is the nature of inquiry? (For example, what purpose(s) does science have? How should we choose what to study, and how should we study it?)

For us, inquiry or research is systematic ways of approaching and attempting to problem solve within social historical contexts. As such, we are informed by pragmatic worldviews. This basically means, for us, that research methods are tools that we use to help answer research questions that are designed to solve problems within social historical contexts.

3

Asking Appropriate Research Questions

Objectives

1. To become familiar with some of the different types of research questions.

2. To identify the characteristics of useful research questions.

3. To develop and construct your own research questions for a mixed methods research proposal.

In the last chapter we focused on the role of theory, which required you to focus on abstract concepts. Now we need you to realign your thinking and move on to an issue that is more concrete—the creation of research questions. Research questions are used to guide your mixed methods inquiry. Before creating research questions, you have to ask yourself: What do I want to know? What am I attempting to investigate in my mixed methods proposal? The answers to these questions will become the building blocks of your research questions. However, crafting quality research questions is more easily said then done. As a result, the main goals of this chapter are to discuss the roles and characteristics of research questions in the mixed methods proposal and to demonstrate how to develop good research questions.

● THE ROLE OF RESEARCH QUESTIONS

It is important to begin the process of developing research questions early in the proposal writing process. This is because you can use your research questions to guide your literature review, the selection of your research methods, and basically the overall organization of your research proposal. In fact, most scholars interested in research methods and methodologies discuss the importance of research questions to the inquiry process. Some have gone as far as labeling research questions the "dictator" of the research process (Tashakkori & Teddlie, 1998). Although we would not go as far as to ascribe ultimate unidirectional control to our research questions, we do see them as a key part of a successful iterative inquiry process. To that end, we agree with Agee (2009), who suggested that "good questions do not necessarily produce good research, but poorly conceived or constructed questions will likely create problems that affect all subsequent stages of a study" (p. 431).

With that in mind, we see research questions as providing important transactional links among your theoretical framework, proposal framework, and proposal research methods—or in other words, all aspects of the research process. As you can see in the Mixed Methods Research Proposal

Figure 3.1 Mixed Methods Research Proposal Framework

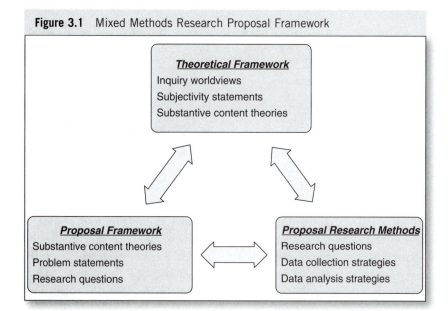

Theoretical Framework
Inquiry worldviews
Subjectivity statements
Substantive content theories

Proposal Framework
Substantive content theories
Problem statements
Research questions

Proposal Research Methods
Research questions
Data collection strategies
Data analysis strategies

Framework in Figure 3.1, which we introduced in Chapter 2, the research questions provide important links among the key components of your proposal. More specifically you can use your research questions to guide your review of the literature (i.e., substantive content theories) and therefore help you to develop understandings of what is known in an area. For example, a preliminary research question such as "Are self-efficacy beliefs about exercise related to college freshmen's *body mass index (BMI)*?" can guide you during your review of the literature to see if there are researchers who have investigated this issue. If you find such studies, they will provide you with information you should use to refine your research questions.

Those same refined research questions will also help you to determine your research methods (i.e., data collection and data analysis strategies). In other words, when you are in doubt at any point in the mixed methods research proposal development process, ask yourself, "What are my research questions?" How you answer that question, in most cases, can refocus and guide you to the next step in the research proposal development process, which might include finding additional scholarly literature, changing your research questions, and/or adjusting your research methods.

It is also important to keep in mind that your research questions emerge, in part, from your theoretical framework (i.e., inquiry worldview, subjectivity statement, and substantive content theory). For example, in Table 3.1 we provide sample research questions that might emerge from the inquiry worldviews we presented in Chapter 2.

Table 3.1   Research Questions From Different Inquiry Worldviews

Inquiry Worldviews	Sample Research Question
Positivism-Postpositivism	What is the relationship between exercise self-efficacy and the amount of time spent exercising per week for mothers who have given birth within the last year?
Interpretivism-Constructivism	How do mothers who have given birth within the last year talk about the amount of time they spend exercising?
Critical Worldview	How do self-perceptions of female body image influence new mothers' confidence about exercising?
Transformative-Participatory Worldview	How can mothers who have given birth in the last year organize and implement programs of exercise in their community?
Pragmatism-Pluralism	How do mothers who have given birth in the past year talk about their problems associated with finding time to exercise?

In reading these questions, you will see how researchers with different worldviews might come up with somewhat different research questions for a similar issue. Thus, the way you look at a problem area has the potential to influence the type of research questions you might ask.

● TYPES OF RESEARCH QUESTIONS

In a mixed methods research proposal, there are potentially three general types of questions: (1) qualitative research questions (i.e., questions that help you investigate meaning or process), (2) quantitative research questions (i.e., questions that help you explain variance or relationships among your variables of interest), and (3) mixed methods research questions (i.e., questions that help you explicate the transactions among process, meaning, and the explanation of variance).

Qualitative Research Questions

Qualitative research questions are written to help you as the researcher understand how your participants talk about, understand, and/or engage in the processes related to the phenomenon of interest (Agee, 2009). From this perspective, as a researcher, you are trying to develop an understanding of the topic of interest from the perspective of an individual or a group of individuals. For example, if you were conducting a research study on emotions in the classroom that focuses on the role of teacher emotions related to classroom management, a qualitative research question might read, "How do high school teachers talk about the emotions they experience while managing their classroom activities?"

The attempt with qualitative research questions is to explore how individuals understand and experience the area or topic of interest. With that goal, it is not unusual for research questions to continue to emerge and be revised throughout the data collection process. In other words, as you begin to develop understandings from local contexts and the individuals involved in that context, your research questions need to reflect the viewpoints, interactions, and processes of the people in your study. This suggests that in some cases it may be useful to begin with more general overarching research questions that provide guidance, and then look to develop more specific research questions as data collection and analysis continue (Agee, 2009). An example of a more overarching research question might be, "How do high school teachers talk about their emotions in the classroom?"

Quantitative Research Questions

Quantitative research questions tend to focus on variation or the relationships among variables of interest. For example, if we give a sample of high school teachers a scale that measures their confidence or self-efficacy in their classroom management ability, quantitatively we may be interested in how other variables might explain those differences (i.e., variance) in the teachers' scores. We would expect that some teachers would score higher on the measure, indicating more confidence in their classroom management ability. On the other end of the continuum, there would also be teachers who were not as confident in their ability to manage the classroom and who therefore score lower on that measure. From a quantitative perspective, the interest would be in what other variables help explain that variance in the scores of a sample of high school teachers. Thus, an example of a potential research question might be, "Are high school teachers' anxiety levels related to their confidence in their classroom management ability?"

It is important to remember that research questions are not the same as research hypotheses. Basically, research questions state what you would like to learn about an area of interest. On the other hand, research hypotheses are your tentative answers to those questions, based on your understanding of the literature (Maxwell, 2013). Thus, for the above research question, a hypothesis might be, "Higher scores on a teacher anxiety measure will be related to lower scores on a classroom management confidence measure." Remember, the key to creating testable hypotheses from research questions is an in-depth understanding of the scholarly literature. As such, when writing your proposal, it is best to work from your research questions and not jump to making hypotheses until the latter stages of your proposal development, when you have a clearer understanding of the literature.

Mixed Methods Research Questions

Mixed methods research questions are developed to provide guidance while investigating relationships between the data collected and/or analyzed qualitatively and the data that is collected and/or analyzed quantitatively. Mixed methods research questions can be stand-alone, used without additional quantitative or qualitative questions. In addition, mixed methods research questions can serve as umbrella questions, helping to organize the quantitative and qualitative components of the research. The mixed methods questions researchers choose to develop depend upon the goals of the research as well as personal preference. Some mixed methods researchers feel that all mixed methods studies need a mixed methods question. However, other mixed methods researchers, including us, feel that mixed methods questions are not always necessary, as long as there are sufficient quantitative and qualitative research questions. Again, the need to use a mixed methods research question may vary by discipline—as such we strongly encourage you to consult the appropriate sources in your area.

The goal of mixed methods research questions is to create deeper understandings of the phenomenon of interest than the understanding a researcher might expect from looking at qualitative or quantitative data separately. For instance, to continue with the aforementioned research example, the researcher might be interested in the following research question: "Do high school teachers who scored high on the classroom management self-efficacy scale perceive teacher anxiety differently than high school teachers who scored low on the classroom management self-efficacy scale?" This would be an example of a mixed method research question. The researcher is attempting to investigate the potential overlap or similarities between teachers' discussions about anxiety (qualitative data) and their levels of confidence in their ability to manage their classroom activities (quantitative data).

Mixed methods research questions tend to be more complicated than either qualitative or quantitative questions. This is because, in order to answer those questions, the researcher is tasked with bringing together data that was collected and/or analyzed from a qualitative perspective with data that has been collected and/or analyzed from a quantitative perspective. This also means that there is always the potential that the data collected in these different ways may or may not agree with each other. Thus, your qualitative data may tell you something different then your quantitative data, which also adds to the potential complexity of the mixed methods research questions. Keep in mind that this potential challenge is also an important opportunity to discover things that you may not even have been able to find with just qualitative data or just quantitative data.

At this point, you have probably noticed that we have not talked much about specific mixed research methods or designs. This has been intentional in that at this point in the process, we want you to keep in mind that as a researcher, you begin the mixed methods research process by crafting useful research questions that are designed to help investigate problems of interest. Once you have developed at least a draft of those useful research questions, then it will be time to investigate which research methods and designs would work best when attempting to answer those questions. Our point here is that we want you to use your research questions to determine your research

methods; we don't want you to use your research methods to determine your research questions. Therefore, we will focus the remainder
of this chapter on creating your own useful research questions, and we
will leave mixed methods research designs to Chapter 6 and research
methods to Chapter 7.

CREATING YOUR OWN RESEARCH QUESTIONS   ●

As indicated, the development of your research questions is an iterative process that continues throughout the writing of your proposal.
This means it is important to begin by drafting research questions early
in the process, as you begin to reflect on what you know about your
research topic and on your research experience, as well as on your own
personal experiences related to your problem of interest. The writing
and rewriting process continues and becomes more refined as you use
your research questions to guide your investigations of the scholarly
literature and begin to develop research methods for data collection
and analysis. Finally, as data is collected and analyzed, your research
questions may continue to be refined in order to best represent the data
being collected and analyzed (Plano Clark & Badiee, 2010), which may
also direct you back to the literature for additional theoretical investigations. As such, your research questions have both a focusing and
guiding role during the research proposal writing process (Maxwell,
2013; Miles, Huberman, & Saldaña, 2013).

In order to guide you through the process of writing useful
research questions, we have provided Table 3.2. The criteria in Table 3.2
will help you to write questions that both focus and guide the development of your research proposal.

To demonstrate, earlier in this chapter we used the research question, "Are high school teachers' anxiety levels related to their confidence in their classroom management ability?" as an example of a
quantitative research question. We will use it again now to provide an
example of the characteristics of a useful research question. First, you
can see that the question is clearly worded and unambiguous. Second,
you can tell that the participants are high school teachers and that the
study would take place in a high school setting. In terms of what is
being studied, you see two variables, "classroom management confidence" and "teacher anxiety." In this case, the data needed would be
survey data from a classroom management confidence scale and a
measure of teacher anxiety. To determine whether the fourth criterion
is met (i.e., interconnection with other research questions), you would

Table 3.2 Criteria for Useful Research Questions

Research questions should be
1. Written clearly so they are easily understood and unambiguous, and so they logically follow from your purpose statement or statement of the problem.
2. Written specifically such that the research concepts or constructs connect to data indicators by showing a. who are your participants, b. where the study will take place, and c. what you will be studying.
3. Answerable, so you can see what data is required and how the data will be obtained and analyzed.
4. Interconnected with each other in some meaningful way, rather than being unconnected.
5. Substantively relevant such that they are interesting and worthwhile questions for the investment of research effort.

need to have the other research questions for this study, and for the fifth criterion (i.e., relevant, interesting and worthwhile), you would need the purpose statement or statement of the problem to be able to accurately judge.

In summary, the creation of quality research questions is an important component of the mixed methods proposal development process. The research questions help to guide the focus of the various components of the proposal, especially the research methods. As such, it is important to take the appropriate time to craft your research questions. Investing this time up front will make crafting the research methods section a lot easier.

PRACTICE SESSION

Guided Questions

1. Based on your reading of the scholarship in your area, what have others suggested as important areas for future research?
2. Look at research articles you have read recently. Do the researchers present their research questions? If they do list their research questions, do the questions meet the criteria listed in Table 3.2?

3. Take a look at your current research questions. Do you have some qualitative questions that focus on the phenomenon of interest? Do you have some quantitative questions that look at the relationships among variables? Do you have any mixed methods questions that focus on both the phenomenon of interest and the relationships among variables?

Activity for Creating Research Questions

1. First, in bold letters at the top of the page, write the word "DRAFT" (or use the watermark function on your computer). The word "DRAFT" is there to remind you that research and the development of research questions is an iterative process, which basically means there is the potential that only a few of the research questions that you start with will actually make it into the final version of the proposal. But don't despair—the hard work you put into your early research questions will lay the foundation for the successful proposal you will be writing.

2. Next, it is time to brainstorm a list of at least 12 to 15 research questions related to your topic area. Remember, while brainstorming you want to avoid making any judgments regarding wording or content. Just try to let the questions flow. What do you want to know about this topic area? Your goal should be to get down as many questions as you can. At this point, 12 to 15 research questions may seem like a lot; however, you never know where your best questions are going to emerge. It could be your 2nd and 3rd question, but it could also be the 13th and 14th questions, or even a combination of your 2nd and 12th questions. So if you stopped at 7, you may not get to your best questions!

3. Once you have your list of 12 to 15 questions, go back and edit your questions. You may find some repetition, some incomplete ideas, or some questions that could be combined. Overall this step is to clean up the wording.

4. Use the criteria in Table 3.2 to edit your research questions so that they begin to meet the criteria for useful research questions. At this point in the process, they do not have to be perfect to help focus and guide your research, so avoid being too critical. Refining the wording is iterative and will continue throughout the mixed methods proposal development process.

5. Identify which questions can be answered with qualitative data, which with quantitative data, and which will require a mixed methods approach.

6. Finally, keep your list of research questions with you as you continue to read the scholarly literature in your area. You may find that you will be answering some of those questions as you read, which will result in revisions in your questions or help you to develop new questions that you had not previously considered—remember, at this stage, they are draft questions.

Additional Readings on Developing Research Questions

Agee, J. (2009). Developing qualitative research questions: A reflective process. *International Journal of Qualitative Studies in Education, 22*(4), 431–447.

Plano Clark, V. L., & Badiee, M. (2010). Research questions in mixed methods research. In A. Tashakkori & C. Teddlie (Eds.), *SAGE handbook of mixed methods in social and behavioral research* (2nd ed., pp. 275–304). Thousand Oaks, CA: Sage.

Maxwell, J. A. (2013). Research questions: What do you want to understand? In J. A. Maxwell (Ed.), *Qualitative research design: An interactive approach* (3rd ed., pp. 73–76). Thousand Oaks, CA: Sage.

Sample Session—Drafting Research Questions

Below is our beginning list of research questions for our research study on racial microaggressions within the college context. The italicized questions are the research questions that were eventually chosen for our investigation.

DRAFT Research Questions

1. How do African American college students talk about their experiences interacting with their college professors?

2. How do African American college students talk about their experiences interacting with other students on campus?

3. How do African American college students talk about their experiences interacting with university staff on campus?

4. How do African American college students talk about their racial microaggression experiences at their college?

5. *What are African American college students' experiences with racial microaggressions?*

6. How does the experiencing of racial microaggressions impact African American college students' sense of belonging?

7. *How does the experiencing of racial microaggressions impact African American college students' sense of racial identity?*

8. How does the experiencing of racial microaggressions impact African American college students' health choices/outcomes (e.g., drug use, sex, overeating)?

9. How do African American college students describe the strategies they use when dealing with microaggressions from faculty, other students, or college staff?

10. How do African American college students cope with the experiencing of racial microaggressions in the college context?

11. *How do African American college students cope with and regulate the emotions associated with the experiencing of racial microaggressions in the college context?*

12. What strategies do African American college students think are most useful when dealing with microaggressions from faculty, other students, or college staff?

13. How do African American college students talk about the role of approach coping while dealing with microaggressions?

14. How do African American college students talk about the role of avoidance coping while dealing with microaggressions?

15. *Where do African American college students see the boundary between microaggressions and nonmicroaggressions?*

16. How does where African American college students see the boundary between microaggressions and nonmicroaggressions influence their sense of belonging to their college?

17. How do African American college students who score high in sense of belonging to their college talk about microaggressions compared to students with a low sense of belonging?

18. What are the psychological needs of African American college students?

19. *What are the psychological need profiles of African American college students?*

20. *How do African American college students who score high on the measure of psychological needs scale address racial microaggressions?*

21. *What is the relationship among racial microaggressions, racial identity, coping and emotional regulation strategies, and psychological needs for African American college students?*

4

The Mixed Methods Proposal Introduction

So far in this book we have focused on some of the things that you need to know or should have prepared before beginning to craft the major components of your mixed methods research proposal. We know that many of you are wondering, "When are we actually going to talk about the major components of a mixed methods research proposal?" Well, the answer is right now! It was necessary to provide a discussion on theory and research questions in order to ensure that you are ready to begin writing your proposal. Now that we have examined the relevant background information needed to begin writing a mixed methods research proposal, it is time to discuss how to actually develop the major components of your proposal. Are you ready? Well, the first major component to be discussed is the mixed methods proposal introduction. Before we begin our discussion, it is necessary to state that several of the terms used in this chapter are not agreed-upon terms within the larger social science research community. For instance, instead of *purpose statement*, researchers in some fields say *problem statement*. As such, it is important for you to identify the appropriate terminology for your field. However, we urge you to focus more on the substance of our discussion of the various components rather than the labels.

● PURPOSE OF THE MIXED METHODS PROPOSAL INTRODUCTION

The mixed methods proposal introduction provides an overview of the research proposal. It is important because it is a summary of the research problem that you plan to study, but it also provides readers with the context for understanding your proposal, including why you are interested in the subject matter, why the study is important, and who is the intended audience (Bui, 2009). The introduction is essential because it serves as a guide for readers to help them understand how you plan to explore the research problem in the study as well as what will not be done in the study. Specifically, the introduction helps to provide parameters and to quell expectations regarding what will be done in the proposed study.

Usually, the introduction is the shortest of the major sections in the mixed methods proposal. However, do not let the brevity trick you into thinking that writing the introduction is a simple task. On the contrary, the introduction can often be the most difficult section to write, because it is the most succinct and sets the tone for the entire proposal. The introduction is generally the first section the reader reads. However, for you as the writer, it may not be the first section you want to write to its completion. Because the introduction describes the research problem and is an overview of what readers will discover as they read the full document, it may be easier to take an iterative approach to writing the introduction. Begin writing some components of the introduction (e.g., background of the study, statement of the problem, inquiry worldview, subjectivity statement, and mixed methods definition and rationale); then wait until your other sections are almost written to go back and continue writing the remaining components of the introduction (e.g., research goals, substantive content theory, and significance of the study). Otherwise, you may find yourself constantly rewriting the introduction in order to match what you have written in the literature review and methods sections. Or you may even find yourself constraining what you write in your literature review and methods section in order to match what you have already written in your introduction. Regardless, before you begin writing your introduction, you need to take some time to think about the major points you will convey to your readers. Use Table 4.1 to help organize your thoughts regarding your introduction. (See Chapter 8 for some general writing tips.)

Table 4.1   What Do You Consider When Developing the Mixed Methods Introduction?

	Questions to Consider	Possible Responses/Approaches
1	What is your study about? What do you want readers to know about your study?	• Research problem • Research goals
2	What are the goals of your study?	• Predict • Explain • Generate theory • Understand phenomena • Test new approach
3	How did you become interested in this research area?	• Personal experience • Previous research experience • Trending issue
4	What theories will you use to help guide your investigation?	• Inquiry worldviews • Substantive content theories
5	How do you define mixed methods research?	• Focus on methods • Focus on methodology • Focus on methods and philosophy • Focus on multiple ways of seeing the social world
6	What mixed methods research design will you use for your study? Why?	• Exploratory sequential • Explanatory sequential • Concurrent parallel • Embedded • Multiphase
7	How does your study fulfill a research need? What makes your research study different from other studies in the field?	• New population of interest • Different theoretical lens • Novel research methods
8	Who is your intended audience?	• Researchers • Policy makers • Practitioners • Funding agency • Dissertation committee

● COMPONENTS OF THE MIXED METHODS PROPOSAL INTRODUCTION

The order in which the components of the introduction appear in a mixed methods proposal may vary depending upon the academic discipline, a person's individual writing style, or the proposal's subject matter. Make sure you consult with your appropriate authorities (e.g., academic advisor) before embarking upon the introduction writing process. As such, the organization and length of introductions will vary. However, all mixed methods proposals should address each of the following components in some way: background of the study, theoretical framework (including subjectivity statement), purpose of the study (statement of the problem, rationale for study), goal of the research, mixed methods definition, mixed methods rationale, and significance of the study. See Table 4.2 for a summary of the components of the mixed methods introduction. A detailed example of the introduction, including all of its components, will be featured at the end of the chapter in the Sample Session section.

Table 4.2 Defining the Components of the Mixed Methods Introduction

Introduction Sections	Introduction Subsections	Descriptions
Background of the Study		A brief history of the research area that generally focuses on big theoretical, empirical, and/or methodological trends. It can also include current events.
Theoretical Framework		A discussion of the inquiry worldview(s), your subjectivity statement, and possible substantive content theories that guide your research study.
	Inquiry Worldview	A description of how you understand and interpret the research process.
	Subjectivity Statement	A description of your personal connection to the research area and topic, and possibly also your experiences utilizing the research methods.
	Substantive Content Theories	A brief discussion of the theories that guide your research.

Introduction Sections	Introduction Subsections	Descriptions
Purpose Statement		A comprehensive, yet succinct, summary of the rationale for the research proposal.
	Statement of the Problem	A description of the issue that you will explore in your research proposal. The reasons for engaging in your research study.
	Goal of the Research	What you would like your research to accomplish.
	Mixed Methods Definition	The definition of mixed methods that will be used in your research proposal.
	Mixed Methods Rationale	A brief description of your mixed methods design and your reason for using a mixed methods design.
Significance of the Study		The reasons the research study is necessary, important, and timely.

Background of the Study

Before you can discuss your research topic, it is necessary to provide some context for your area of interest. The *background of the study* allows you to discuss the big issues that are related to your topic. You should think of this section as a brief history of the subject that you are interested in exploring. It is also important for you to provide a brief summary of how the research problem has been explored in the research literature. The background is necessary because it helps the readers to better understand the larger historical issues that are associated with your research topic. For instance, if your research study explores closing the achievement gap and school policy, it may be useful for you to provide a discussion of the implementation of the No Child Left Behind Act (2001) and the recent Common Core State Standards initiative (http://www.corestandards.org/) in order to demonstrate the various ways in which policy has been used to attempt to address the achievement gap. Doing so would allow you to easily explain why your proposed study is necessary and is a logical extension of the research literature.

Theoretical Framework

As discussed in Chapter 2 of this book, the *theoretical framework* provides a conceptual foundation for your study; it consists of your inquiry worldview, your subjectivity statement, and the substantive theories used in your study. Within the introduction, it is necessary for you to describe the role that theory will play in your study, particularly how it will be used in conjunction with your research design and data analysis. It is important to note that the placement of the theoretical framework discussion in a research proposal varies by discipline. Some fields prefer this discussion to occur within the introduction, while others discuss the theoretical framework within the literature review or methods sections. However, for our discussion throughout this book, the theoretical framework is placed within the introduction and revisited within the literature review and methods sections.

Inquiry Worldview

The first component of the theoretical framework is the inquiry worldview, your beliefs about how you see, understand, and interpret how research investigations work. As we discussed in Chapter 2, the inquiry worldview can be seen as a global or umbrella theory that guides your general understanding about knowledge and impacts all elements of the research proposal. The inquiry worldview helps to frame your thinking and provides readers with a general template of how you will address the components of the research study. For example, if using a transformative/participatory lens, this indicates that you believe that your participants will play an active role in guiding the research process. In addition, a goal of your study will be to make change(s). Thus, if you were studying the impact of the closing of rural hospitals and the subsequent creation of medical deserts, using a transformative/participatory lens would suggest that you would be actively engaged with members of the rural communities that have been impacted by the closing of the hospitals. In addition, an ultimate goal of your research might be to help find/create alternate means for the participants to access health care.

Subjectivity Statement

When choosing a research topic, we generally think about our own personal experiences. We then use those experiences to connect to a particular issue. The subjectivity statement is a personal explanation of how you are connected to your research topic and is part of your theoretical framework. In particular, it highlights any experiences you may have with the subject area. It also serves as a means of disclosing any relationships you may have with the topic being explored. For example, if you were interested in studying group counseling techniques for adults who are suffering from depression, it would be important to discuss why you are interested in that topic. In your subjectivity statement, you may describe how you or a family member suffered from depression or how you worked at a clinic that treated veterans suffering from depression. Your experience with depression could potentially serve as a hindrance or a benefit to your research study. This disclosure is important because it helps to reveal any biases, attachments, or insights you may have to the topic and research study.

Substantive Content Theories

The last important aspect of the theoretical framework is substantive content theories, which are the specific theories you will use to help guide your inquiry. Substantive content theories are derived from your larger research literature and are used to help explain phenomena. It is important to include substantive content theories within your theoretical framework in order to provide a connection to a particular research literature and to help situate your study within it. For example, if you were examining the spiritual development of emerging adults, it would be important for you to include a discussion of a relevant theory or theories on spirituality, such as Fowler's stages of faith development (Fowler, 1981). It is important to include a discussion of such a theory within the theoretical framework, because the theory will play an integral role in your data collection (i.e., collecting data from participants who represent the various stages) and data analysis (i.e., analyzing the data and categorizing the participants according to the stages of development) while making a connection to the research literature.

Purpose Statement

Within the introduction of the mixed methods research proposal, it is imperative that you clearly describe why you are proposing this particular research study. This description is known as the research *purpose statement* (or statement of the problem in some fields). The purpose of the study summarizes the problem area, the reasons your study is needed, the goals of your study, and how you will accomplish your goals. The purpose statement can be viewed as the most succinct summary of your mixed methods research proposal, suggesting that readers should be able to read your purpose statement and have a general understanding of your entire proposal. See Table 4.3 for general

Table 4.3 Characteristics of the Purpose Statement

1.	Written in clear, nontechnical language, avoiding jargon.
2.	Stimulates the reader's interest.
3.	Succinct and limited in scope for a manageable research study.
4.	Clearly describes the general goals of the study, including research design.

characteristics of a purpose statement. When discussing the purpose, it is also necessary to provide specific information, including a statement of the problem, the goal of the research, your definition of mixed methods, and your rationale for using mixed methods.

Statement of the Problem

The *statement of the problem* draws upon the background of the study (as well as the extant research literature) and describes the main issue(s) to be explored in your mixed methods research study. In other words, the statement of the problem succinctly states your research problem(s) or the issues/areas of concern that you would like to investigate. The statement of the problem also discusses gaps in the research literature as well as the consequences for not addressing the problem, helping make the case for why your study is needed.

Goal of the Research

The *goal of the research* (also referred as the purpose statement or research aims in some fields) is closely aligned with the statement of the problem. In developing the goal of the research, it is necessary for you to directly address the issue that is outlined in the statement of the problem. Your goal statement will explain how your study will attempt to address the need that you described in the statement of the problem. There are various ways in which any particular problem can be explored and examined. As previously mentioned, according to Newman et al. (2003), there are eight reasons for conducting research: to predict, add to knowledge, measure change, understand phenomena, test new ideas, generate new ideas, inform constituencies, and examine the past. Thus, it is important for you to decide upon the reason(s) for engaging in the research study and specify the reason(s) within your proposal.

Defining Mixed Methods

In the purpose statement, it is important to provide a brief description of how you are *defining mixed methods*. (For various definitions of mixed methods research, see Johnson, Onwuegbuzie, & Turner, 2007.) There exists a variety of viewpoints on the definition and implementation of mixed methods. For example, some researchers view mixed methods in terms of multiple ways of seeing the social world (Greene, 2007) while others focus on methodology including the roles of quantitative and qualitative research (Johnson et al., 2007). Thus, it is essential that you choose the definition that most closely aligns with your own perspectives regarding mixed methods research. It is not expected that you will go into detail, as such a discussion should be saved for your research methods section (to be discussed in Chapter 7). However, it is important for you to disclose to the readers how you are conceptualizing mixed methods. This will allow you to provide a methodological context for your readers.

Mixed Methods Rationale

In addition to providing your definition of mixed methods research, it is also necessary for you to briefly mention your *mixed methods rationale*, or the specific mixed methods design that you anticipate using and why this mixed methods design is most relevant for your study. In doing so, it would be helpful to consider Greene, Caracelli, and Graham's (1989) reasons for conducting mixed methods research as discussed in Chapter 1:

- triangulation (using quantitative and qualitative methods to demonstrate convergence or explain a lack of convergence),

- complementarity (using qualitative and quantitative methods to examine overlapping but different aspects),

- development (using quantitative and qualitative methods sequentially with one method informing the other method),

- initiation (using one method to discover or explore contradictory findings that resulted from the other method), and

- expansion (using one method to extend a study).

Again, it is not expected that you go into detail, as such a discussion is most necessary in the methods section (to be discussed in Chapter 7). However, this approach will allow you to provide a sneak peak into your research methods as well as give insight into the thought processes behind your choice of a mixed methods design. Writing the mixed methods rationale can be difficult if you have not already planned out your research methods. This is another reason why you should take an iterative approach to writing your introduction, and not complete it until after you have carefully thought out your methods section.

Significance of the Study

The *significance of the study* provides the answer to the infamous phrase, "So what?" Your readers will want to know if engaging in this research is really worth your time conducting, and more important, worth their time reading. As such, the significance of the study serves to provide a rationale as to why your proposed research topic is worthy of being explored. In describing your significance, you must state how your research study is novel as well as how it will make a significant contribution to your field. In addition, this statement serves as the closer for your introduction. You want your readers to walk away from your introduction knowing that your study is relevant, timely, and necessary for your field.

Other Potential Components

There are some other potential components of the introduction that we have not discussed including research questions, definitions, ethical considerations, limitations, and delimitations. We did not include these topics in our discussion, because they are not always included in the introduction. The inclusion of such topics is variable, depending upon the requirements of external authorities (e.g., discipline, funding agency, advisor). However, we do recognize that the inclusion of research questions, definitions, ethical considerations, and limitations are standard practice for many research fields, particularly within dissertations. Specifically, some research fields encourage the initial presentation of the research questions within the introduction in order to help provide the readers with a better understanding of the overall purpose of the study. The research questions are then later explored in detail within the literature review and methods section. We prefer to rely on the purpose statement to provide the initial description, with a detailed discussion of the research questions within the methods section. Likewise, some fields prefer to provide definitions for difficult terms and constructs within the introduction. We prefer to provide detailed definitions within the proposal in context. In other words, whenever you introduce a term, you should provide a proper definition for your readers.

Also, in some fields it is common to discuss ethical considerations (e.g., personal connections with participants, deception within an experiment, medical side effects) within the introduction. We do think that it is important to discuss ethical considerations; however, we feel that such a discussion should be intertwined within other sections such as the subjectivity statement (e.g., personal connections), research methods (e.g., participant description, procedures), or even the appendices (e.g., copy of institutional review board research application). In addition, many people like to discuss the research limitations within the introduction. We do not find it helpful to include the limitations within the introduction, because the reader has not yet had a chance to see the full research study. Discussing the limitations within the introduction is premature and can potentially provide readers with a negative perception before they get the chance to actually read your full proposal. You do not want your readers to be biased against your work before they get a chance to read about it! Similarly, it is better to discuss the delimitations—boundaries of the study—in later sections as well. Again, the manner in which the introduction is composed varies greatly by discipline, department, funding agency, and/or advisor.

PRACTICE SESSION

Guided Questions

The following questions will assist you in thinking about several components of the introduction of the mixed methods proposal. Specifically, we want you to think about the background of the study, the theoretical perspective (subjectivity statement), the purpose statement (research problem area), and the significance of the study, three of the more important components of the introduction.

Background of the Study

1. What does the literature say about your research area?
2. What are the current research trends surrounding your area?
3. What are the big issues associated with your topic?

Subjectivity

1. How do you identify yourself in relation to your research?
2. What identities do you bring to the topic with regard to who you are (e.g., age, race/ethnicity, gender, abilities, personal experiences, cultural history) that will help readers understand your thinking?
3. What perspectives do you bring to your writing and research?
4. Which inquiry worldviews most closely align with your way of thinking?

Problem Area

1. What is the problem area?
2. What brought the problem area to your attention?
3. Is the problem area in the mainstream of your field of study? Explain.
4. Is there a substantial body of literature on the problem area? Explain.
5. Is the problem timely? Explain.

Significance

1. Why does this area need exploration?
2. Why is the proposed study important?
3. What potential impact would this research have in your field?

Mixed Methods Introduction Writing Activity

Now that you have had time to think about the various components of the introduction of your proposal, we would like you to begin drafting these various components. First, we would like you to draft an abbreviated discussion on the background of the study. Next, we would like you to draft your theoretical framework, including a discussion of the inquiry worldview, subjectivity statement, and substantive content theories. Third, we would like you to begin working on your purpose statement, including a statement of the problem, goals of the research, mixed methods definition, and mixed methods rationale. Last, we would like you to draft a discussion regarding the significance of the study.

Additional Readings on Writing the Mixed Methods Proposal Introduction

Bloomberg, L. D., & Volpe, M. (2012). *Completing your qualitative dissertation: A road map from beginning to end* (2nd ed.). Thousand Oaks, CA: Sage.

Booth, W. C., Colomb, G. G., & Williams, J. M. (2008). *The craft of research* (3rd ed.). Chicago, IL: University of Chicago Press.

Queen's University, Belfast. (n.d.). *The research proposal*. Retrieved from http://www.qub.ac.uk/schools/SchoolofEducation/Research/Doctoral ResearchCentre/PhD/TheResearchProposal/

University of Southern California. (n.d.). *Writing guide*. Retrieved from http://libguides.usc.edu/writingguide

Sample Session—Mixed Methods Introduction

Below are our responses to the mixed methods introduction writing activity regarding our racial microaggressions study. Because the subjectivity statement is based upon personal experiences, each author provided his or her own statement. However, the remaining components are joint statements, because they focus specifically on the topic of the research study.

Background of the Study

On October 1, 1962, President John F. Kennedy federalized the Mississippi National Guard to help escort James Meredith, an African American, onto the University of Mississippi campus. Upon Meredith's arrival, he found an angry mob shouting a series of racial slurs. He continued to receive this type of treatment until he graduated in 1963 (McGee, 2013). Because of Meredith's sacrifice, as well as the sacrifices of many others, African Americans and other racial/ethnic minority groups can now enroll and matriculate in predominately White universities without the fear of being accosted by the racial slurs of racist angry mobs. However, students of color can still be subjected to more subtle forms of racism. Recently, expressions of racism on college campuses, and in society in general, have become more sophisticated, morphing from overt expressions that are relatively easy to detect to more muted forms of racism that are subtle and often overlooked. One aspect of this contemporary form of racism is known as racial microaggressions.

Racial microaggressions can be defined as "brief, everyday exchanges that send denigrating messages to people of color because they belong to a racial minority group" (Sue, Capodilupo, Torino, Bucceri, Holder, Nadal, & Esquilin, 2007, p. 273). Racial microaggressions are further described as being frequently and automatically expressed by majority group members and manifested as "subtle snubs or dismissive looks, gestures, and tones" (Sue et al., p. 273), such as telling an African American that "I don't think of you as Black," suggesting that you are denying this person's racialized experience as an African American.

Racial microaggressions are present in all contexts, including the educational context. Studies have examined racial microaggressions in a variety of educational contexts, including high school (Allen, 2010) and college (Yosso, Smith, Ceja, & Solórzano, 2009). Racial microaggressions have been negatively associated with the emotional well-being of students of color (Wang, Leu, & Shoda, 2011), often causing extreme stress (Smith, Hung, & Franklin, 2011). A growing area of research has focused on racial microaggressions within the college environment, particularly among college students. The experiences of students of color on college campus are even receiving national attention. Recently, *Time* magazine featured an article by John McWhorter (2014) titled "Microaggression Is the New Racism on Campus." Similarly, the *New York Times* featured an article by Tanzina Vega (2014) called "Students See Many Slights as Racial Microaggressions." Because microaggressions are becoming pervasive on college campuses,

(Continued)

(Continued)

it is important to better understand how African Americans experience and are being impacted by racial microaggressions.

Theoretical Framework

The following theories and experiences have shaped our perspective and help guide our approach to this research study. These theories and experiences will be used to assist us in better understanding African American college students' experiencing of racial microaggressions within the PWI context.

Inquiry Worldview

Our work is situated within a critical framework. Specifically, we are guided by critical race theory (CRT), which places race as the center of focus and explores the transformations of the relationships among race, racism, and power (Bell, 1992; Delgado & Stefancic, 2012). CRT is composed of six tenets:

- *Counterstorytelling* is the use of narratives that challenge majority perspective by focusing on the experiences of marginalized groups (Delgado, 1989).
- The *permanence of racism* investigates the pervasiveness of racism (Bell, 1992).
- The *critique of liberalism* challenges liberal discourses regarding colorblindness (not seeing race), meritocracy (beliefs of equal access and opportunity), and incremental change (the need to make small changes rather than systematic changes) (Gotanda, 1991).
- *Interest convergence* explores how racial progress occurs only when it is beneficial to Whites (Bell, 1980).
- *Intersectionality* examines the intersection of identities, specifically race and gender (Crenshaw, 1989).
- *Whiteness as property* explores White privilege (Harris, 1993).

Within the educational system, CRT is frequently used to expose African Americans' experiences of racism in the educational context, both blatant and subtle, as well as used to make change and bring about equity (DeCuir & Dixson, 2004; Ladson-Billings & Tate, 1995). We will use a CRT lens to help guide our research process, including the data collection and analysis processes.

Subjectivity Statement

I (Jessica DeCuir-Gunby) attended predominately White universities in the South, where it was common for African American students to experience racial microaggressions from both their peers and professors. As an African American, I too experienced racial microaggressions in those contexts. Because of my personal experience, I am very sensitive to issues of race and racism with the college context. As such, I am interested in learning how African American students on predominately White college campuses experience and deal with racial microaggressions in this supposed postracial context. I am a trained social scientist with research and methodological interests in racial identity development and mixed methods research. In addition, the CRT perspective informs my approach to research.

As a White male, who is progressively getting older, I (Paul Schutz) have tried to unpack the "gifts" that I have received due to my birth in this particular social historical context. Thus, for the most part, my life is one where I have played the role of being the "norm," while also attempting to problematize that "norm-ness" wherever possible. To that end, I am also informed by CRT, which for me brings important understanding to the racial microaggressions experienced by college students. In addition, I am a trained social scientist with interests in learning, motivation, and emotion. As such, I bring to this research project an interest in research as problem solving within a social historical context, with a focus on social justice.

Substantive Content Theories

In addition to being guided by CRT and our personal experiences, we are also guided by theories and their associated assumptions. One theory is the multidimensional model of racial identity (MMRI) (Sellers, Smith, Shelton, Rowley, & Chavous, 1998). The MMRI conceptualizes Black racial identity as a multidimensional construct. It assumes that racial identity is situationally influenced yet somewhat stable. One assumption of this theory is that every individual has multiple identities within some type of hierarchical structure, and that some identities are more important than others. Another assumption is that personal perception of racial identity is the most valid indicator of identity. The MMRI focuses on the current status of an individual's racial identity rather than on the development of identity over time.

A theorist with an MMRI perspective attempts to explain the variety of ways in which Black racial identity is manifested. In order to empirically test the theory, the MMRI has been operationalized through the creation of several inventories, including the *Multidimensional Inventory of Black Identity* (MIBI) (Sellers, Rowley, Chavous, Shelton, & Smith, 1997) and the *Multidimensional Inventory of Black Identity–teen* (MIBI-t) (Scottham, Sellers, & Nguyen, 2008). We intend to utilize the MMRI in the creation of our research study focusing on African American college students' experiences of racial microaggressions.

A second theory that informs our work is self-determination theory (SDT). Researchers who are informed by SDT tend to assume that the roots of human motivation and well-being are tied to innate psychological needs for autonomy, competence, and relatedness (Deci & Ryan, 2000; Ryan, Huta, & Deci, 2008). Specifically, *autonomy* refers to the human need to determine, control, and organize your own behavior and goals, or to see yourself as having control in your world. *Competence* refers to the human need to learn and master challenging tasks or to be good at some activities. Finally, *relatedness* refers to the human need to feel attached to others or to be meaningfully involved in relationships with other humans.

(Continued)

(Continued)

From this perspective, having these needs met within the college context is a necessary condition for psychological growth, integrity, and well-being. This would suggest that within social historical contexts, activities and individuals who provide support to college students in meeting those basic needs will help the natural growth processes, whereas contexts and individuals who constrain or inhibit the meeting of those needs (e.g., through the use of racial microaggressions) tend to be associated with lower motivation, performance, and psychological well-being (Deci & Ryan, 2000; Ryan et al., 2008).

Purpose Statement

The following discussion describes what we intend to do in our study as well as why our study is relevant.

Statement of the Problem

African American students frequently experience racial microaggressions within predominately White university settings. These experiences can impact their emerging racial identity as well as require them to develop appropriate coping and emotional regulation skills for dealing with racism. Ultimately, experiencing racial microaggressions can impact their ability to meet their psychological needs for autonomy, competence, and relatedness within the college context (Deci & Ryan, 2000; Ryan et al., 2008).

Goals of the Research

The purpose of this research project is four-fold. The first goal is to better understand how African American students experience racial microaggressions within the college context. The second goal is to explore how students' racial identity influences their experiencing of racial microaggressions. The third goal is to explore how students cope with and regulate the emotions associated with experiencing racial microaggressions within the college context. The final goal is to investigate the relationships among racial microaggressions, racial identity, coping and emotional regulation, and innate psychological needs for autonomy, competence, and relatedness during their college experience. We will draw implications to help students to better recognize and more positively address racial microaggressions within the college context.

Mixed Methods Definition and Rationale

In order to engage in this study, we will be taking a mixed methods approach. We will be guided by Tashakkori and Creswell's (2007) definition of mixed methods as "research in which the investigator collects and analyzes data, integrates the findings, and draws inferences using both qualitative and quantitative approaches or methods in a single study or program of inquiry" (p. 4). A mixed methods approach will be used for our study because we will explore both the breadth and depth of African American college students' experience with racial microaggressions. Mixed methods research allows us to access a large number of participants through surveys and engage in in-depth interviews with a smaller number of participants. The integrated findings will provide for a more nuanced interpretation of the participants' experiences.

Significance of the Study

The proposed study is significant in the field of educational psychology in various ways. First, little research examines how issues of racism, or racial microaggressions specifically, impact the coping skills, emotional regulation, and basic psychological needs of African American students at college. Second, there is a paucity of race-focused research (i.e., research focused on racial constructs) in the larger area of motivation in education; this study would be able to make a significant contribution to the motivation literature. Last, there are a limited number of research studies within the area of racial microaggressions and psychological needs at college that have been conducted using mixed methods approaches; this study will make a significant methodological contribution.

INTRODUCTION REFERENCES   ●

Allen, Q. (2010). Racial microaggressions: The schooling experiences of Black middle-class males in Arizona's secondary schools. *Journal of African American Males in Education, 1*(2), 125–142.

Bell, D. (1992). Racial realism. *Connecticut Law Review, 24*(2), 363–379.

Bell, D. (1993). *Faces at the bottom of the well: The permanence of racism.* New York, NY: Basic Books.

Bell, D. A. (1980). *Brown v. Board of Education* and the interest-convergence dilemma. *Harvard Law Review, 93*(3), 518–533.

Crenshaw, K. (1989). Demarginalizing the intersection of race and sex: A Black feminist critique of antidiscrimination doctrine, feminist theory and anti-racist politics. *University of Chicago Legal Forum,* 139–167.

Deci, E. L., & Ryan, R. M. (2000). The "what" and "why" of goal pursuits: Human needs and the self-determination of behavior. *Psychological Inquiry, 11,* 227–268.

DeCuir, J., & Dixson, A. (2004). "So when it comes out, they aren't that surprised that it is there": Using critical race theory as a tool of analysis of race and racism in education. *Educational Researcher, 33*(5), 26–31.

Delgado, R. (1989). Storytelling for oppositionists and others: A plea for narrative. *Michigan Law Review, 87,* 2411–2441.

Delgado, R., & Stefancic, J. (2012). *Critical race theory: An introduction* (2nd ed.). New York: New York University Press.

Gotanda, N. (1991). A critique of "Our constitution is color-blind." *Stanford Law Review*, *44*, 1–68.

Harris, C. (1993). Whiteness as property. *Harvard Law Review, 106*(8), 1707–1791.

Ladson-Billings, G., & Tate, W. F. (1995). Towards a critical race theory of education. *Teachers College Record, 97*(1), 47–68.

McGee, M. C. (2013). *James Meredith: Warrior and the America that created him.* New York, NY: Praeger.

McWhorter, J. (2014, March 21). Microaggression is the new racism on campus. *Time.* Retrieved from http://time.com/32618/microaggression-is-the-new-racism-on-campus/

Ryan, R. M., Huta, V., & Deci, E. L. (2008). Living well: A self-determination theory perspective on eudaimonia. *Journal of Happiness Studies, 9*, 139–170.

Sellers, R. M., Rowley S. A. J., Chavous, T. M., Shelton, J. N., & Smith, M. A. (1997). Multidimensional Inventory of Black Identity: A preliminary investigation of reliability and construct validity. *Journal of Personality and Social Psychology, 73*, 805–815.

Sellers, R. M., Smith, M. A., Shelton, J. N., Rowley, S. A. J., & Chavous, T. M. (1998). Multidimensional Model of Racial Identity: A reconceptualization of African American racial identity. *Personality and Social Psychology Review, 2(1)*, 18–39.

Smith, W. A., Hung, M., & Franklin, J. D. (2011). Racial battle fatigue and the miseducation of Black men: Racial microaggressions, societal problems, and environmental stress. *Journal of Negro Education, 80*(1), 63–82.

Sue, D., Capodilupo, C., Torino, G., Bucceri, J., Holder, A., Nadal, K., & Esquilin, M. (2007). Racial microaggressions in everyday life: Implications for clinical practice. *American Psychologist, 62*(4), 271–286.

Tashakkori, A., & Creswell, J. W. (2007). The new era of mixed methods. *Journal of Mixed Methods Research, 1*, 3–7.

Vega, T. (2014, March 21). Students see many slights as racial microaggressions. *New York Times.* Retrieved from http://www.nytimes.com/2014/03/22/us/as-diversity-increases-slights-get-subtler-but-still-sting.html

Wang, J., Leu, J., & Shoda, Y. (2011). When the seemingly innocuous "stings": Racial microaggressions and their emotional consequences. *Personality and Social Psychology Bulletin, 37*(12), 1666–1678.

Yosso, T. J., Smith, W. A., Ceja, M., & Solórzano, D. G. (2009). Critical race theory, racial microaggressions, and campus racial climate for Latina/o undergraduates. *Harvard Educational Review, 79*(4), 659–691.

5

The Literature Review

Situating Your Mixed Methods Study in the Larger Context

Objectives

1. To develop an understanding of the role of the literature review in a mixed methods proposal.

2. To identify ways to prepare, organize, and write your literature review.

3. To identify what components you will need for your literature review.

4. To learn how to create a detailed outline for your literature review.

In the last chapter we focused on developing the introduction of your research proposal, the section where you will talk about the importance and purpose of your mixed methods study. Now it is time for you to begin to think about your research problem within the context of the existing scholarly literature. In order to do so, we will ask you to address the following questions: What do scholars say about the research on your topic? What methodological approaches have been used to address your research problem? Where does your research study fit within the current research literature? The answers to these questions are essential to crafting a relevant and thorough literature review for your mixed methods proposal. Remember, your goal for your literature review is to make the case for why your research study is needed and how your mixed methods study will add to the literature in your area of interest.

● THE ROLE OF THE LITERATURE REVIEW

As a completed document, the literature review section of a proposal is the place where you review, critique, and synthesize the literature for your topics of interest with the goal of generating new perspectives related to your research problem(s) (Torraco, 2005). Thus, the literature review plays an important role in the mixed methods proposal. It helps to identify and explain the major themes associated with your research topic. Moreover, the literature review synthesizes and extends the literature in your topic area and leads the reader to the research questions you will attempt to answer using your mixed methods design. Thus, the literature review is where you develop your substantive content theory (see Chapter 2). Basically this involves developing, understanding, and synthesizing a unique look at how others have talked about and researched your problem of interest. To help you with the creation of your literature review, we have divided the rest of this chapter into three sections: (1) preparing and organizing your research literature, (2) the components of the literature review, and (3) writing your literature review.

● PREPARING AND ORGANIZING YOUR RESEARCH LITERATURE

Before you begin writing your literature review, it is important for you to search for literature in a variety of outlets as well as develop a plan for organizing that literature. In addition, it is important to make a distinction between (1) the act of reviewing the literature and (2) what will actually be written in the literature review section of your proposal. For example, as you are reviewing the literature, you will discover what methods other researchers have used to investigate your problem of interest, but unless you are doing a study on research methods, most of what you find out about research methods will end up in your methods section, not in the literature review section of your proposal.

However, your synthesis of the research results using those methods will be included in your literature review section. With that in mind, in this section we provide you with strategies regarding ways of searching your literature, what to look for in that literature, and how to organize what you find.

How to Search for Literature

One of the most challenging aspects of writing a literature review is knowing where and how to begin. The first place to begin is to actually locate the relevant literature in your research topic area. In Table 5.1

Table 5.1 What Do You Look for While Preparing Your Literature Review?

Topic Areas	What do you look for while preparing your literature review?
What writing should you look for?	• Theoretical writings that address different theoretical frameworks (e.g., thought pieces, theoretical reviews)
	• Data-driven empirical research writings: quantitative (e.g., descriptive, inferential), qualitative (e.g., interview, ethnographic), and mixed methods (e.g., interviews + survey data)
	• Review writings (e.g., meta-analysis, reviews of the literature)
How do you identify and clarify your topic area?	• Key constructs and how different scholars define constructs. Are there meaningful differences in how particular or similar constructs are defined? What definitions fit with your emerging conceptual framework? Where are the gaps and limitations in the literature?
	• What researchers have found about your constructs of interest and their relationships with other constructs. What constructs appear not to be applicable? Why might they not be related?
	• Trends, patterns, and themes in your readings. How have the constructs emerged and changed and over time? Where do you think the trends, patterns, and themes are headed in the future?

(Continued)

Table 5.1   (Continued)

Topic Areas	What do you look for while preparing your literature review?
How do you organize your database?	• Develop a system for organizing the material (i.e., chapters, articles, books) that you collect and a system for organizing the content of your review.
	• Develop a system for keeping track of the references you will be using in your proposal.

we highlight some of the things you should be looking for while searching your literature, beginning with the type of readings to look for. Generally, the readings you will be using to create and organize your literature will tend to fall into three basic categories: theoretical writings, empirical studies, and reviews.

First, there are theoretical writings. These writings generally focus on the development of new theoretical ideas that explain the results of a number of studies. As such, they usually do not concentrate on the results of single studies but on using the results of a number of studies to critique or improve particular theoretical frameworks. In most disciplines there are journals that publish theoretical articles in addition to empirical articles as well as some journals that are dedicated to publishing only theoretical or conceptual articles. Another resource for more theoretical pieces would be books and chapters in edited books. The focus in these writings is the development or explication of theoretical positions related to particular topic areas. These writings are useful to help you identify and create your own substantive content theory. They are also helpful in locating a variety of resources on your topic. The reference sections of such writings can be tremendous resources.

The second type of literature is data-driven research writings or empirical studies. Generally, these are journal articles that focus on a single study or a series of studies dealing with a particular set of research questions. When reading such articles, keep track of what constructs researchers are investigating, the consistent findings across studies you review, and the unique findings from particular studies. In addition to the research findings, these articles will also include the researchers' methods sections, which will describe what the researchers did to examine their phenomenon of interest (what procedures, measures, methods, etc. were used). Pay special attention to the research methods and methodologies used in research articles: What do the researchers identify as the strengths and weakness of the methods they used? What approaches seem useful or problematic? What approaches may be useful to answer the current version of your research questions? Also keep track of what the researcher found. Are different researchers coming up with similar findings? Is there agreement? Are researchers coming up with different findings? Is there disagreement? How do researchers talk about the agreement or disagreement? Your answers to those questions may help you to find a place where you can add to the literature.

The researchers' discussion of their research methods and results will help you to think about your own research questions. In addition, keep track of any measures or instruments that were developed or used. What reliability and validity evidence about those instruments was provided? Are the characteristics of their participants similar to those of the participants you would like to use? For quantitative approaches, what measures were used, what validity and reliability information was provided, and how were their measures aligned with your definition of the constructs? For qualitative approaches, what types of data were collected, how was the data collected and analyzed, and what methodological perspectives informed the scholars' work? For mixed methods approaches, how did they talk about their mixed methods study, and how did they integrate the quantitative and qualitative data in both the data collection and analysis stages? How did theory inform both their data collection and analysis?

These articles are also helpful because they can serve as models for how you will eventually write up the findings for your proposed study. Again, remember you will use your research questions to guide your research methods and methodology decisions. As such, you should always keep an updated draft of your research questions close by. So keep that file open on your computer, print them out and tape them to your computer monitor, or do whatever works for you. To reiterate, as you are working on your literature review, the draft of your research questions should always be within arm's reach. This way you can see if other researchers are researching similar research questions, or you may find information that will help you to revise your research questions.

Finally, the third type of literature to locate is the available reviews of existing literature on topics. There are generally two types of these writings—a review of the literature and a meta-analysis. There are journals in some areas that will publish reviews of the literature articles, where the authors review and extend the research in a particular topic area. You may also find such reviews in edited book chapters as well. In essence, the authors of these publications, guided by their theoretical frameworks, synthesize the literature in an area, much like you will be doing for the literature review part of your proposal. As such, if you can find one that is well thought out and well written, you can also use it as a model for how your literature review should look.

The meta-analysis is a particular type of review article, where the goal is to examine a number of research articles, dissertations, and other potentially unpublished research by converting the researchers' findings from different studies to a common effect size statistic allowing comparisons across studies. Recently, some have also attempted to include qualitative and mixed methods research in these review articles (Sandelowski & Barroso, 2006; Timulak, 2014). This allows the author(s) to make comparisons across studies. Thus, in addition to the findings, meta-analyses can help you to get an understanding of what effect sizes you might expect for the quantitative part of your mixed methods study, which will help you with your power analysis. However, it is important to keep in mind that in order for a meta-analysis to be written, there would need to be a sufficient amount of research in a topic area. This means that if you are looking into an area where there is not a lot of research, it may be hard to find a meta-analysis. (For full discussions of meta-analyses, see Glass, MacGaw, & Smith, 1984; Lipsey & Wilson, 2001.)

How to Identify and Clarify Your Topic Area

With the aforementioned types of readings in mind, we next provide you with some suggestions for how to proceed with your literature review. To begin with, you have probably already accumulated some literature. To put it another way, what got you interested in this problem? So, check the papers you have written for classes or other course assignments and the readings that might be related. What did you read for those assignments? Also, remember that from this point on, when possible, try to write class papers, unpublished conference proposals, or draft papers on topics that are related to your research problem of interest. Your goal is to become an expert in your topic area as well as other related areas. So read, read, and then read some more.

You may remember in Chapter 2 we suggested that the process of writing a literature review is somewhat like joining a conversation that has been going on for some time. In using that analogy, it is important to remember that as a new person in the conversation, it is your responsibility to develop an understanding of what has been discussed, who are the key players in the discussion, and where the discussion might be headed. To do so we suggest you start with the most current research and work your way back to origins of the key constructs and people in your topic area and related areas. In other words, how are the scholars defining the key constructs? Who is doing the defining? What are the research methods and methodologies they are using in your topic area? As you are reading, identify what seem to be the major themes and key issues related to your topic. As you do so, work to reduce those themes to key words and phrases that you can use to search electronic databases for additional readings. Meanwhile, remember it will be important to develop a search plan. For your search plan, you want to make sure you are covering all the potential literature, so be systematic in your approach.

During this phase of the process, it may be useful to use a mining analogy. For example, when mining for silver, if you are skilled miner, you may find a rich vein of silver that you want to follow wherever it might take you. This is also the case when doing a literature review. You may find a scholar or a group of scholars who are doing research that is related to your interests. These researchers will also cite other researchers who may be of interest. Thus, one article, chapter, or book may lead you to a number of other publications of interest. Thus, the process tends to be multiplicative. This means that just as a miner would follow a rich vein of silver, you will also need to follow the "rich vein" left by researcher(s) you have found. In addition, as you are following a particular vein, you will begin to find overlapping veins. It is through this process that you begin to map the research in your area of interest. The result of this process is that you will most likely begin to see that some scholars and particular written works are cited by a number of other scholars. Those articles and scholars may represent the landmark, classic studies, or seminal writings that you will need to develop the range and depth required for your comprehensive substantive content theory. You may also begin to find researchers who are working in slightly different fields of study being cited in the writings you find. It will be important to follow those veins as well. They may not only provide valuable insight to your understanding of your problem area but also provide you with invaluable ideas about research methods that you may not have found by just staying with your own topic area of interest.

For example, our own study focuses on racial microaggressions. In exploring this topic area, we have generally consulted the research literature in education, counseling, and psychology. One example of a rich vein in this research area would be the work of Sue and colleagues

(2007) in the area of counseling. However, it will be important for us to consult the work in the business literature on microinequities, a similar and related construct that focuses on the differential treatment of people of color in the workplace (Rowe, 1990). Again your job is to become an expert on your chosen topic area and to become cognizant of its sister research areas.

How to Organize Your Database

Due to the multiplicative nature of the literature review search process (i.e., in one article you may find the citations for three additional useful articles, etc.), your organization skills will be tested. Think about the organization of your literature searches on two levels. At one level is the organization of the material (i.e., chapter, articles, books) that you collect as you are reviewing the literature. At a second level is the organization of the content of your review. Your ability to organize your literature will prove to be crucial to successfully writing your literature review.

In terms of the organization of materials, things have changed over the years. In the past, many of us used our own elaborate systems, where we would pile printed copies of articles, chapters, and books based on some content categories that we developed through reading, thinking, and writing about those articles, chapters, and books. Now, we tend to do that organization via the use of electronic folders with electronic versions of our readings. The key point here is that in the beginning, when you have 5 to 10 readings, it may be fairly easy to keep track of what you have read. However, that 5 to 10 will quickly become 50 to 100 or more readings. Thus, useful organization of those documents has the potential to save you a lot of time. Whatever organizational system you use for your readings, your goal is to be able to access any piece of information that you need in a timely manner. To reach that goal, the development of a useful organization system for your readings is critical. For some people this involves using an open-source or commercial reference management software package. (For software reviews, see Gilmour & Cobus-Kuo, 2011.) For others it may mean developing their own electronic folder system. The key is finding something that works for you.

To organize the content of your review, it is important to keep in mind that it will be useful for you, as much as possible, to combine the reading of the literature with the writing about the literature. Try to be consistent in the format of your notes and writing. Look for ways of rearranging the elements derived from your analysis to identify relationships, show the main organizing principles, or show how these principles could be used to make different constructs. For some, the development of a model where you can visually diagram your constructs and the transactions among those constructs is a good way to help you organize and clarify your thinking. Many commercial writing software packages have such functionality. Again the key is finding something that works for you.

THE COMPONENTS OF THE LITERATURE REVIEW   ●

In order to prepare for the writing of your literature review, it will be important to develop an understanding of what areas should be addressed in your literature review. In Table 5.2, we describe the general areas that tend to be covered in a literature review. The areas include revisiting the statement of the problem, covering the topic, synthesizing the literature into your substantive content theory, discussing the significance of your research, and generally presenting your research questions. Before beginning our discussion, we have two points of clarification. First, Table 5.2 is not intended to suggest the order in which you would address these issues but only that these are issues that should be addressed somewhere in this section of your proposal. Second, as always, remember to be aware of your local norms (i.e., college, department, and/or advisor preferences) before you begin and as you work your way through this process.

Revisiting Your Statement of the Problem

Here, in the literature review, it can be useful to remind the reader about the importance of the problem that you would like to research. In essence, what you are attempting to do is generally set the stage for the importance of your work as you lead into your finer-grained analysis of the literature. So it may be useful to begin the literature review by revisiting your statement of the problem to set the stage and reiterate the importance of the research you are proposing.

Covering the Topic

It will also be important to situate your problem area so the reader develops a clear idea of not only what will be addressed in the proposal but also what will not be addressed, with clear rationales for the decisions you have made. As such, one goal for the literature

Table 5.2 General Areas to Cover in Your Literature Review

Areas	Issues to be Addressed in the Literature Review
Revisiting Your Statement of the Problem	• Remind the reader of your problem to set the stage for your approach to the problem.
Covering the Topic	• Clarify what has been investigated, what has not been investigated, and what could use a fresh perspective. Describe your decisions for inclusion and exclusion of literature from your review.
Synthesizing the Literature Into Your Substantive Content Theory	• Situate your research within the broader social-historical context. • Clarify what you see as the important constructs in your topic area. • Address how the key constructs are defined in the literature, and clarify how you will be defining those constructs. • Critique and synthesize the key literatures you have identified into a coherent perspective on your problem of interest. • Develop the themes and patterns that you have discovered in the readings.
Discussing the Significance of Your Research	• Argue and establish the importance of the problem area you are investigating. • Discuss what you are adding to the literature. • Discuss the potential practical significance of your proposed research. How might your study help (practically and/or theoretically) with the problem you are attempting to address?
Presenting Your Research Questions	• State the research questions you plan to investigate with the research methods you will talk about in the next section of your proposal.

review is to make sure that on the one hand you cover the important issues associated with your research topic area (e.g., key constructs, theories, and researchers as well as any conflicting theories); yet, on the other hand, it is important to understand that most likely you will not be able to cover everything related to your topic in your literature review. This suggests that you will need to make decisions about what to include in this proposal and what you will want to address in your future research and publications. One strategy for helping you make those decisions is to remember that in the final document you prepare after completing your study, what you talk about in your literature review should also be addressed in your methods, results, and discussion sections. So for example, in the literature review you will define and talk about the important constructs in your research topic area and the mixed methods you will be using to investigate that topic. Then, in the methods section you will talk about how you will collect data to study those important constructs. In the results section you will talk about what you found related to those constructs, and finally in the discussion section you will talk about the importance of what you found related to those important constructs. This makes the synthesis of your literature a key step in the process.

Synthesizing the Literature Into Your Substantive Content Theory

To develop a convincing argument, your overall goal for the literature review is to synthesize the relevant literature you have accumulated into your substantive content theory. Basically, what synthesizing involves is a combining of the theories, research, and other information you have investigated into a unique way of looking at the problem(s) you have identified. Through this process you are also critiquing the literature you are reading. For example, what is missing in the literature? What could have been done differently?

In the beginning phases of pulling the information together, you may feel like you are simply summarizing what others have thought and written about. At that point, remind yourself that you need to be able to describe and understand what others have written before you will be able to synthesize what you have found into something new. As such, in most cases, think of your early summaries as signposts on the road to a useful synthesis of the literature, but also remember they are only signposts, suggesting that more work is to be done.

The literature review is also the section where you situate your proposal within the broader social historical context. In other words, why is your study important to the overall history of issues related to your topic? Generally, you can think of your literature review as a funnel (see Figure 5.1) where you begin broadly, then work your way toward more specificity (e.g., how particular constructs are related), and finish by leading the reader to the logical conclusion, which is the importance of your approach to the problems and the research questions you have developed. As you are doing that, it is also useful to identify and define the key constructs in your topic area and how they relate to each other. In addition, you will want to clarify how you plan to use those concepts and why.

Discussing the Significance of Your Research

Also in your literature review, you will establish the significance of your research by developing and providing evidence for the importance of the problem area you are investigating and the potential practical significance of your approach to the problem. In other words, by the time the readers have finished your literature review (when they get to the bottom of the funnel), you should have convinced them that the research you are planning is exactly what should be done next to address the problem area you have identified, clarified, and defined. In essence, making the case for your mixed methods study basically

Figure 5.1   A Literature Review Funnel

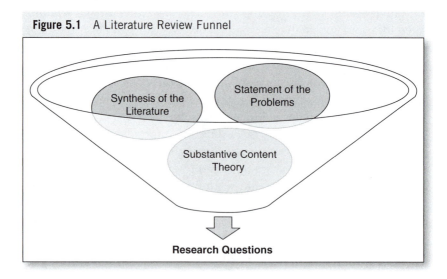

involves answering the "so what" question. To answer that question,[1] it will be useful to think in terms of three key areas: (1) How will your study add to the literature in this area? (2) What practical applications might emerge as the result of your study? (3) Why is it important to use mixed methods to answer your research questions?

Presenting Your Research Questions

Finally, it will be useful to state the research question that you plan to address in the methods section. Keep in mind that the next section of your mixed methods research proposal will be your methods section. Thus, the end of your literature review will be a great place to list or remind the reader generally about the research questions that you intend to address and how your mixed methods approach will be discussed in the methods section of your proposal.

WRITING THE LITERATURE REVIEW ●

Earlier in this chapter we reminded you that there is a difference between what you do during the process of reviewing the literature and what you actually write in the literature review section of your proposal. In the previous section, we talked a bit about the components that should appear in the research proposal, and now we will talk about some strategies for or ways of creating that text.

Identifying Patterns and Themes in the Literature

In order to identify patterns and themes in your literature, we would suggest that you borrow from a grounded theory approach and think in terms of a constant comparative analysis of the literature you are reviewing. The focus in a constant comparative, grounded theory approach is to attempt to identify the essence of the phenomenon or the area of interest (Glaser & Strauss, 1967). Thus, for our purposes here, what you would try to do is to identify the patterns and associations in the readings and attempt to synthesize and represent those finding to your committee (Maykut & Morehouse, 1994). To do this,

---

[1]The "so what" question is one you may be asked at your proposal meeting—so take care of it in the actual proposal.

generally the process is to use "open coding" to break the data—in this case your reading—into basic categories, and then to use "axial coding" to synthesize those key concepts and categories back together in new ways (Strauss & Corbin, 1990). In other words, as you are reading, thinking, and writing about the literature in your area, try to answer these questions:

- What constructs tend to keep reappearing among the scholars you are reading? How do scholars talk about the relationships among those constructs? What processes are involved in those transactions? What models are being used to explain those processes?

- What are the areas where there is agreement among the scholars you are reading? What are some areas of disagreement? How are those differences talked about in the literature?

Overall the key goal for the process of identifying patterns and themes in the literature is to develop an understanding of the literature. This simply means that in order to get to the point where you can synthesize the literature to come up with something new, you need to know and understand your research topic area of interest. The way you get to that point is through reading, thinking, and writing about what you have read and thought about. Thus effort, useful strategies, and a level of persistence are keys to success at this phase of the process.

Making Conceptual Connections With the Literature

As you are identifying patterns and themes in the literature, you should also begin the process of making new or unique connections within the literatures you are reading, thinking, and writing about. This is the creative part of the writing process, and it involves making unique claims regarding the transactions or relationships among the patterns and themes you have identified. Here are some questions to help guide you through this process:

- What are the issues, conflicts, and/or problems that scholars continue to identify? Based on your understandings, what issues, conflicts, and/or problems are the scholars missing?

- What are the gaps in the literature, or what is missing? Are there other constructs that are not being considered that may help explain the processes involved? Are there other, related areas of study that have approached these issues differently?

- What do the scholars suggest as the next area to investigate? Based on your understandings, what do you think is the next area to investigate?

Evaluating and Interpreting Literature

Throughout the process of identifying patterns and themes and making conceptual connections in your literature, it is also critical that you develop your skills at evaluating and interpreting what you are reading, thinking, and writing about. Thus, part of what is involved in synthesizing the literature is critically evaluating what you read. These questions may guide that process:

- What are the scholars claiming as the key constructs needed to explain what they are researching? What evidence do they use to support those claims?

- What do the scholars claim are the relationships among those key constructs? What evidence do they use to support those claims?

- How do the scholars situate the key constructs and relationships in the wider social historical context? What evidence do they use to support those claims?

- What are the limitations of the methods that have been used in previous research?

It is also important to keep in mind that as you are writing your literature review, you will also be making claims regarding your own substantive content theory. This means that you will be required to provide logical and/or empirical evidence for the claims you have made. Critiquing others, and seeing how they are justifying their claims, are excellent ways of honing your skills at making claims and providing evidence for those claims.

One way of getting started on this process of developing your literature review section is to develop and use a detailed outline. As you will see shortly, this involves developing, over time, a thorough plan. Remember, throughout the process of writing the literature review, the outline will be an emerging draft that will change as you read and think more about what you read. However, the value of the outline is that it will give you direction. The outline will help you to understand where you are and where you need to go.

PRACTICE SESSION

Guided Questions

As you begin to reflect upon your mixed methods study and ways you can situate your work within the research literature, think about the following questions.

1. Who are the key scholars in your topic area?
2. What are the keys constructs researchers talk about in your area?
3. What are the key theories in your area?
   a. What are the key areas of agreement regarding key constructs?
   b. What are the key areas of disagreement regarding key constructs?
4. What do the key scholars in your topic suggest as a need for future research?

Activity for Writing a Literature Review

The purpose of this activity is to help you to think critically about the literature in your area of research as well as to situate your work into that context of scholarly literature. For this activity, we would like you to create a detailed outline of your literature review.

Your outline should address the following:

- Create topic sentences for each main area of your literature review. (Keep in mind that as you continue the review process, the main areas may change.)
- Create supporting statements under each topic sentence.
- Make sure that your topic sentences and supporting statements have citations in the proper format (e.g., APA, Chicago, MLS).
- Include references within your outline. Also it is never too early to start creating your reference section, so make sure that your references are in the proper format (e.g., APA, Chicago, MLS).

Additional Readings on Writing a Literature Review

Boote, D. N., & Beile, P. (2005). Scholars before researchers: On the centrality of the dissertation literature review in research preparation. *Educational Researcher, 34*(6), 3–15.

Hart, C. (1998). *Doing a literature review: Releasing the social science research imagination.* Thousand Oaks, CA: Sage.

Hart, C. (2001). *Doing a literature search: A comprehensive guide for the social sciences.* Thousand Oaks, CA: Sage.

Glass, G. V., MacGaw, B., & Smith, M. L. (1984). *Meta-analysis in social research.* Beverly Hills, CA: Sage.

Machi, L. A., & McEvoy, B. T. (2009). *The literature review: Six steps to success.* Thousand Oaks, CA: Corwin Press.

Maykut, P. S., & Morehouse, R. E. (1994). *Beginning qualitative research: A philosophic and practical guide* (vol. 6). London, UK: The Falmer Press.

Randolph, J. J. (2009). A guide to writing the dissertation literature review. *Practical Assessment, Research & Evaluation, 14*(13), 2.

Ravitch, S. M., & Riggan, M. (2012). *Reason and rigor: How conceptual frameworks guide research.* Thousand Oaks, CA: Sage.

Sandelowski, M., & Barroso, J. (2006). *Handbook for synthesizing qualitative research.* New York, NY: Springer.

Timulak, L. (2014). Qualitative meta-analysis. In U. Flick (Ed.), *The SAGE handbook of qualitative data analysis* (pp. 481–496). Thousand Oaks, CA: Sage.

Torraco, R. J. (2005). Writing integrative literature reviews: Guidelines and examples. *Human Resource Development Review, 4*(3), 356–367.

Sample Session

Below is our example of a detailed outline that we have developed and will use to help guide us during the writing of our literature review for our racial microaggressions study.

African American College Students' Experiences With Racial Microaggressions

I. African American students are increasingly enrolling at predominately White institutions (PWIs) of higher learning.
   a. Recent statistics on African Americans attending PWIs (Harper, 2012)
   b. Growing incidents of racism on PWIs (Baber, 2012; Cabrera, 2014; Johnson-Ahorlu, 2012)
   c. Purpose of the literature review

II. African American students often experience racial microaggressions at PWIs (Sue, Capodilupo, Torino, Bucceri, Holder, Nadal, & Esquilin, 2007).
   a. College students' experiences with racial microaggressions (Gomez, Khurshid, Freitag, & Lachuk, 2011; Harwood, Hunt, Mendenhall, & Lewis, 2012; Yosso, Smith, Ceja, & Solórzano, 2009)
      i. Experiences with professors (Kohli & Solórzano, 2012)
      ii. Experiences with peers (Torres, Driscoll, & Burrow, 2010)
   b. Impact of racial microaggressions on students' health (Paraides, 2006)
      i. Social/emotional impact (Constantine, 2007; Wang, Leu, & Shoda, 2011)
      ii. Physical impact (Harrell, 2000)

III. Enduring racism within the college context requires African American students to engage in specific coping and emotional regulation

(Continued)

(Continued)

strategies (Brondolo, ver Halen, Pencille, Beatty, & Contrada, 2009; Brown, Phillips, Abdullah, Vinson, & Robertson, 2011).

   a. Coping strategies (Thomas, Witherspoon, & Speight, 2008)

      i. Avoidance coping (Lazarus & Folkman, 1984; Suls & Fletcher, 1985)

      ii. Approach coping (Lazarus & Folkman, 1984; Suls & Fletcher, 1985)

      iii. Coping with racism (Forsyth & Carter, 2012; Lewis, Mendenhall, Harwood, & Huntt, 2012; Melor, 2004)

   b. Emotional regulation strategies (Folkman & Moskowitz, 2004; Gross & John, 2003; Utsey, Giesbrect, Hook, & Stanard, 2008)

      i. Affective approaches

      ii. Cognitive approaches

      iii. Social approaches

IV. Attending a PWI and experiencing racial microaggressions impacts African American students' sense of self, particularly their racial identity (Smith, Hung, & Franklin, 2011).

   a. Racial identity (Sellers, Rowley, Chavous, Shelton, & Smith, 1997)

   b. Relationship between racial identity and healthy outcomes (Helms, Jernigan, & Mascher, 2005; Thomas, Caldwell, Faison, & Jackson, 2009)

V. Ultimately African American college students' experiencing of racial microaggressions within the college context, their means of coping with racism, and their racial identity beliefs impact their motivation, particularly their self-determination.

   a. Self-determination theory (Deci & Ryan, 2000; Ryan, Huta, & Deci, 2008)

      i. Need for autonomy

      ii. Need for competence

      iii. Need for relatedness

   b. Relationship between racial microaggressions, coping, racial identity, and self-determination

● REFERENCES FOR LITERATURE REVIEW OUTLINE EXAMPLE IN APA FORMAT

Baber, L. D. (2012). A qualitative inquiry on the multidimensional racial development among first-year African American college students attending a predominately White institution. *The Journal of Negro Education, 81*(1), 67–81.

Brondolo, E., ver Halen, N., Pencille, M., Beatty, D., & Contrada, R. (2009). Coping with racism: A selective review of the literature and a theoretical and methodological critique. *Journal of Behavioral Medicine, 32,* 64–88.

Brown, T. L., Phillips, C. M., Abdullah, T., Vinson, E., & Robertson, J. (2010). Dispositional versus situational coping: Are the coping strategies African Americans use different for general versus racism-related stressors? *Journal of Black Psychology, 37*(3), 311–335.

Cabrera, N. L. (2014). Exposing Whiteness in higher education: White male college students minimizing racism, claiming victimization, and recreating White supremacy. *Race Ethnicity and Education, 17*(1), 30–55.

Constantine, M. G. (2007). Racial microaggressions against African American clients in cross-racial counseling relationships. *Journal of Counseling Psychology, 54,* 1–16.

Deci, E. L., & Ryan, R. M. (2000). The "what" and "why" of goal pursuits: Human needs and the self-determination of behavior. *Psychological Inquiry, 11,* 227–268.

Folkman, S., & Moskowitz, J. T. (2004). Coping: Pitfalls and promise. *Annual Review of Psychology, 55,* 745–774.

Forsyth, J., & Carter, R. (2012). The relationship between racial identity status attitudes, racism-related coping, and mental health among Black Americans. *Cultural Diversity and Ethnic Minority Psychology, 18*(2), 128–140.

Gomez, M. L., Khurshid, A., Freitag, M. B., & Lachuk, A. J. (2011). Microaggressions in graduate students' lives: How they are encountered and their consequences. *Teaching and Teacher Education, 27,* 1189–1199.

Gross, J. J., & John, O. P. (2003). Individual differences in two emotion regulation processes: Implications for affect, relationships, and well-being. *Journal of Personality and Social Psychology, 85,* 348–362.

Harper, S. R. (2012). *Black male student success in higher education: A report from the national Black male college achievement study.* Philadelphia: University of Pennsylvania, Center for the Study of Race and Equity in Education.

Harrell, S. P. (2000). A multidimensional conceptualization of racism-related stress: Implications for the well-being of people of color. *American Journal of Orthopsychiatry, 70,* 42–57.

Harwood, S. A., Huntt, M. B., Mendenhall, R., & Lewis, J. A. (2012). Racial microaggressions in the residence halls: Experiences of students of color at a predominantly White university. *Journal of Diversity in Higher Education, 5*(3), 159.

Helms, J., Jernigan, M., & Mascher, J. (2005). The meaning of race in psychology and how to change it: A methodological perspective. *American Psychologist, 60*(1), 27–36.

Johnson-Ahorlu, R. N. (2012). The academic opportunity gap: How racism and stereotypes disrupt the education of African American undergraduates. *Race Ethnicity and Education, 15*(5), 633–652.

Kohli, R., & Solórzano, D. (2012). "Teachers, please learn our names!": Racial microaggressions and the K–12 classroom. *Race Ethnicity and Education, 15*(4), 441–462.

Lazarus, R. S., & Folkman, S. (1984). *Stress, appraisal, and coping.* New York, NY: Springer.

Lewis, J. A., Mendenhall, R., Harwood, S., & Huntt, M. B. (2013). Coping with racial microaggressions among Black women. *Journal of African American Studies, 17,* 51–73.

Mellor, D. (2004). Responses to racism: A taxonomy of coping styles used by Aboriginal Australians. *American Journal of Orthopsychiatry, 74,* 1, 56–71.

Paradies, Y. (2006). A systematic review of empirical research on self-reported racism and health. *International Journal of Epidemiology, 35*(4), 888–901.

Pieterse, A. L., Todd, N. R., Neville, H. A., & Carter, R. T. (2012). Perceived racism and mental health among Black American adults: a meta-analytic review. *Journal of Counseling Psychology, 59*(1), 1–9.

Ryan, R. M., Huta, V., & Deci, E. L. (2008). Living well: A self-determination theory perspective on eudaimonia. *Journal of Happiness Studies, 9,* 139–170.

Sellers, R. M., Smith, M. A., Shelton, J. N., Rowley, S. A., & Chavous, T. M. (1998). Multidimensional model of racial identity: A reconceptualization of African American racial identity. *Personality and Social Psychology Review, 2*(1), 18–39.

Smith, W. A., Hung, M., & Franklin, J. D. (2011). Racial battle fatigue and the miseducation of Black men: Racial microaggressions, societal problems, and environmental stress. *Journal of Negro Education, 80*(1), 63–82.

Sue, D., Capodilupo, C., Torino, G., Bucceri, J., Holder, A., Nadal, K., & Esquilin, M. (2007). Racial microaggressions in everyday life: Implications for clinical practice. *American Psychologist, 62*(4), 271–286.

Suls, J., & Fletcher, B. (1985). The relative efficacy of avoidant and nonavoidant coping strategies: A meta-analysis. *Health Psychology, 4,* 249–288.

Thomas, O. N., Caldwell, C. H., Faison, N., & Jackson, J. S. (2009). Promoting academic achievement: The role of racial identity in buffering perceptions of teacher discrimination on academic achievement among African American and Caribbean Black adolescents. *Journal of Educational Psychology, 101*(2), 420–431.

Torres, L., Driscoll, M. W., & Burrow, A. L. (2010). Racial microaggressions and psychological functioning among highly achieving African-Americans: A mixed-methods approach. *Journal of Social and Clinical Psychology, 29*(10), 1074–1099.

Utsey, S. O., Giesbrecht, N., Hook, J., & Stanard, P. M. (2008). Cultural, sociofamilial, and psychological resources that inhibit psychological distress in African Americans exposed to stressful life events and race-related stress. *Journal of Counseling Psychology, 55*(1), 49–62.

Wang, J., Leu, J., & Shoda, Y. (2011). When the seemingly innocuous "stings": Racial microaggressions and their emotional consequences. *Personality and Social Psychology Bulletin, 37*(12), 1666–1678.

Yosso, T. J., Smith, W. A., Ceja, M., & Solórzano, D. G. (2009). Critical race theory, racial microaggressions, and campus racial climate for Latina/o undergraduates. *Harvard Educational Review, 79*(4), 659–691.

6

Mixed Methods Designs

Frameworks for Organizing Your Research Methods

Objectives

1. To become familiar with the major types of mixed methods designs.

2. To understand the methodological emphases of mixed methods designs.

3. To learn how to choose a mixed methods design.

4. To learn how to create a visual model for your mixed methods design.

Now that you have started on your introduction and literature review sections, you are well on your way to developing your mixed methods research proposal. We know that you are ready to begin drafting the research methods section of your proposal, but before you get started, we need to have a conversation regarding mixed methods designs. In this chapter, we provide a discussion of how the type of mixed methods design informs the organization of the research methods. In doing so, we will focus on the most commonly used mixed methods designs.

● LEARNING THE LANGUAGE OF MIXED METHODS DESIGNS

Since you are embarking upon a mixed methods study, you have probably taken numerous courses or participated in several workshops on various quantitative and qualitative methods. Again, as a reminder, this book is not designed to provide a full discussion of mixed methods research designs. For more in-depth descriptions, you will need to consult other mixed methods resources (e.g., Creswell & Plano Clark, 2011; Greene, 2007; Hesse-Biber, 2010a; Ivankova, 2015; Morgan, 2014; Teddlie & Tashakkori, 2009). In those courses and workshops, you were exposed to words and phrases that were unique to each approach. Mixed methods research is similar in that it has its own language, more specifically its own notation system or nomenclature (see Morse, 2003, 2010). In order to engage in a mixed methods research study, it is essential that you master the mixed methods language. Table 6.1 provides a summary of the mixed methods nomenclature.

The mixed methods nomenclature is relatively simple and straightforward. It largely consists of the use of the terms *qualitative* and *quantitative*, along with various symbols. The terms *qual* and *quan* are used to indicate qualitative and quantitative methods, respectively. The capitalization of *QUAL* or *QUAN* suggests where emphasis is being placed in the study or

Table 6.1   Mixed Methods Notation System

Notation	Definition/Explanation	Examples
qual	Qualitative methods. (Lower case letters indicate lack of emphasis.)	qual
quan	Quantitative methods. (Lower case letters indicate lack of emphasis.)	quan
QUAL	Qualitative methods where emphasis is placed on the qualitative aspect. (Capital letters suggest emphasis.)	QUAL
QUAN	Quantitative methods where emphasis is placed on the quantitative aspect. (Capital letters suggest emphasis.)	QUAN
+ (plus sign)	Simultaneous or concurrent design, where quantitative and qualitative data are collected at the same time.	• QUAN + qual (emphasis on quantitative aspect) • QUAL + quan (emphasis on qualitative aspect) • QUAN + QUAL (equal emphasis on both methods)

Notation	Definition/Explanation	Examples
→ (single arrow)	Sequential design where quantitative and qualitative data are collected in phases.	• QUAN → qual (emphasis on quantitative aspect, with quantitative leading to qualitative) • QUAL → quan (emphasis on qualitative aspect, with qualitative leading to quantitative) • QUAN → QUAL (equal emphasis on both methods, with quantitative leading to qualitative) • QUAL → QUAN (equal emphasis on both methods, with qualitative leading to quantitative)
→← (double arrow)	Quantitative and qualitative methods are used in a recursive manner, often through phases.	• QUAN →← QUAL (quantitative and qualitative methods collected in a recursive manner with equal emphasis on both methods)
( ) (parentheses)	Embedded design where one method is embedded within another method.	• QUAN(qual) (emphasis on quantitative aspect with embedded qualitative component) • QUAL(quan) (emphasis on qualitative aspect with embedded quantitative component)

Source: Adapted from Creswell and Plano Clark (2011, Table 4.1) with permission of SAGE Publications, Inc.

indicates which approach is dominant. Likewise, the use of lowercase letters, *qual* and *quan*, indicates less emphasis. Mixed methods studies can be either qualitative- or quantitative-dominant (see Hesse-Biber, 2010b). Although it is possible for a study to have an equal emphasis on quantitative and qualitative approaches, taking an equal approach is difficult. Generally, most research slants qualitatively or quantitatively. In terms of symbols, a plus sign (+) indicates that the research components are conducted simultaneously or currently (e.g., QUAN + qual or QUAL + quan), whereas a single arrow (→) indicates that the research components are conducted sequentially (qual → QUAN or quan → QUAL). Double arrows (→←) suggest that quantitative and qualitative data are being collected in a recursive or multiphased fashion (QUAN→←QUAL).

On the other hand, parentheses ( ) imply that one method is embedded or entrenched within another method [QUAN(qual) or QUAL(quan)].

UNDERSTANDING MIXED METHODS DESIGNS

Now that you understand the language of mixed methods, it is time to delve into the various mixed methods designs. There are more complex mixed methods designs than those we are discussing in this chapter (see Bergman, 2008; Leech & Onwuegbuzie, 2009; Teddlie & Tashakkori, 2009; Vrkljan, 2009); however, for ease of discussion and because you are new to mixed methods research, we will focus on the core mixed methods designs. As suggested by Creswell and Plano Clark (2011), there are five basic designs within mixed methods research: explanatory sequential design, exploratory sequential design, convergent parallel design, embedded design, and multiphase design. (See Table 6.2 for brief explanations.) It must be stated that the framework used by Creswell and Plano Clark (2011) is compatible with the frameworks described in other major mixed methods textbooks (e.g. Greene, 2007; Hesse-Biber, 2010a; Ivankova, 2015; Morgan, 2014; Teddlie & Tashakkori, 2009). Thus, the information provided in this chapter, and throughout this book, can be easily used as a supplement to any of the major mixed methods textbooks.

Explanatory Sequential Design

An explanatory sequential design (QUAN → qual) is a two-phase research design where quantitative data are collected initially and is used to identify the qualitative data to be collected. In such designs, the qualitative data serve to explain the quantitative data. In using this design, you have to actually analyze the quantitative data before you can collect the qualitative data. The quantitative data help to inform what is done in the qualitative component. You should use this design if you want to use qualitative data to help further explore interesting patterns in the quantitative data or even help explain patterns that are contradictory to the research literature. After both sets of data are collected and analyzed, the findings are integrated and interpreted (see Figure 6.1).

For example, let's say you are interested in exploring veterans' experiences with reacclimatizing to civilian life. In order to examine this phenomenon, you decide to conduct a survey featuring Likert-format items with the goal of using the quantitative findings to help shape how you will design the qualitative portion of your study. After analyzing the quantitative data, you find that there was a statistically significant difference between the men's and women's responses. As a

Table 6.2 Descriptions of Mixed Methods Designs

	Explanatory Sequential →	Exploratory Sequential →	Convergent Parallel +	Embedded ( )	Multiphase →←
Definition	This is a sequential two phase design where quantitative data are initially collected and analyzed in Phase 1. Using the results of Phase 1, qualitative data are collected in Phase 2.	This is a sequential two phase design where qualitative data are initially collected and analyzed in Phase 1. Using the results of Phase 1, quantitative data are collected in Phase 2.	Quantitative and qualitative data are collected concurrently but separately; the data analyses are merged.	Qualitative data is collected within a traditional quantitative design, or quantitative data is collected within a traditional qualitative design.	Quantitative and qualitative data are collected and analyzed sequentially and/or concurrently in a recursive fashion over multiple phases.
Purpose	Enables the qualitative data to be used to expand upon or explore an aspect that was identified by the quantitative data. This approach is often used to expand upon interesting or perplexing results.	Enables the quantitative data to be used to expand upon the qualitative data. This approach is often used in scale development studies.	Enables the combining of related data that has been collected and analyzed separately. Also, this approach is often used to collect quantitative and qualitative data using one instrument.	Allows the collection of data within a traditional framework. This approach is often used in experimental and quasi-experimental designs as well as case studies.	Allows quantitative and qualitative data to be collected and analyzed in various phases. Often used in program development and evaluation.

(Continued)

Table 6.2 (Continued)

	Explanatory Sequential →	Exploratory Sequential →	Convergent Parallel +	Embedded ( )	Multiphase →←↑
Data Mixing/ Integration	The quantitative data are analyzed, leading to collection of the qualitative data. Mixing occurs through the creation of Phase 2 and during the analysis and discussion.	The qualitative data are analyzed, leading to the collection of the quantitative data. Mixing occurs through the creation of Phase 2 and during the analysis and discussion.	The quantitative and qualitative data are analyzed separately and then merged to create a comprehensive analysis and discussion.	The data are mixed during or after the data of emphasis has been collected and analyzed, depending upon the purpose of the study.	Quantitative and qualitative data can be merged at any stage, depending upon the data type and the purpose of the study.
Example Studies	• Buck et al. (2009) • Fetters et al. (2007)	• Stoller et al. (2009) • Hayden & Chiu (2015) • Durham et al. (2011)	• Kerrigan (2014) • Henwood et al. (in press) • Rosenberg et al. (2013)	• Quinlan & Quinlan (2010) • Brady & O'Regan (2009) • Weaver-Hightower (2014) • Marshall et al. (2015)	• Chilisa & Tsheko (2014) • Youngs & Piggot-Irvine (2012)

Sources: Adapted from Creswell and Plano Clark (2011, Table 3.3) and Ivankova (2015, Table 5.1) with permission of SAGE Publications, Inc.

Figure 6.1   Explanatory Sequential Design

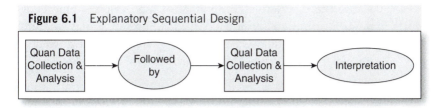

result you decide to design your qualitative aspect of the study in order to better understand why there was a difference between the two groups. In doing so, you choose your participants based upon the quantitative findings. You may decide to hold focus groups that are organized by gender. In other words, you can select participants for interviews based upon specific characteristics or patterns found in your data. In addition, you can use the quantitative findings to help create specific interview questions. You should begin the study with some questions planned for the qualitative phase, because you always knew that you would utilize a qualitative component. The findings from the quantitative analysis simply provide you with the opportunity to adapt your interview questions to reflect your quantitative data.

As described by Creswell and Plano Clark (2011), there are several benefits and challenges of using an explanatory sequential design:

Benefits of the Explanatory Sequential Design

- The design is relatively easy to implement and write up because of its two phases.

- Its quantitative dominance is appealing to quantitative-oriented researchers.

- The design is data driven and emergent, in that the qualitative component is dictated by the quantitative component.

Challenges of the Explanatory Sequential Design

- Like all mixed methods designs, this design can be time consuming. You cannot begin the qualitative component of the study until after the quantitative data has been collected and analyzed. In addition, the qualitative component will take additional time.

- There is always a chance that the qualitative findings may contradict the quantitative findings. Such paradoxical findings may make some researchers uncomfortable, whereas for others it is a welcome challenge to try to explain the different results.

- Because the qualitative component of the design is emergent, gaining institutional review board (IRB) approval may be difficult, in that all details of a study are needed in order to receive approval, particularly when human subjects are involved.

- Some researchers are uncomfortable with the emergent nature of such a design, preferring to use more prescribed research designs that feature definitive approaches.

Exploratory Sequential Design

An exploratory sequential design is similar to an explanatory sequential design, except the components are reversed. In an explanatory sequential design (qual → QUAN), qualitative data is initially collected, followed by quantitative data. In such designs, the reason for collecting quantitative data is to explore the themes that are found in the qualitative data. You can focus on exploring any of qualitative findings, including interesting or contradictory patterns. Like the explanatory design, this design requires that you actually analyze the first phase of the data, the qualitative component, before you can collect the quantitative component. The qualitative data helps to shape what is done in the quantitative component. After both sets of data are collected and analyzed, the findings are integrated and interpreted (see Figure 6.2). For instance, let's say you would like to better understand the experiences of children who are suffering from food insecurity. In order to explore their experiences, you would first engage in a qualitative component (e.g., individual interviews, focus group interviews, observations). You would then use the results of your qualitative findings to help you to determine what types of quantitative data should be used and how you should use the quantitative component. The qualitative data can suggest that you focus on particular constructs or even recommend specific contexts or populations for the quantitative exploration. In addition, you could use an exploratory sequential design to create a scale (see DeCuir-Gunby, 2008;

Figure 6.2 Exploratory Sequential Design

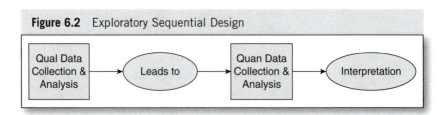

Onwuegbuzie, Bustamante, & Nelson, 2010). Using the aforementioned example regarding food insecurity, the qualitative component would help you to determine the major themes (factors) that should be captured in the scale and will enable you to create the items for your scale. The quantitative component of the study would involve the testing of the items in a specific context with a particular population.

As described by Creswell and Plano Clark (2011), there are several benefits and challenges of using an exploratory sequential design:

Benefits of the Exploratory Sequential Design

- The design is relatively easy to implement and write up because of its two phases.

- The design can be either qualitative- or quantitative-dominant (e.g., instrument design); thus it appeals to both qualitative- and quantitative-oriented researchers.

- The design is data driven and emergent, in that the quantitative component is dictated by the qualitative component.

Challenges of the Exploratory Sequential Design

- Like all mixed methods designs, this design can be time-consuming. You cannot begin the quantitative component of the study until after the qualitative data has been collected and analyzed. In addition, if this approach is used to engage in instrument development, additional time will be needed, particularly to establish reliability and validity (to be discussed more in Chapter 7).

- Because the quantitative component of the design is emergent, gaining institutional review board (IRB) approval may be difficult, in that all details of a study are needed in order to receive approval, particularly when human subjects are involved.

- Some researchers are uncomfortable with the emergent nature of such a design, preferring to use more prescribed research designs that feature definitive approaches.

Convergent Parallel Design

A convergent parallel design (QUAN + qual), also known as a triangulation or concurrent mixed methods design, allows you to collect quantitative and qualitative data at the same time or in a parallel fashion. In this type of design, the quantitative and qualitative components do not impact each other during data collection and analysis. It is not until after the data is analyzed separately that you integrate the findings (see Figure 6.3). The quantitative and qualitative data are designed to support each other, or rather the design enables you to triangulate the findings (see Jick, 1979), demonstrating that you are making the same claims using different types of data. For example, you are interested in exploring the leadership styles of women executives. In using a convergent parallel design, you could send out a survey featuring both Likert items (quantitative) and open-ended questions (qualitative), a process known as intramethod mixing (Johnson & Turner, 2003). You would analyze the quantitative and qualitative responses separately and then integrate. Or you may simply give out a Likert-item survey to women executives and during the same time frame collect focus group interviews with women executives. Once the data has been collected and analyzed separately,

Figure 6.3   Convergent Parallel Design

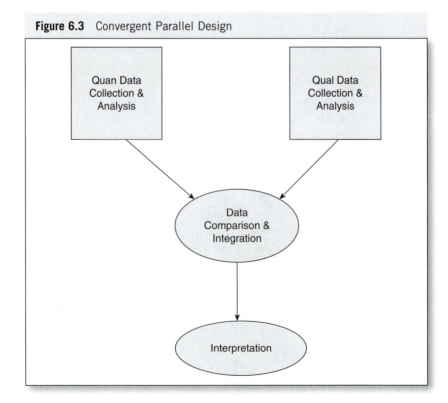

you would then integrate the results and make appropriate conclusions.

As they do for the sequential designs, Creswell and Plano Clark (2011) suggest that there are several benefits and challenges to using a convergent parallel design:

Benefits of the Convergent Parallel Design

- The design is relatively easy to implement, because data is collected in one phase. This design is less time consuming than some of the other mixed methods designs.

- The quantitative and qualitative data are collected separately, and this approach most easily adheres to traditional quantitative and qualitative data analysis approaches.

Challenges of the Convergent Parallel Design

- Merging the separate analyses can be difficult because of the differences in the types of data.

- The quantitative and qualitative findings may not always converge seamlessly. There is always the chance of contradictions being found in the data. This will require the researcher to make decisions about potential immediate next steps that need to be taken, including the need to collect additional data.

Embedded Design

An embedded design involves the collection of quantitative and qualitative data within either a traditional quantitative (e.g., experimental) or qualitative (case study) design (see Figure 6.4). The word *embedded* suggests that one data type is nested within another data type. In terms of the more traditional experimental approach, the secondary data are collected before, during, or after the implementation of the primary data collection. However, in terms of a case study, the quantitative and qualitative approaches are collected together or embedded. For instance, let's say that you are interested in studying the use of electronic tablets to modify the behavior of students in a special education classroom. In using an embedded design, you would design an intervention using electronic tablets. You would then collect pre and post observations of classroom

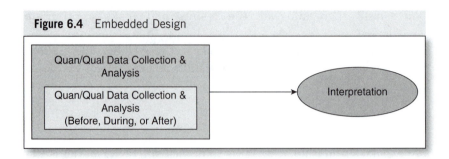

Figure 6.4   Embedded Design

behavior (quantitative), while engaging in think-aloud protocols (qualitative) during the intervention to understand how students are learning to modify their behavior. In this same example, instead of conducting the qualitative component during the intervention, you could conduct interviews before or after the intervention. However, if you wanted to take more of the case study approach to the embedded design, you could focus on the modification of one student's behavior over time and collect both quantitative and qualitative data.

As described by Creswell and Plano Clark (2011), there are several benefits and challenges of using an embedded design:

Benefits of the Embedded Design

- The design is relatively easy to implement and write up because the quantitative and qualitative results are distinct from one another.

- The design can be either qualitative- or quantitative-dominant (e.g., quasi-experimental design, case study); thus it appeals to both qualitative- and quantitative-oriented researchers.

Challenges of the Embedded Design

- It can be difficult to determine when the best time is to collect the qualitative data (beginning, during, or after the quantitative data has been collected).

- Integrating the results can be challenging, because the quantitative and qualitative components are addressing two different research questions.

Multiphase Design

A multiphase design (quan→←QUAL) combines many of the elements found in the sequential and convergent designs. The purpose of this design is to combine a variety of quantitative and qualitative approaches over time in a manner that resembles separate research studies (see Figure 6.5). Multiphase designs are often recursive, employing quantitative and/or qualitative approaches in a spiraling manner. An example would be the design, implementation, and evaluation of a program/curriculum designed to teach nurses how to care for patients with highly infectious and deadly diseases. In this example, you will need to create the curriculum, implement the curriculum, and evaluate the curriculum. Your data collection and analysis will focus on the curriculum development and the evaluation processes. Creating the curriculum and evaluating the curriculum could both involve a variety of qualitative and quantitative approaches.

Creswell and Plano Clark (2011) provide several benefits and challenges of using a multiphase design:

Benefits of the Multiphase Design

- It is a flexible design in that you have the opportunity to engage in a variety of phases in order to examine a phenomenon.

- The design fits well with program design and evaluation.

- It is a good way to develop a program of research.

Challenges of the Multiphase Design

- This can be the most time consuming of all of the designs. Because the multiphase design is essentially a series of studies, it will take substantial time and effort to implement.

Figure 6.5   Multiphase Design

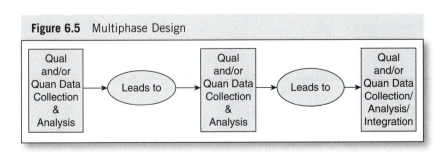

- Since there are so many stages within any individual phase, it may be difficult to connect the various components of the design.

- Because this is a potentially lengthy design, it is possible that institutional review board (IRB) approval may have to be sought on multiple occasions.

● CHOOSING A MIXED METHODS DESIGN

Now that you have a good understanding of the basic mixed methods designs, it is time for you to think about which design works best for your study. The explanatory and exploratory sequential designs are typically the easiest designs to implement. If you are new to mixed methods research or research in general, you may want to focus on one of these designs. In fact, these designs are quite popular among doctoral students. On the other hand, the embedded and multiphase designs are more complicated and can be quite nuanced. (The multiphase design may also be extremely time consuming.) These are better suited for more seasoned researchers. The specific design that you choose is dependent upon your research questions and the overall purpose of your research study. It is also dependent upon your skill and experience levels.

At this time it is important for you to revisit your research questions and your purpose statement in order to assist with choosing the best design for your study. In choosing a mixed methods design, you need to consider the order in which the data will be collected, the interdependency between the quantitative and qualitative data, the type of quantitative and qualitative designs being used, whether or not your study will require several phases of data collection, and your ability to carry out the design. Table 6.3 provides some questions for you to consider when choosing a design.

The first question you need to ask yourself is this: In what order will the data be collected? Specifically, you should consider whether your research questions will be best answered by collecting data sequentially, concurrently, or in some combination of both. If your questions are best answered by collecting data sequentially, you should focus on exploratory sequential designs, explanatory sequential research designs, embedded designs, or multiphase designs. However, if your questions are best answered by collecting data concurrently or simultaneously, you should focus on the convergent parallel design. Consider the aforementioned study on the leadership

Table 6.3   How to Choose a Mixed Methods Design

Issues to Consider	Possible Mixed Methods Design
1. Will your quantitative and qualitative data be collected at the same time?	• Convergent Parallel Design
2. Will your quantitative and qualitative data be collected in sequence?	• Exploratory Design • Explanatory Design
3. Will the collection of one type of data be dependent upon the collection of another type of data?	• Exploratory Design • Explanatory Design • Multiphase Design
4. Will you collect quantitative and qualitative data within an experimental, quasi-experimental, or case study design?	• Embedded Design
5. Will you collect data in multiple phases?	• Multiphase Design
6. Will you have substantial time to collect and analyze the data?	• Multiphase Design

styles of women executives. In such a study, using a convergent parallel design, you could use a survey featuring both Likert items and open-ended questions.

The second question you should consider concerns the relationship between the quantitative and qualitative data. In other words, what roles do the various data types play? Does the qualitative data support or extend the quantitative data? If so, you should focus on the explanatory sequential design. Using the earlier discussed example on veterans' transition from military to civilian life, an explanatory sequential design would consist of giving recent veterans a battery of psychological assessments and then using interviews to further explore some of the findings.

As you do with the explanatory sequential design, you have to consider the order in which the data are to be collected with the exploratory sequential design. Does the quantitative data expand the qualitative data? If so, you should consider the exploratory sequential design. In the example on children suffering from food insecurity, you would focus on collecting in-depth data, such as observations and interviews, from a small sample, and then use the information gained to inform the implementation of a Likert-item survey to be administered to a larger sample.

The third question that needs to be addressed is whether or not you are embracing a mixed methods approach within a traditional quantitative or qualitative design. Are you using an experimental design? Are you utilizing case study methodology? If you are taking either approach, you should consider the embedded research design. Consider exploring the use of electronic tablets to modify the behavior of students in a special education classroom. In such a study, you would conduct pre and post surveys (quantitative data), with interviews and observations (qualitative) embedded within the quantitative data collection.

The last question involves whether or not you will engage in several phases of data collection. How many phases will you use to collect data? Will you engage in three or more phases of data collection? Will you collect quantitative and qualitative data in a recursive manner? If you are planning a series of data collection phases, you should consider a multiphase mixed methods design. For example, if you are developing and evaluating a curriculum designed to teach nurses how to care for patients with highly infectious and deadly diseases, this would require a multiphase design, in that you will have to engage in curriculum development, implement the curriculum, and conduct the evaluation, using a combination of quantitative and qualitative methods.

After you have asked yourself the above questions, you need to think about the many ways in which your research questions could potentially be answered. Research questions can be answered using multiple mixed methods research designs. Before committing to a particular design, it is important for you to consider which one works best for answering your specific research questions. In determining the best mixed methods research design, it may be helpful for you to consider how your research questions would look if answered using each of the five mixed methods designs. See Table 6.4 for an example of potential designs to address the following research question: What impact does social media have on adolescent girls' self-esteem?

As illustrated by Table 6.4, each mixed methods design requires a different use of quantitative and qualitative data. In the different designs, the data is analyzed at different phases, which will result in different findings. Thus, when choosing a design, it is imperative that you also consider the types of claims that you potentially would like to make with your study. As a researcher, it is important for you to contemplate the potential impact your research study will have in your field.

Table 6.4   Potential Mixed Methods Research Designs Using the Same Research Question: What Impact Does Social Media Have on Adolescent Girls' Self-Esteem?

Mixed Methods Design	Description	Conclusions Drawn From Data
Explanatory Sequential	Conduct a survey on social media usage and self-esteem. Using the findings from the survey, conduct interviews to follow up on general findings from the survey.	Further explain the general trends on how social media impacts the self-esteem of adolescent girls
Exploratory Sequential	Conduct interviews regarding social media usage and self-esteem. Using the findings from the interviews, use a survey to examine social media usage and self-esteem in a larger sample.	Discuss general trends on how social media impacts the self-esteem of adolescent girls, based upon earlier findings
Convergent Parallel	Collect interview data and survey data on social media usage and self-esteem during the same time frame. (One means of data collection is not dependent upon the other.)	Describe how the social media impacts the self-esteem of adolescent girls. Possibly demonstrate how the data sources serve to corroborate or contradict each other.
Embedded	Use a quasi-experimental design featuring pre and post surveys on self-esteem (quantitative) with an intervention focusing on social media usage using a focus-group approach (qualitative).	Explain whether an intervention was successful in positively impacting adolescents' self-esteem
Multiphase	Phase 1: Collect quantitative surveys on social media usage and self-esteem. Phase 2: Conduct focus group interviews on social media usage and self-esteem.	Discuss the utility of a curriculum that was designed to positively impact adolescents' self-esteem

(Continued)

Table 6.4 (Continued)

Mixed Methods Design	Description	Conclusions Drawn From Data
	Phase 3: Design a curriculum on social media usage and self-esteem based upon the results of phases 1 and 2.	
	Phase 4: Implement the curriculum.	
	Phase 5: Evaluate the curriculum using quantitative and/or qualitative approaches.	

● VISUALLY REPRESENTING YOUR MIXED METHODS DESIGN

In addition to choosing a mixed methods design, it is also important to visually represent your design. In mixed methods research, it is common to provide a visual representation or diagram of your design. Because mixed methods designs are often complex, diagrams help to simplify the steps of your study for your readers. As a beginning mixed methods researcher, it is essential that you develop an appropriate diagram for your research study. Doing so will help you to better articulate the steps of your research study and will allow you to create a more explicit methods section for your proposal (to be discussed in Chapter 7).

Creating a Basic Diagram

Before you begin to create your diagram, it is important for you to consider a few issues as recommended by Creswell (2015), Creswell and Plano Clark (2011), and Ivankova, Creswell, and Stick (2006). First, sketch your diagram using pencil/pen and paper. Take this time to try out various possibilities for representing your design.

After you have decided upon the general design for your diagram, you should next consider what software package you will use to create your diagram. Many mixed methods researchers find that PowerPoint is sufficient. However, there is more sophisticated software that you can use to create the diagram, particularly concept mapping or graphics software. Use the software that you feel the most comfortable using. The diagram does not have to be complicated. Try to keep it as simple as possible. You do not want to spend an inordinate amount of time working on the diagram; that time can be used on more important tasks.

Third, become familiar with the diagram symbols. For the diagram, boxes are used to represent data collection and analysis, circles indicate interpretation, and arrows show the flow of the design.

Fourth, consider the orientation you will use to create your diagram. Do you want to use a vertical or horizontal orientation? The choice depends upon personal preference as well as your ability to fit all of the appropriate details on one page. Yes, the diagram is to be only one page, so you have to be concise! It is okay if you begin with one orientation and then decide to use the other orientation somewhere in the process.

Last, become familiar with the formats associated with the basic mixed methods designs (review Figures 6.1–6.5). You will use the format associated with the mixed methods design that you have chosen for your study as the foundation for your diagram.

Adding Details to Your Diagram

Once you have your foundational design, it is essential to begin filling in the necessary details. Creating the diagram is a great way to brainstorm or even outline your research methods. It is important to put as much essential detail on the diagram as possible. First, it is necessary to think about your data collection procedures. When are you going to collect data? What type of data will you collect? Who are your participants? What is your context? Next, you need to think about data analysis procedures. When will you conduct your analyses? What types of analyses will you conduct? After you have added those details, you should focus on the type of products you will have. Products are the outcomes you will gain after engaging in the data collection and data analysis steps. After data collection, what will you have in terms of raw data? After data analysis, what specific analyses and outcomes will you have? Once this is done, you then need to think about data integration. When will you integrate the data? How will you integrate the data? Last, although this is not mandatory, it is helpful to include details of your timeline in your diagram. How long will it take to implement each component of your design? What is your expected timeline for the entire project?

PRACTICE SESSION

Guided Questions

Use the following questions to guide your thinking on how to choose the best design for your mixed methods research study.

1. What design works best for your study? Why?
2. Are there other designs that could be used to answer your study's research questions? What would your study look like using the other designs?
3. Will your study be quantitative- or qualitative-dominant? How does the emphasis impact your overall design choices?

Choosing a Mixed Methods Design

Think about the research design that you have chosen for your study. For this activity, we would like you to attempt to visually represent your mixed methods design and to create your own diagram. (See examples throughout the chapter.) First, decide on whether you want to use a vertical or horizontal orientation. Then within your diagram, make sure to include adequate details regarding your data collection, analysis, and interpretation procedures. Don't be afraid to be creative and colorful!

Additional Readings on Mixed Methods Designs

Brady, B., & O'Regan, C. (2009). Meeting the challenge of doing an RCT evaluation of youth mentoring in Ireland: A journey in mixed methods. *Journal of Mixed Methods Research*, *3*(3), 265–280.

Buck, G., Cook, K., Quigley, C., Eastwood, J., & Lucas, Y. (2009). Profiles of urban, low SES, African American girls' attitudes toward science: A sequential explanatory mixed methods study. *Journal of Mixed Methods Research* (2009), 386–410.

Chilisa, B., & Tsheko, G. N. (2014). Mixed methods in indigenous research: Building relationships for sustainable intervention outcomes. *Journal of Mixed Methods Research*, *8*(3), 222–233.

Durham, J., Tan, B. K., & White, R. (2011). Utilizing mixed research methods to develop a quantitative assessment tool: An example from explosive remnants of a war clearance program. *Journal of Mixed Methods Research*, *5*(3), 212–226.

Fetters, M. D., Yoshioka, T., Greenberg, G. M., Gorenflo, D. W., & Yeo, S. (2007). Advance consent in Japanese during prenatal care for epidural anesthesia during childbirth. *Journal of Mixed Methods Research*, *1*(4), 333–365.

Hayden, H. E., & Chiu, M. M. (2015). Reflective teaching via a problem exploration–teaching adaptations–resolution cycle: A mixed methods study of preservice teachers' reflective notes. *Journal of Mixed Methods Research*, *9*(2), 133–153.

Henwood, B. F., Rhoades, H., Hsu, H. T., Couture, J., Rice, E., & Wenzel, S. L. (in press). Changes in social networks and HIV Risk behaviors among homeless adults transitioning into permanent supportive housing: A mixed methods pilot study. *Journal of Mixed Methods Research*.

Hesse-Biber, S. (2010). Qualitative approaches to mixed methods practice. *Qualitative Inquiry, 16*(6), 455–468.

Ivankova, N. V., Creswell, J. W., & Stick, S. L. (2006). Using mixed-methods sequential explanatory design: From theory to practice. *Field Methods, 18*(1), 3–20.

Kerrigan, M. R. (2014). A framework for understanding community colleges' organizational capacity for data use: A convergent parallel mixed methods study. *Journal of Mixed Methods Research, 8*(4) 341–362.

Marshall, P. L., DeCuir-Gunby, J. T., & McCulloch, A. W. (2015). *When critical multiculturalism meets mathematics: A mixed methods study of professional development and teacher identity.* New York, NY: Rowman & Littlefield.

Morse, J. (2010). Procedures and practice of mixed method design: Maintaining control, rigor, and complexity. In A. Tashakkori & C. Teddlie (Eds.), *SAGE handbook of mixed methods in social and behavioral research* (2nd ed., pp. 339–352). Thousand Oaks, CA: Sage.

Quinlan, E., & Quinlan, A. (2010). Representations of rape: Transcending methodological divides. *Journal of Mixed Methods Research, 4*(2), 127–143.

Rosenberg, B. D., Lewandowski, J. A., & Siegel, J. T. (2013). Goal disruption theory, military personnel, and the creation of merged profiles: A mixed methods investigation. *Journal of Mixed Methods Research, 9*(1), 51–69.

Stoller, E. P., Webster, N. J., Blixen, C. E., McCormick, R. A., Hund, A. J., Perzynski, A. T., ... Dawson, N. V. (2009). Alcohol consumption decisions among nonabusing drinkers diagnosed with hepatitis C: An exploratory sequential mixed methods study. *Journal of Mixed Methods Research, 3*(1), 65–86.

Weaver-Hightower, M. B. (2014). A mixed methods approach for identifying influence on public policy. *Journal of Mixed Methods Research, 8*(2), 115–138.

Vrkljan, B. H. (2009). Constructing a mixed methods design to explore the older driver copilot relationship. *Journal of Mixed Methods Research, 3*(4), 371–385.

Youngs, H., & Piggot-Irvine, E. (2012). The application of a multiphase triangulation approach to mixed methods: The research of an aspiring school principal development program. *Journal of Mixed Methods Research, 6*(3), 184–198.

Sample Session—Mixed Methods Visual Model

In order to best answer our research questions regarding African American college students' experiences with racial microaggressions, we are using an explanatory sequential mixed methods design. We felt that this design would best address our various research questions, in that our data will be collected in sequence, and one data source is dependent upon another. In addition, the qualitative data will help to *explain* the quantitative data. We will conduct surveys featuring Likert items, and then we will conduct interviews to explore/explain significant findings. On the following two pages are two sample diagrams for our study.

Figure 6.6 Diagram Example 1

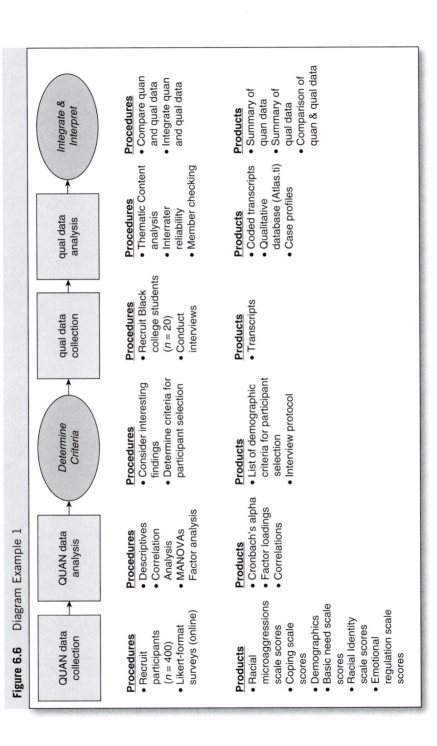

Figure 6.7 Diagram Example 2

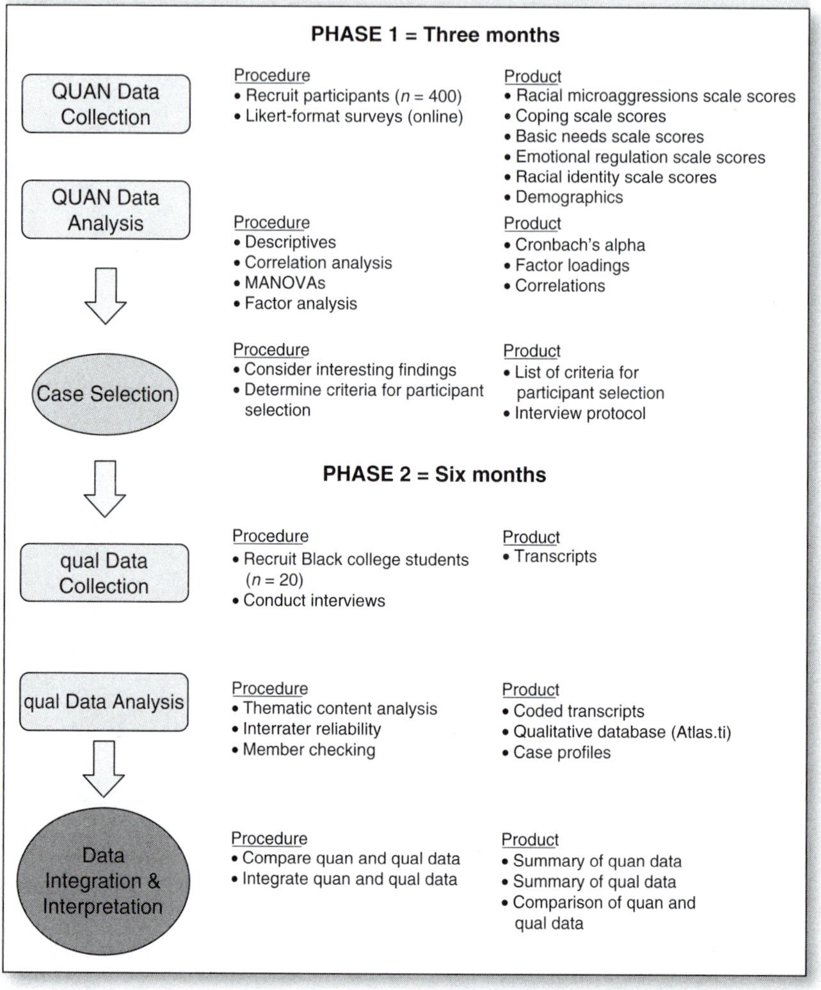

PHASE 1 = Three months

QUAN Data Collection

Procedure
• Recruit participants (n = 400)
• Likert-format surveys (online)

Product
• Racial microaggressions scale scores
• Coping scale scores
• Basic needs scale scores
• Emotional regulation scale scores
• Racial identity scale scores
• Demographics

QUAN Data Analysis

Procedure
• Descriptives
• Correlation analysis
• MANOVAs
• Factor analysis

Product
• Cronbach's alpha
• Factor loadings
• Correlations

Case Selection

Procedure
• Consider interesting findings
• Determine criteria for participant selection

Product
• List of criteria for participant selection
• Interview protocol

PHASE 2 = Six months

qual Data Collection

Procedure
• Recruit Black college students (n = 20)
• Conduct interviews

Product
• Transcripts

qual Data Analysis

Procedure
• Thematic content analysis
• Interrater reliability
• Member checking

Product
• Coded transcripts
• Qualitative database (Atlas.ti)
• Case profiles

Data Integration & Interpretation

Procedure
• Compare quan and qual data
• Integrate quan and qual data

Product
• Summary of quan data
• Summary of qual data
• Comparison of quan and qual data

7

The Heart of the Mixed Methods Research Plan

Discussing Your Methods Section

Objectives

1. To understand the various components of the research methods section of a mixed methods research proposal.

2. To understand the purpose of the research methods section for your mixed methods research proposal.

Every chapter thus far in this book has led up to this moment—the discussion of the research methods section of the mixed methods research proposal. Chapter 1 provided a discussion on mixed methods research and encouraged you to reflect upon your level of preparedness for engaging in a mixed methods study. Chapter 2 discussed the importance of the theoretical framework and how it influences all aspects of the research process. Chapter 3 introduced research questions/hypotheses and how they guide your investigation. Chapter 4 explained how to compose the introduction to your mixed methods proposal. Chapter 5 instructed you on how to construct your literature review by situating your research within the larger research context. Last, Chapter 6 gave an overview of the most common mixed methods designs and helped you to identify a design for your study. Now it is time to discuss a key element of the mixed methods research proposal—the research methods section.

● THE ROLE OF THE RESEARCH METHODS SECTION

The research methods section of your mixed methods proposal is where you lay out the steps you will take to conduct the study you designed to answer your research questions. Although your goal should be to implement the steps described in your research methods section, it is important for you to remember that the research methods section is a tentative plan. We say *tentative* because research plans often change for a variety of reasons, most of which are unforeseen circumstances (e.g., difficulty gaining access to participants, delayed approval from the IRB, requested changes from your supervising authority). If it appears that you may need to augment your research plans, it is imperative that you consult with your supervising authority (e.g., dissertation chair, committee, grantor) regarding the potential modifications before any changes are actually implemented. Some changes may be considered minor modifications (e.g., adding a research question). Other changes may be more involved (e.g., changing target population, changing the manner of data collection) and will require subsequent steps such as resubmitting to the IRB in order to implement the changes. Regardless, it is necessary that you approach the development of the research methods section with the understanding that you will need to be flexible and that your study may indeed have emergent elements. However, you should try your best to stick to the original plan if possible.

Also, it is important for you to make the research methods section as detailed as possible. The more specific you are, the more feedback you can receive from your reviewers. In addition, being specific will help you to be better prepared for the actual implementation of your study. On the other hand, if you are too vague with your descriptions, you will potentially open yourself up to unnecessary critique from your readers. In other words, take the time to write a thoughtful and detailed research methods section!

Before we begin to discuss the specific components of a research methods section, it is essential to gauge your readiness for composing the research methods section. In order to begin, we would like for you to revisit Table 4.1 in Chapter 4, which discussed your readiness for writing

Table 7.1   What to Consider When Writing the Research Methods Section

1. What are your research questions/hypotheses? How will they guide your research process?
2. What mixed methods research design will you use for your study? Why?
3. Who are your study participants? How will you access your participants?
4. What are your data sources? How will you collect your data?
5. How will you analyze your data?
6. How will you integrate the quantitative and qualitative components of your data?
7. What role will your theoretical framework play in your data analysis?
8. How will you address reliability/credibility?
9. How will you address validity/trustworthiness?

your introduction section. This table asked pertinent questions regarding the overall purpose of your research study. Revisiting the purpose of your study will help you to better clarify your thoughts regarding what you intend to do in your proposal and should thus guide the creation of your methods section. Table 7.1, on the other hand, helps you to consider your readiness to develop the research methods section, specifically. Before you begin writing your research methods section, you need to take some time to think about your overall methods strategy. Use Table 7.1 to help organize your thoughts regarding your research methods section. The questions raised in the table will be addressed in the following sections.

THE COMPONENTS OF THE RESEARCH METHODS SECTION   ●

As indicated in previous chapters in this book, there is no standard way to compose and organize the research methods section. The components of the section can vary by discipline and/or research purpose (e.g., dissertation, grant). However, there are some standard aspects that should be included in the research methods section. The components of the section include research questions/hypotheses, mixed methods definition, mixed methods design, sample/participants, data collection, and data analysis. See Table 7.2 for a summary of the components of the research methods section. An abbreviated example of the research methods section, including all of its components, will be featured at the end of the chapter in the Sample Session section.

Table 7.2 Defining the Components of the Research Methods Section

Components	Subcomponents	Descriptions
Research Questions/ Hypotheses		The questions that are guiding your inquiry.
Mixed Methods Definition		The definition of mixed methods that will be used in your research proposal and the rationale for choosing a mixed methods approach.
Mixed Methods Design		The approach to collecting, analyzing, and integrating your quantitative and qualitative data.
Sample/ Participants		The descriptions of sampling procedures as well as the context.
	Context	The place in which the study occurs.
	Sampling	The process used to gain access to the participants in the study.
Data Collection		The process used to gather the data for the study.
	Instrumentation	The description of the tools used to obtain the information that will be used for the data analysis.
	Procedures	The specific steps taken to use the instruments to gather data.
Data Analysis		The means of making sense of your data.
	Procedures	The specific steps taken to analyze your data.
	Data Integration	The manner in which the quantitative and qualitative findings are compared and/or combined.
	Role of Theoretical Framework	The way in which the theories used to guide and create your study will be used to help to analyze your data.
	Reliability/ Credibility	The consistency of the responses in your data.
	Validity/ Trustworthiness	The degree to which you are studying what you think you are studying. In mixed methods research, this includes examining the quality of inferences being made from your data.

Research Questions/Hypotheses

The research questions/hypotheses are the first components of the research methods section. As described in Chapter 3 of this book, research questions state what you would like to learn about a phenomenon and are used to guide the mixed methods inquiry. Research questions can be quantitative, qualitative, or mixed methods. Similarly, hypotheses are statements that are generated to test your thoughts regarding a phenomenon. Your discussion of the research questions will serve as the core for the entire research methods chapter. Thus, the research methods section is largely organized around the discussion of the research questions/hypotheses. Every other component of the research methods section addresses how it will be used to help answer the research questions/hypotheses.

Mixed Methods Definition

After describing your research questions, it is important to tell your audience that you will take a mixed method approach to examine those research questions as well as explain why this approach is necessary. In order to do so, it is important for you to provide a definition of mixed methods research. As you recall in Chapter 1, we described that there are various definitions of mixed methods research. We also reiterated this in Chapter 4 when discussing the introduction section of the mixed methods proposal. Although we recommend that you provide a definition of mixed methods research in your introduction, it is important for you to remind your readers of your mixed methods definition again in your research methods section. Doing so in conjunction with your research questions/hypotheses will help to create context for your readers. In addition, it will help you to set up your discussion and description of your mixed methods design.

Mixed Methods Design

The description of the mixed methods design is the third component of the research methods section. As previously described in Chapter 6 of this book, there are five common mixed methods designs: explanatory sequential design, exploratory sequential design, convergent parallel design, embedded design, and multiphase design. It is important for you to describe the design of your study as well as how it relates to your research questions/hypotheses. Do not forget to include a diagram or illustration of your design. Although the diagram is generally placed within the appendix, it is important to use it as a guide while you are working on the research methods section, particularly while writing your description of the mixed methods design. However, do not be surprised if through the writing process you realize that you may need to edit your diagram. Again, proposal development is an iterative process!

Sample/Participants

Now that you have described the questions that you would like to answer, provided a definition of mixed methods research, and given a description of your research design, it is time for you to talk about the people who will participate in your research study. The participant description helps to provide a context in which the study will take place. Also, the description of your research participants is important because it depicts the qualities/characteristics you would like your study participants to possess. Moreover, the description of the research participants helps to determine sampling procedures, including the number of participants needed, who is eligible and ineligible for your study, and the means for gaining access to the participants.

Context

It is important to understand the environments in which you want to understand your participants. As such, providing a description of the research context is an important aspect of the participant description component. For example, if you are conducting a case study on the incorporation of an organic lunch program within a particular school context, the school environment itself is central to your investigation. You cannot understand how the lunch program has been implemented without understanding the school environment. As such, the more details you can provide about your preferred research context(s), the better your readers will be able to understand the possible outcomes for your study.

Sampling

In addition to understanding where you want your research to occur, an essential question that you will need to address is this: How many participants do I need for my study? Unfortunately, there is no easy answer to this question. There are, however, some general guidelines that you should consider. For the quantitative components, there are several ways to consider the number of participants. In quantitative research, generally larger tends to be better. You usually strive for a large number of participants. But in real-world research, this is not always feasible. Therefore, you should always consider the assumptions for the specific statistics that you are using in order to determine the minimum number of participants needed. Each statistic has a minimum number of cases needed in order for a model to converge without violating normality. In order to determine this, you have to conduct a power analysis, which determines the probability of making a Type 2 error (i.e., not rejecting the null hypothesis, when you should) (Gall, Gall, & Borg, 2007). Generally, there is a good chance that someone on your committee will want you to conduct a power analysis—so just do it! Luckily, there are many online tools that you can use to calculate sample size based on the expected effect size as well as previously calculated effect size tables. You can also calculate this the old-fashioned way—by hand.

In determining sample size, we generally follow what we call the factor analysis rule. In general, when conducting factor analysis, you should have at least 8 to 10 cases per item, although this is debatable (Benson & Nasser, 1998; Williams, Brown, & Onsman, 2010). This means that if you have a 20-item scale, you will need at least 160–200 participants. Following the factor analysis heuristic may allow you to have sufficient explanatory power to conduct your analyses.

Determining the number of participants for the qualitative aspect, on the other hand, requires a different approach. Choosing the number of participants for the qualitative component is an emergent process and operates under the notion of "saturation," which means the point at which you no longer gain any additional information (Merriam, 2009). You continue to add more participants until you no longer discover anything new. However, you do want to begin with a number of participants that is representative of the larger goals of your study. For instance, if you are studying low-SES pregnant women, it will be important to make sure that you have participants of varying races/ethnicities, from various regions, with varying access to insurance, et cetera. Also, you should keep the number of participants manageable. For example, although it may be tempting to interview 40 participants, do keep in mind that you will have to transcribe and code all of those interviews. You may need only 20 interviews to provide the pertinent information or to reach saturation (Guest, Bunce, & Johnson, 2006).

Now that you have figured out the number of participants that you need, it is imperative that you consider your sampling strategy. You have to have a plan to determine how you will best choose the participants for your study. Our discussion here is not to elaborate on the different types of sampling procedures but to inform you of the importance of describing your sampling strategy procedures in your research methods section. There are quantitative, qualitative, and mixed methods sampling strategies. Quantitative sampling strategies include probability, non-probability sampling, and purposeful sampling (see Gall, Gall, & Borg, 2007). There are also numerous qualitative sampling strategies; the most common include purposive, quota, and snowball sampling (see Mack, Woodsong, MacQueen, Guest, & Namey, 2005; Patton, 2002). Last, mixed methods sampling has four types: identical sampling, parallel sampling, nested sampling, and multilevel sampling (Collins, Onwuegbuzie, & Jiao, 2007; Mertens, 2014). Table 7.3 provides brief descriptions of several common types of mixed methods sampling strategies.

Table 7.3   Mixed Methods Sampling Strategy

Sampling Strategy	Description	When to Use in a Study	Most Appropriate Mixed Methods Designs
Identical Sampling	Using the same people in both the quantitative and qualitative components of the study.	When you want to understand the experiences of a single group of people in your sample.	• Convergent Parallel • Embedded
Parallel Sampling	Using different people, from the same population, in the quantitative and quantitative components of the study.	When you want to make claims about a population, but using the same sample for the quantitative and quantitative components is not necessary for your research purpose or feasible to accomplish.	• Convergent Parallel • Exploratory Sequential • Explanatory Sequential
Nested Sampling	Taking a subset of those in one method of the study to participate in the other method of the study.	When you want to further explore the experiences of a smaller group of participants.	• Exploratory Sequential • Explanatory Sequential
Multilevel Sampling	Different people from different populations are used for the various components of the study.	When you would like to obtain different but relevant perspectives regarding the same issue or different components of a project.	• Multiphase Design

Source: Adapted from Collins, Onwuegbuzie, and Jiao (2007).

Identical sampling involves using the same people in both the quantitative and qualitative components of the study. Such a sampling approach would allow you to make direct comparisons between participants' quantitative and qualitative responses. The second type, *parallel sampling*, involves using different people, from the same population, in the quantitative and quantitative components of the study. You can choose this approach if do not have access to or do not want to utilize the participants from the first component of the study for the second component. The third type, *nested sampling*, involves using a subset of those in one method of the study to participate in the other method of the study. In this type of sampling, you could choose a small number of participants to engage in interviews based upon their responses to a survey. Last, in *multilevel sampling*, different people from different populations are used for the various components of the study. This approach is best used if you are interested in examining how similar groups of people view or experience the phenomenon that is being explored. Overall, it is important to align your sampling strategy with your mixed methods design in the best way possible. Refer to Table 7.3 for sampling recommendations for specific mixed methods designs.

Although we have discussed distinct quantitative, qualitative, and mixed methods sampling strategies, it must be noted that convenience sampling cuts across approaches. Although we may start off with a plan to use a particular sampling approach, many of us end up obtaining samples of convenience. For instance, you may want to have a sample that resembles the general population and want to use random sampling techniques, but you end up having to conduct your study using willing participants from the psychology research pool. Regardless of the sampling strategy you end up using, it is essential that you consider and write about the pros and cons of that strategy in your proposal.

While thinking about your sampling strategy, you will also need to determine how you will actually gain access to your participants. You should really take considerable time to figure out whether or not you can realistically get access to your population of interest. For instance, do you have an "informant" or "gatekeeper," someone who can get you access to your population of interest? If not, do you have a strategy to cultivate a relationship with someone in order to develop someone into a gatekeeper? Or are you your own informant or gatekeeper? Do you have a relationship with the population of interest? Another question you should ask concerns time: How long will it take you to gain access to this population? How much time do you have to invest in recruiting participants? In addition, you should ponder the tactics you will use to recruit participants for your study. Although you may find your study to be the most interesting project in the world, it does not mean that everyone else will think about it in the same way. What will you do to encourage people to participate? Are you considering using incentives (e.g., gift cards) in order to entice people to participate? It is important to consider the number of incentives as well as the cost of using incentives while creating your participant description component.

Data Collection

The data collection component of the research methods section describes all of the steps you will take to procure the data. It is what you intend to do to collect the data as well as what you expect from your participants. In the data collection section, you need to focus on *what* data you plan on collecting, *when* you plan on collecting the data, *where* you will collect the data, *how* you will collect the data, and *why* you will collect the data. You address these questions within the instrumentation and data collection procedures subcomponents. Keep in mind that your approach to data collection should coincide with your mixed methods design. For instance, if you are utilizing an exploratory or explanatory sequential design, this suggests that you will collect one type of data before collecting another type of data. A convergent parallel design, on the other hand, implies the quantitative and qualitative data are collected simultaneously. With the embedded design, the secondary data can be collected before, during, or after the collection of the primary data from the traditional design. Likewise, the multiphase design consists of collecting data at various points in time.

Instrumentation

Within the instrumentation subcomponent, you focus on the types of data to be collected (the *what*), specifically the instruments you will use to collect the data. You need to describe all of the instruments, both quantitative and qualitative. If you are using surveys or tests, you should provide a brief explanation of the purpose of the survey/test, the structure of the survey/test (e.g., number of items), and the reliability and validity of the survey/test. Likewise, if you are conducting interviews or observations, you should describe your interview protocol/observation rubric. You should include complete copies of all instruments in the appendix section of your proposal.

Data Collection Procedures

The data collection procedures subcomponent focuses on the *when*, *where*, *how*, and *why*. You should discuss *when* data will be collected (e.g., time of day, month, year). Additionally, it is necessary to discuss *where* the data will be collected (e.g., on campus, in a hospital, in the participants' homes). Most important, you have to explain *how* you will collect the data. This requires you to provide explicit descriptions of the steps that you will take to collect the data and how the participants will be involved. In other words, what will your participants be doing from the beginning to the end of the data collection period? You have to provide a realistic description about how long the participants will be involved in the study. Keep in mind that if you are requiring too much from your participants (e.g., providing blood and urine samples, journaling, taking medications, participating in multiple interviews, taking a large number of surveys) or requiring too much of a time commitment, you may not get quality results or may have an attrition problem. Last, it is necessary for you to provide an explanation as to *why* you made your procedural choices. Your explanation is important for readers to better understand the choices that you made.

Data Analysis

After describing the data collection, it is necessary for you to discuss how you will approach data analysis in your study. Data analysis is the process of making sense of your data. The data analysis component of the research methods section is a discussion of the procedures and steps that you plan to take to analyze your data. Remember that your data analysis approach should align with your mixed methods design. For instance, if you are utilizing an exploratory or explanatory sequential design, you will analyze one type of data before collecting another type of data; the analysis of the first type of data often determines who will be in the sample for the second type of data or what second type of data will be collected. In a convergent parallel design, on the other hand, the quantitative and qualitative data are analyzed separately. With the embedded and multiphase designs, the quantitative and qualitative data can be analyzed sequentially or simultaneously, depending upon the purpose of the study.

The data analysis component involves a variety of subcomponents, including the analysis procedures, plan for data integration, reliability/credibility, and validity/trustworthiness.

Data Analysis Procedures

The procedures subcomponent describes the specific steps you will take to analyze the data. Within this subcomponent, you should focus on data organization, basic data analysis procedures, advanced analysis procedures, and how you will use specific software (Creswell, 2015). When discussing data organization, you should discuss how you plan to catalog your data (e.g., create a database storage system), clean your data (e.g., find missing data points, correct transcripts), and store your data (e.g., computer filing system, filing cabinets). For basic data analysis, you should focus on finding basic trends in your data. For quantitative data this would involve conducting descriptive statistical analysis, while for qualitative data this would involve conducting initial readings of your data and the possible creation of codes, books, or manuals to use for later analysis (see DeCuir-Gunby, Marshall, & McCulloch, 2011).

The discussion of the advanced analysis procedures is where you go into detail about the sophisticated analyses you will use to analyze your data. When discussing quantitative data, you will describe the various descriptive and inferential statistics that you will conduct and why you are using those particular analyses. When discussing the qualitative analysis, you will provide details as to how you will code the data, organize the codes, combine the codes into larger themes, and use those themes to create narratives (Strauss & Corbin, 1990). It is also important for you to discuss whether you are going to engage in *data transformation*, the converting of one form of data to another form of data (qualitative data to quantitative data or quantitative data to qualitative data) for the means of analysis (Onwuegbuzie & Teddlie, 2003). Data transformation is not required in order for a study to be considered mixed methods. However, data transformation is a common approach to mixed methods analysis.

Last, it is necessary for you to discuss the types of software you will use for your study. There are numerous software packages that can be used to analyze quantitative data (e.g., SPSS, SAS, R). In addition, there is software for the analysis of qualitative data (e.g., Atlas.ti, HyperRESEARCH, NVivo). There is even software designed to analyze both quantitative and qualitative data (e.g., MAXQDA and Dedoose). Being transparent about the use of software is important so that your readers can have a clearer understanding of your analysis process.

Data Integration

An important aspect of analyzing data in a mixed methods research study is the process of data integration, which involves the mixing of quantitative and qualitative data. In the data integration subcomponent, it is important for you to discuss how you will combine the quantitative and qualitative components of your data. According to Creswell (2015), data integration can occur in a variety of ways, including *merging* (combining the quantitative and qualitative data), *explaining* (using one form of data to explain another form), *building* (using one form of data to expand another form), or *embedding* (one form of data is a subset of the other). With a convergent parallel design, data integration is achieved through the process of merging (i.e., combining and comparing/contrasting the results of interviews and surveys that were collected/analyzed separately). The explanatory design uses the explaining form of data integration (i.e., findings from interviews will be used to explain findings from surveys). The exploratory sequential design uses the building form of data integration (i.e., findings from surveys will be used to expand upon the findings from interviews). With the embedded design, the data are integrated through embedding (i.e., findings from interviews will be used to support the findings from pre/post tests). With a multiphase design, data integration could consist of merging, explaining, and/or building.

Data integration is essential, because it showcases why the combination of quantitative and qualitative data was necessary for your study. However, at the data interpretation and reporting level, it can be difficult to demonstrate how you will integrate your data. There are three ways to engage in data integration at the data interpretation and reporting level that can be used in all mixed methods designs: narrative, data transformation, and joint displays (Fetters, Curry, & Creswell, 2013).

In the *narrative* approach, the quantitative and qualitative findings are integrated within a narrative or account. The quantitative and qualitative findings can be discussed together thematically, separately within the same document, or separately in different documents. The *data transformation* approach, on the other hand, requires more planning. With this approach, one form of data is transformed into another form of data. Then the transformed data is integrated into the dataset that has not been transformed. For example, interviews can be transformed into frequency counts and then integrated into the original interviews; thick rich descriptions from the interviews can serve as support for the frequency counts. The *joint display* approach involves using visuals as a means of integrating the data. In this approach, quantitative and qualitative data are organized using a visual in order to highlight a new perspective. Data displays can be used as a standalone means of demonstrating data integration, but they are often used in conjunction with the narrative and the data transformation approaches. While writing your mixed methods proposal, it is important for you to consider how you will engage in data integration at the data interpretation and reporting level. Will you use the narrative, data transformation, or joint display approach? Will you use a combination?

Role of Theoretical Framework

The theoretical framework helps to shape your overall research study and should play an important role in your data analysis. As such, it is necessary for you to discuss how your theoretical framework will be used in the data analysis process. Your inquiry worldview and substantive content theories should be essential to your analysis. For instance, if you are examining children's coping with the loss of loved ones using a poststructural inquiry worldview and Kübler-Ross's stages of grief as your substantive content theory, it is expected that your data analysis will require focusing on the children's use of language (poststructural inquiry worldview) while using Kübler-Ross's stages of grief to help analyze participants' interviews (substantive content theory). Using the theoretical framework in your discussion of the data analysis helps to reconnect your readers to the introduction section of your research proposal.

Reliability/Credibility

Within the data analysis component, it is also necessary for you to discuss how you will ensure that you are capturing consistency in the data. In this subcomponent, you should discuss the steps you will take to establish reliability/credibility. In quantitative research, there are four types of reliability (Gall, Gall, & Borg, 2007): interrater (raters giving consistent estimates), test-retest (consistency of measurement over time), parallel forms (consistency of results on two tests), and internal consistency (consistency of results across items within a test). In qualitative research, establishing credibility means demonstrating the believability of the results. Among the many ways of achieving this are triangulation, prolonged engagement in the field, and negative case analysis (see Lincoln & Guba, 1985). In order to have a reliable/credible study, it is expected that you will address as many forms as feasible. It is not expected that you will address every form of reliability/credibility in your study. However, the more evidence that you can provide, the more reliable or credible your results will be. It is important to state in your methods section what you plan to do and explain why. Avoid going into discussion about the approaches you do not plan to use.

Validity/Trustworthiness

The last subcomponent to be addressed in the research methods section concerns how you will address validity/trustworthiness. It is essential that you address validity in terms of both your quantitative and qualitative components. Again, as mentioned in the discussion on reliability, it is not expected that you will address every form of validity in your study. However, the more aspects you can address, the more believable your results will be.

In quantitative research, validity examines whether you are measuring what you say you are measuring. A traditional way to address validity is to examine separately content validity, criterion-related validity, and construct validity. A more modern way to examine validity is to use a unified approach, where construct validity encompasses content and criterion-related validity (Messick, 1995; Shepard, 1993). Taking this approach suggests establishing internal evidence (e.g., theoretical rationales for items, scale structures) and external evidence (e.g., relationships to other constructs). In qualitative research, trustworthiness involves determining "whether or not research findings seem accurate or reasonable to the people who were studied" (LeCompte, 2000, p. 152). With qualitative data, according to Lincoln and Guba (1985), establishing trustworthiness means that you have to establish credibility (believability of the results), transferability (research can be transferred to other contexts), dependability (findings are consistent and repeatable), and confirmability (findings are supported by the data). Trustworthiness can be addressed in a variety of ways, including using thick rich descriptions, member checking, audit trails, peer debriefing, and many other techniques (see Lincoln & Guba, 1985).

In mixed methods research, validity and trustworthiness are often discussed in terms of *inference making*. It is essential to address the quality of the metainferences that are being made from your combining of quantitative and qualitative data (Teddlie & Tashakkori, 2009). One way to assess the quality of metainferences is to use the *legitimation* model (Onwuegbuzie & Johnson, 2006), which suggests that issues of validity should be continuously evaluated throughout a research study. Types of legitimation include sample integration, inside-outside, weakness minimization, sequential, conversion, paradigmatic mixing, commensurability, multiple validities, and political legitimation. In addition, in the validation framework by Dellinger and Leech (2007), it is recommended that you also consider a *consequential* aspect to your study. What are the consequences of your study being conducted? How will your findings be used? It is very important to consider the potential impact of your research study, specifically how others will use it.

PRACTICE SESSION

Guided Questions

The following questions will assist you in thinking about several components of the research methods section of the mixed methods proposal.

1. What are your current research questions? What research methods will help you to answer those questions?

2. What is your research context?

3. How many participants will you need?

4. What types of data will you collect?

5. What software packages will you use for your data analysis?

6. What types of data analysis will you conduct?

Writing Activity for the Research Methods Section

The purpose of this activity is to enable you to think deeply about the data collection and analysis processes to be used in your proposal. For this activity, you will provide a detailed summary of the methods that will be used in your research proposal. The idea is that your summary will be expanded to create your research methods section. Focus on the following questions:

1. What research questions/hypotheses are guiding your inquiry? State your research questions/inquiry.

2. How will you define mixed methods? State your rationale for using a mixed methods approach.

3. What mixed methods design will you use? Explain the mixed methods design that is being employed.

4. Who are your participants? Describe your context, participants, and the recruitment strategies used to gain access to participants.

5. What instruments (data sources) will you use in your study? Describe the instruments used to address each research question.

6. What are your data collection strategies? Describe data collection procedures for each research question.

7. How will you analyze your data? Describe the data analysis strategies for each research question.

8. What is your strategy for data integration? Discuss how you will integrate the quantitative and qualitative data.

9. How will you address reliability/credibility and validity/trustworthiness? Provide reliability/credibility and validity/trustworthiness techniques to be used for each research question.

Additional Resources on Developing the Research Methods Section of the Mixed Methods Research Proposal

Locke, L. F., Spirduso, W. W., & Silverman, S. J. (2013). *Proposals that work: A guide for planning dissertations and grant proposals* (6th ed.). Thousand Oaks, CA: Sage.

Ogden, T. E., & Goldberg, I. A. (2002). *Research proposals: A guide to success* (3rd ed.). Waltham, MA: Academic Press.

Punch, K. F. (2006). *Developing effective research proposals* (2nd ed.). Thousand Oaks, CA: Sage.

Sample Session—Research Methods Summary

The following is an example of a research methods summary that is based upon our racial microaggressions study. This summary can be used as a model to help develop your own outline for your proposal.

Research Questions

RQ #1: What are African American college students' experiences with racial microaggressions? (Quantitative & Qualitative)

RQ #1A: How do African American college students cope with and regulate the emotions associated with the experience of racial microaggressions? (Quantitative & Qualitative)

RQ #1B: How is their experience of racial microaggressions related to African American college students' sense of racial identity? (Quantitative)

RQ #1C: Where do African American college students see the boundary between microaggressions and nonmicroaggressions? (Qualitative)

RQ #2: What are the psychological need profiles of African American college students? (Quantitative)

RQ #2A: How do African American college students who score high on the measure of psychological needs scale address racial microaggressions? (Quantitative)

RQ #3: What is the relationship among racial microaggressions, racial identity, coping and emotional regulation strategies, and psychological needs for African American college students? (Quantitative)

Mixed Methods Definition

- Mixed methods is defined as "research in which the investigator collects and analyzes data, integrates the findings, and draws inferences using both qualitative and quantitative approaches or methods in a single study or program of inquiry" (Tashakkori & Creswell, 2007, p. 4).

- We are using a mixed methods approach because it will allow us to capture the breadth of students' experiences as well as provide in-depth descriptions of students' experiences with racial microaggressions.

Research Design

We will use an explanatory sequential mixed methods design (QUAN → qual). See Chapter 6 for our research diagram.

Sample/Participants

A total of 400 African American students who are currently enrolled in predominately White colleges and universities (PWIs) will be recruited to complete an online survey. We will recruit participants from a variety of PWIs throughout the United States. Participants for the quantitative part of the study will be recruited by accessing personal connections via e-mail and Facebook. Invitations for participation will also be sent to several organizational discussion lists. After the quantitative data has been analyzed, a subset of participants (n = 20) will be selected to participate in the qualitative portion of the study. Participants will be chosen based upon their scores on various instruments used in the study.

Data Collection

Instruments/Data Sources

- Racial and Ethnic Microaggressions Scale (Nadal, 2011)
- Coping With Discrimination Scale (Wei, Alvarez, Ku, Russell, & Bonett, 2010)
- Emotional Regulation Questionnaire (Gross & John, 2003)
- Multidimensional Inventory of Black Identity (Sellers, Smith, Shelton, Rowley, & Chavous, 1998)
- Basic Psychological Needs at College Scale (Deci & Ryan, 2000)
- A semistructured interview schedule (Moustakas, 1994) featuring broad, open-ended questions will be used to capture the participants' experiences with racial microaggressions, their coping ability, and their sense of racial identity. All interviews will be audio-taped and later transcribed for data analysis.

Data Collection Procedures

- Potential participants will be recruited using e-mail, Facebook, and discussion lists. In the recruitment letter, participants will be provided a direct hyperlink to a Qualtrics-based survey.
- Once participants click on the survey hyperlink, they will be redirected to the consent form, where they will be explicitly asked if they are interested in participating in the survey. If they choose "yes,"

they will be confirming that they do consent to participate in the study and will be directed to the survey questions. If they choose "no," they will be directed to a page that thanks participants for their interest in the survey.

- After consenting, the participants will be asked to complete a demographics survey as well as surveys concerning racial microaggressions, coping, emotional regulation, racial identity, and psychological needs. Once the surveys have been completed, participants will be asked if they are willing to participate in an interview. If so, they will be asked to give their contact information (name and e-mail address). If not, their participation in the survey will be completed and the survey will be ended. The data collected will be confidential; IP addresses will not be collected.

- Once the survey information has been collected, the data will be analyzed using SPSS. We will conduct descriptive statistical analysis as well as perform exploratory factor analysis. Next we will conduct inferential statistical analyses such as correlations, regressions, and ANOVAs. More advanced analyses may also be conducted using other software packages such as LISREL.

- The results of our quantitative analyses will help dictate our initial selection of the participants for the interviews that will be later collected. We will use the qualitative data to further explore the quantitative findings. For example, if we find that African American men experienced the most racial microaggressions on campus, we may choose to focus our interviews on that subgroup. Once the interviewees have been chosen, we will send them invitations to participate in the study. Before the interviews are conducted, participants will be asked to complete a consent form. The interviews will be conducted using a semistructured interview guide over the telephone, via Skype videoconference, or in person at an agreed upon, neutral location. All interviews will be audio-recorded using a digital recording device. If the interview is a videoconference, only the audio portion will be recorded. Although we are planning to interview 20 participants, it is possible that we will stop conducting interviews once we have reached saturation, or when the interviews no longer produce any new information. All interview participants will be informed that they may be contacted for follow-up interviews if necessary.

- After the interviews have been conducted, they will be transcribed. We will then use Atlas.ti, a qualitative software package, to help analyze and sort the data. We will code the data, organize the data into themes, and connect the data to the larger research literature.

- Once we have finished analyzing the quantitative and qualitative data, we will combine the findings. We will use this information to create manuscripts that will be submitted to research journals as well as national conferences.

Data Analysis

Procedures

- For the quantitative data, several analyses will be conducted:
  - o Basic descriptive statistics (means, standard deviations, etc.) will be calculated in order to help describe the data.
  - o Inferential statistical analyses will be conducted (ANOVAs, MANOVAs, multiple regression, cluster analyses, confirmatory factor analysis, etc.).
- The interviews will be analyzed using thematic content analysis (Coffey & Atkinson, 1996).
  - o We will begin with open coding at the sentence/paragraph level (Corbin & Strauss, 2015).
  - o Next, we will list all of the codes and organize them into categories (Corbin & Strauss, 2015).
  - o We will then utilize the statements that best illustrate these categories to construct each participant's counterstory (Solórzano & Yosso, 2002).
  - o In order to explore their counterstories, we will use the analysis of narratives approach (see Polkinghorne, 1995). In the analysis of narratives approach, the goal is to find common themes across participants' stories (Polkinghorne, 1995).
  - o Critical race theory (CRT) will serve as the lens of analysis (DeCuir & Dixson, 2004).

Data Integration

The quantitative data will help determine how the qualitative data are collected. Once all data are collected and analyzed, the quantitative and qualitative findings will be discussed together. The qualitative data will be used to support, contradict, or expand the quantitative findings.

Reliability/Credibility

- In order to address reliability for the quantitative component, reliability analyses (Cronbach's alpha) will be conducted on the surveys.
- To address credibility for the qualitative component, the following techniques will be used:
  - o The interviews will be coded at least twice in order to ensure that we do not miss any significant findings and to check our interpretations.
  - o Peer reviewers/debriefers will code a subset of the interviews.

Validity/Trustworthiness

- In order to address validity for the quantitative components, exploratory factor analysis/confirmatory factor analysis will be conducted on the surveys.
- Trustworthiness will be addressed using thick rich descriptions and member checking with the participants (Merriam, 2009).

REFERENCES FOR RESEARCH METHODS SUMMARY ●

Coffey, A., & Atkinson, P. (1996). *Making sense of qualitative data: Complementary research designs.* Thousand Oaks, CA: Sage.

Corbin, J. M., & Strauss, A. L. (2015). *Basics of qualitative research: Techniques and procedures for developing grounded theory* (4th ed.). Thousand Oaks, CA: Sage.

Deci, E. L., & Ryan, R. M. (2000). The "what" and "why" of goal pursuits: Human needs and the self-determination of behavior. *Psychological Inquiry, 11,* 227–268.

DeCuir, J. T., & Dixson, A. (2004). "So when it comes out, they aren't that surprised that it is there": Using critical race theory as a tool of analysis of race and racism in education. *Educational Researcher, 33*(5), 26–31.

Gross, J. J., & John, O. P. (2003). Individual differences in two emotion regulation processes: Implications for affect, relationships, and well-being. *Journal of Personality and Social Psychology, 85,* 348–362.

Merriam, S. B. (2009). *Qualitative research: A guide to design and implementation.* San Francisco, CA: Jossey-Bass.

Moustakas, C. E. (1994). *Phenomenological research methods.* Thousand Oaks: Sage.

Nadal, K. (2011). The racial and ethnic microaggressions scale (REMS): Construction, reliability, and validity. *Journal of Counseling Psychology, 58*(4), 470–480.

Polkinghorne, D. E. (1995). Narrative configuration in qualitative analysis. *Qualitative Studies in Education, 8*(1), 5–23.

Sellers, R. M., Smith, M. A., Shelton, J. N., Rowley, S. A., & Chavous, T. M. (1998). Multidimensional model of racial identity: A reconceptualization of African American racial identity. *Personality and Social Psychology Review, 2*(1), 18–39.

Solórzano, D. G., & Yosso, T. J. (2002). Critical race methodology: Counterstorytelling as an analytical framework for education research. *Qualitative Inquiry, 8*(1), 23–44.

Wei, M., Alvarez, A., Ku, T., Russell, D., & Bonett, D. (2010). Development and validation of a coping with discrimination scale: Factor structure, reliability, and validity. *Journal of Counseling Psychology, 57*(3), 328–344.

8

A Little *Lagniappe* ...
A Little Something Extra

Objectives

1. To develop an understanding of the supporting components of a mixed methods proposal.

2. To develop ways of writing and talking about your mixed methods proposal.

3. To understand additional issues that extend beyond the mixed methods proposal.

In the Gulf Coast region of the United States, primarily in Louisiana, as well as in other places across the world, it is common for vendors to show appreciation to their customers by providing some *lagniappe* or a little something extra for *gratis* or good measure. It is similar to the concept of a baker's dozen (i.e., 13 instead of 12 donuts). Now that we are at the end of the book, we would like to provide you with a little *lagniappe*. Specifically, we want to talk to you about how to bring the components of the proposal together, give you some general writing tips, and help you to think beyond your mixed methods proposal.

● THE SUPPORTING SECTIONS OF THE MIXED METHODS PROPOSAL

As previously discussed, the mixed methods proposal consists of three major sections (introduction, literature review, and methods sections) and two supporting sections (references and appendices). We have discussed the three major sections in Chapters 4, 5, and 7. Now it is important for us to have a discussion regarding the two supporting sections, the references and the appendix, as well as two other components, the title and the abstract. We will present our discussions of these components in the order in which they appear in the mixed methods proposal.

The Mixed Methods Title

An important component of the mixed methods research proposal is the title, which should be a synopsis of your research proposal. According to Creswell and Plano Clark (2011), a good title should do the following: (1) be short and succinct; (2) describe the topic being addressed, including the participants and location; (3) include the term "mixed methods"; and (4) reflect the type of mixed methods design that is being used in the study. Creswell (2015) also suggests that titles should be kept as short as possible, using a colon when necessary to separate two components. As such, titles for mixed methods studies are distinctive and tend to place emphasis around the methods. We, however, suggest that your title capture the main topics or constructs that are being explored as well as the population of interest, which will help the reader to better contextualize your study. Your title should be a brief synopsis of your proposal. You can emphasize your methodological design, but from our perspective, doing so is not mandatory. It really depends upon the purpose of your study. See Table 8.1 for examples of mixed methods research titles according to research topic and design.

Although *how* to write the title is important, it is also necessary to consider *when* to write the title. Some researchers prefer to write their titles before beginning to write; they cannot start their proposal unless they have a title, because they believe that a title will help guide the writing process. However, others like to write their titles once the introduction section (or even the whole proposal) has been completed. Our suggestion is that you think of any title that you use as a *working title* in that it will most likely be revised some time within the proposal writing process. Do not be afraid to develop several alternative titles. Just be flexible in that whatever serves as the initial title will most likely

Table 8.1   Sample Mixed Methods Research Titles by Research Topic and Design

Sample Research Topics	Mixed Methods Design	Sample Mixed Methods Research Proposal Titles
Veterans' experiences with reacclimatizing to civilian life	Explanatory Sequential	Becoming a Civilian Again: A Mixed Methods Explanation of the Experiences of Veterans' Reacclimation to Civilian Life
The experiences of children who are suffering from food insecurity	Exploratory Sequential	Understanding What It Is Like to Be a Child Suffering From Food Insecurity: A Mixed Methods Study
An exploration of the leadership styles of women executives	Convergent Parallel	Women Executives as Organizational Leaders and Change Agents: Integrating Qualitative and Quantitative Methods
The impact of the use of electronic tablets for modifying the behavior of students in a special education classroom	Embedded	Using Electronic Tablets to Help Modify Behavior in Special Education Classrooms: A Mixed Methods Experiment
The development and evaluation of a curriculum designed to teach nurses how to care for patients with highly infectious and deadly diseases	Multiphase	The Mixed Methods Design and Evaluation of a Training Program to Teach Nurses How to Care for Patients With Ebola

go through several iterations. Therefore, do not feel pressured to develop a title when you begin developing your proposal. Instead, write your title when you feel able to craft a title, all the while knowing that it will only be tentative.

The Abstract

Although it is not a requirement for all mixed methods proposals, many disciplines recommend that you include an abstract. An *abstract* is a short summary or synopsis of your research study or proposal. The abstract focuses on all of the important elements of your study, including the topic, context, participants, methods, findings, and conclusions. In the proposal stage, the abstract summarizes what you *intend* to do in your study. However, after you have finished your study, the abstract summarizes what you *actually did* and *found* in your study. Abstracts vary in length depending upon discipline and can be anywhere from 150 to 500 words. Although relatively short, abstracts are often difficult to write. It can be very challenging to summarize your research study in so few words. Thus, be prepared to write multiple drafts and do a lot of editing. Like writing the title, we find that it is often easiest to write the abstract in the later stages of the proposal writing process.

The References

The reference section is the listing of all of the sources that you used to write your mixed methods proposal. The reference section is listed at the end of the proposal, usually after the methods section. There are multiple ways of generating the reference section. Some people like to compile the reference list as they write, while others prefer to wait until the manuscript is completed before attempting to compile the references. Some rely on the assistance of a commercial computer database system (for examples see Gilmour & Cobus-Kuo, 2011), while others prefer the manual listing of references. Regardless of the approach you take, it is imperative that you be systematic with the recording of your references. In addition, it is necessary for you to use the appropriate publication writing style (e.g., APA, MLA, Chicago) for your particular field, and many university graduate schools also have their own style requirements. So make sure you have those guidelines as well. The bottom line is that however you approach this task, strategy wise, it will be important to keep up with your reference section throughout the writing process. Keep in mind you may end up with hundreds of citations, so doing a little at a time will help to maintain your sanity.

The Appendix

Last, the appendix is the true *lagniappe* section of your mixed methods proposal, in that it can potentially feature a variety of documents. This is where you place supporting documents that would break up the flow of your proposal if they were inserted in the text, yet that are important to the overall understanding of the research you are proposing. Make sure to reference the documents you put in the appendix in the actual proposal. Common documents to be included in the appendix section include research instruments (e.g., surveys, tests, interview protocols, observation protocols), mixed methods research design diagrams, human subjects ethics documents (e.g., recruitment scripts, informed consent and assent forms), and research timelines, among many others. Basically, the appendix is used to show-case any additional information that you want your readers to know about that you could not place within the text of the proposal. Also make sure to organize your appendix logically; for example, order the documents in the appendix in the same order they appear in the proposal.

For information that absolutely needs to be read, make sure that you do *not* put it in the appendix. Readers often have the tendency to overlook the appendix section. On the other hand, if they are looking for a particular item (e.g., the items on a survey you plan to use) and it is not anywhere in the document, you will make the readers a bit unhappy. Remember happy graders/reviewers will more likely lead to happy grades/reviews.

WRITING AND TALKING ABOUT YOUR MIXED METHODS PROPOSAL

Now that we have reviewed the major components as well as intro-duced you to supporting components of the mixed methods proposal, we would like to switch gears a bit and provide you with some general advice. Specifically, we would like to talk to you about how to approach writing your mixed methods proposal as well as how to talk about your mixed methods proposal.

General Writing Tips

Writing a research proposal can be a daunting task. Because of this, you need to approach writing with a clear but flexible plan in mind. First, remember, when writing, there is a difference between compos-ing and editing. Composing involves getting your words down on paper. Editing, on the other hand, involves making sure those words say what you want them to say. We have found that it is useful to try to keep these two writing processes separate, especially as you begin writing the different sections of your proposal, particularly the litera-ture review. In essence, writing your literature review may be the most creative part of your research proposal. It is where you synthesize what you have read into a unique way of looking at your problem area. This is where you are trying to get your ideas out, so anything that slows that process down has the potential to interfere with the process of formulating your ideas. For example, as we are composing this paragraph in a word processing program, we can see a few words that are underlined in red (i.e., misspelled words) and some in green (i.e., grammar or sentence structure problems). However, the act of stopping our composing to make those changes breaks the flow in our ideas and getting them out. Thus, we have found that it is more useful to separate composing from editing our writing. Once we complete this sentence, we can go back and edit this paragraph and make sure it says what we want it to say.

Second, it is also important to keep in mind that sometimes you need to be patient while writing. Some days you may only be able to squeeze out a paragraph, while other days you may get pages. That is part of the process and why it is important to expand your ideas about what counts as writing. Let us give you a few examples of tasks that can also be considered parts of the writing process: (1) developing and continuing to work on an outline for your review of the literature; (2) editing a section you wrote earlier; (3) making sure your references are updated; (4) reading a research article (one thing that we have found is that sometimes when you are struggling with your composing, it may simply mean that you need to read more); (5) creating diagrams, models, or tables for your proposal. So remember, writing a research proposal involves a lot of different activities, including composing, editing, updating references, making tables and figures, and developing models to represent your theoretical framework or the data you have previously analyzed. Keep in mind that if you are doing these things, you are still writing and still on task.

Third, you need to plan when you will write or engage in writing activities. Before you do so, you need to remember there is no right way to engage in writing processes. Some people write best early in the morning, while others are better writers late at night. Some people like to write in environments where there is background noise (e.g., at home with music, at a coffee shop) while others prefer complete silence (e.g., at a cubby at the library). However, planning when you will write helps to make writing routine and mandatory. You should set aside a specific amount of time to write on a regular basis. It helps to even mark it on your calendar. That way, writing is seen as just as important as any other appointment that you have scheduled. The big issue to figure out is when you should schedule your writing sessions. Some experts suggest that you should set aside time to write daily (which is the goal of Paul, the second author of this book). This allows you to stay current with what you are writing and contemplating. However, writing every day generally means writing for small periods of time every day. Not everyone is able to or likes to write in short time frames. Many people, including Jessica, the first author of this book, prefer to write in blocks. The goal here is to try to schedule several hours a day on multiple days a week for writing. Using this approach allows you to write on a regular basis but within large chunks of time. Either approach will enable you to take a task-based approach to writing. Sometimes instead of focusing on the amount of time you want to write each week, it is better to focus on the specific tasks you want to accomplish (e.g., finish a conclusion or create a diagram). Setting specific writing goals each week helps you to progress in a systematic manner.

Fourth, it is imperative that you are familiar with the writing styles of your discipline. Even after you have composed your proposal in terms of content, you will still need to edit in terms of style. Every discipline has a common style or way of writing. Most disciplines prefer the use of specific language or terminology, and it is important for you to become familiar with your field's preferences. When writing your proposal, it would be useful for you to examine the writings in your top journals to explore the writing styles of the researchers in your field. This will help you to craft a proposal that more resembles the writings of others in your discipline. Also, it is imperative that your writing is consistent with the publication styles most commonly used in your field (e.g., APA, Chicago, or MLA). Each publication style differs from the others and features various idiosyncrasies that are not easily remembered, especially for formatting headings, tables, and figures. It often takes practice in order to master the use of any publication style. In fact, we have been using the most current American Psychological Association (2009) format since its publication, and we still have to refer to the manual on a regular basis in order to double check formatting issues. Our advice is that you should get familiar with your respective publication manual as soon as possible (long before you begin developing your proposal).

Last, while writing your proposal, it is important to have some established deadlines in order to help create accountability. It is difficult to write without knowing when something is due or needs to be completed. As such, it is helpful to have some self-imposed and/or external deadlines to help motivate your writing. In order to do so, we suggest that you develop a timeline and do your best to stick to it. You can develop your own internal deadlines, or you can get someone else to help create those deadlines. For example, you can suggest that your dissertation chair create dates for when he or she would like to see drafts. You can also join a writing group where each member is expected to present work on a particular day. A third option is to become a member of a writing accountability group. Such groups meet weekly or biweekly to discuss members' writing goals and progress toward those goals. Members of the group help to motivate each other to make reasonable writing goals and to continue to achieve the writing goals. Jessica, the first author of this book, is a member of a writing accountability group and utilized the group throughout the writing of this book. The process indeed works! Whatever method you use, just make sure that you use the method that best works for your approach to writing and helps to keep you accountable for your writing.

Talking About Your Mixed Methods Proposal

Although the mixed methods proposal really is about the written document, it is also important to discuss how to talk about your research study. Inevitably and continually, you will be asked, "What is your study about?" When you are asked this question, you are not being invited to provide a lecture on your entire proposal. Instead, you are really being asked to provide a brief snapshot of your proposal. As such, you have to figure out what you should say, in the smallest amount of words possible. In other words, you need to have an abbreviated oral description of your mixed methods research proposal.

The Elevator Speech

A short oral description, sometimes referred to as an elevator speech, is a 30- to 60-second pitch or description of an issue of interest, or in your case, a description of your research study. It is called *the elevator speech* because you want to be able to tell someone about your study in the time it would take to ride an elevator several floors. Thus, the purpose of the elevator speech is to provide your listeners, who presumably have limited time, with a broad overview of your study. The goal is for them to walk away with a good understanding of your study and be convinced that you are planning a good study. In addition, the listeners should also be able to remember the details of your speech and easily repeat them to others. In giving an elevator speech, you do not have a lot of time for details, so focus on the bigger picture.

Your elevator speech should include a broad overview of the study, explain what you are doing, and discuss why the study is important. Because a period of 30 to 60 seconds goes by quickly, it is important that you practice your elevator speech. The more you practice, the more natural your speech will become. See Box 8.1 for an example of an elevator speech.

Alternative Presentations

Luckily you will not have to adhere to such a severe time crunch every time you are asked to talk about your mixed methods proposal. However, you will be expected to learn to talk about your proposal (and even your research) in short time frames. For instance, when you present at conferences, it is very common to have only 10–15 minutes allotted for your entire presentation, including results. As such, many universities and programs are beginning to require their students to be able to present their research in short time segments of 3–5 minutes. One common approach is to use the 3-minute thesis (see http://three minutethesis.org/), where you have to present your proposal (or entire research study) to an audience that is outside of your academic area. This approach requires you to hone your communication skills and

---

Box 8.1   **Racial Microaggressions Study Elevator Speech**

As highlighted by the many recent race-related events, racial microaggressions are prevalent in our society, even on college campuses. Our study examines how African American college students experience racial microaggressions in the college context. Using an explanatory sequential mixed methods design featuring Likert-item surveys and interviews, we explore how African American college students cope with experiencing racial microaggressions and regulate their emotions. We also examine how experiencing racial microaggressions impacts their sense of racial identity and self-determination (autonomy, competence, and relatedness). Our study findings will have implications for helping African American college students to better cope with the emotional labor associated with experiencing racial microaggressions, as well as give suggestions to universities to help make their environments more receptive to students of color.

necessitates that you focus on the most crucial elements of your proposal. Another form of presentation that is becoming popular is the PechaKucha style (http://www.pechakucha.org/). The format of PechaKucha is to create and present your work using 20 images (20 slides) for 20 seconds each (20x20). The images represent aspects of your study. This approach is another way for you to practice your communication skills and to learn how to succinctly describe your research.

In short, in addition to writing about your mixed methods study, you have to learn to be able to talk about your mixed methods proposal in a variety of ways. There will be opportunities for you to have extended discussions with lengthy time frames. Other times you will be expected to be quite succinct. As such, it is important for you to practice describing your mixed methods proposal using various time frames and in a variety of formats.

● ISSUES BEYOND WRITING THE MIXED METHODS RESEARCH PROPOSAL

In the beginning of this chapter we talked about how we wanted to provide you with more than a discussion on how to prepare a mixed methods research proposal. We would like to discuss some issues that expand beyond the proposal. These issues include creating your committee (if you are a doctoral student), communicating with the institutional review board (IRB), publishing mixed methods research, and procuring grants using mixed methods approaches.

Creating Your Committee

The members of your dissertation/thesis committee are important players in the development of your mixed methods proposal. However, it is also important to keep in mind that the key word in the previous sentence is *your*; in other words, remember this is *your* committee, and it is important that you take ownership of your committee. That ownership begins with the selection of your committee members, which begins with the selection of your chair(s). There are people in the academy who refer to their dissertation chairs as their academic mothers or fathers, which is an indication of the potential nature and importance of the relationship between you and your chair. This means that before you ask someone to be your chair, do your homework. Talk to students who are further along in the program or students who have already graduated. Take classes from the faculty you might be interested in. Ask yourself the guiding questions in Table 8.2.

Table 8.2   Committee Chair and Committee Members Questionnaire

Key Areas	Guiding Questions
Chair and committee content and research skills	Do they have at least some content expertise?
	Do they have research methods expertise?
	Are they open to approaching your research from a mixed methods perspective?
Chair and committee interactions with students	Do they make themselves available to students?
	Do they have a record of publishing with students?
Chair and committee personal characteristics	Do they seem to have good relationships with other faculty members?
	Are they organized yet flexible?
	Do they have a sense of humor?
	Do they enjoy their work?

Source: Adapted from the Committee Member Selection Guide (Rossman, 2002), with permission of SAGE Publications, Inc.

The first question you may want to ask yourself is, "Do they have sufficient content knowledge in your area of interest?" Remember your goal is to develop subject matter expertise; therefore it will be helpful if your chair and at least some of the other committee members have expertise they can use to guide you on your path to become an expert. For the most part, it is probably unlikely that every member of your committee will be an expert in your particular area of interest, but it will be important that at least some members have some expertise even if it is in a slightly different area. You should also have at least one member of your committee who will provide you with research methods expertise. Ideally you would like to have someone who has expertise in quantitative, qualitative, and mixed methods. Unfortunately, that is not always possible, so you may need multiple people with research methods skills. But at a minimum, you will need a chair who is open to the idea of exploring your research questions within the context of a mixed methods proposal.

The next set of guiding questions deals with how the chair and other potential members of the committee interact with students.

Access to your committee will be important. So the next question is, "Do they make themselves available to meet with their students on a regular basis (i.e., weekly or biweekly)?" Remember you will want to meet regularly with your advisor—so accessibility is useful and important. Also keep in mind that you should construct an agenda for each meeting, and you should communicate that agenda to your advisor ahead of time. That way, your advisor will know what you want to talk about at each meeting. Ideally you would also like to find a chair and other committee members who have a track record of publishing with their students. This demonstrates willingness and some experience working with and helping students along their paths of becoming professionals.

The third set of questions basically asks about some of the personal characteristics of your potential committee members. First of all, do they "play well with others"? The chair's role is more than just helping you with your proposal. The chair will also need to be an advocate for you inside and outside of your university. Therefore chairs need to have contacts and connections, and this is more likely if they play well with others! You can also benefit by finding someone who is organized, yet has some flexibility of thought, who will allow you to be creative. For example, if committee members want you to work *only* with the ideas and methods they are comfortable with, trying to do something different could be a problem. Next, do they have a sense of humor? Researching and writing a dissertation is a challenging process, which means that having members who can make you laugh during the process can be very helpful. Finally and quite simply, do they enjoy their work? Like people in every other occupation, there are people in the academy who, for various reasons, simply do not like what they do. As you know, if you do not like what you do, you most likely will not do a good job at it. So find people who enjoy what they do.

Gaining Approval From the Institutional Review Board (IRB)

Another important area to discuss is getting permission to conduct your study. If you are conducting research with human or animal subjects, you have to obtain permission or approval from the IRB before you can begin your research. The IRB is a committee that monitors and reviews biomedical and behavioral research and your institution (Enfield & Truwit, 2008). Numerous countries have their own regulations and guidelines regarding the ethical conduct of research with human subjects. In the United States, research on human subjects must follow regulations from the Food and Drug Administration (FDA) and the Department of Health and Human Services (DHHS), while research on animals follows regulations from the Institutional Animal Care and Use Committee (IACUC). Specifically, IRBs in the United States follow the *Code of Federal Regulations* Title 45, Part 46, which details the policies and procedures for conducting research with human subjects. Most, if not all, academic institutions have their own IRBs. However, private companies often do not have their own IRBs and instead use independent IRBs that are located in the local community. All IRBs are subject to the same rules and regulations. Not following the policies and procedures that have been approved in your IRB application puts you in violation of or noncompliance with IRB rules and regulations. You will have to immediately stop all research activities until all violations have been corrected. Institutions having a history of severe ethics violations can even be punished, resulting in everyone associated with an institution not being able to conduct research involving human subjects. Needless to say, adhering to IRB protocols is a mandatory requirement.

Crafting an IRB application for a mixed methods research study requires substantial attention; thus it is important for you to be knowledgeable about the IRB application process. When creating your overall research timeline, make sure that you take into consideration the amount of time it will take to prepare your IRB application and have it reviewed, as well as any additional time associated with making revisions to your application. Any research involving vulnerable populations (e.g., children, pregnant women, the incarcerated) will take longer to review, because the IRB will need to make sure that protections are in place to ensure that subjects will not be harmed or exploited. Similarly, research that requires invasive procedures such as being exposed to chemicals or taking medications will involve extra scrutiny and will take more time to be approved. Keep in mind that if you intend to conduct research in public schools, for instance, you may have to complete separate protocols for each school district, adding time to your overall research timeline.

In addition, a mixed methods study often consists of complicated data collection procedures because of the use of both quantitative and qualitative methods. Because of this, you will need to be careful to write your procedures in a clear manner. It is also important to keep in mind that different ethical issues can emerge based on the design you decide to use. For example, in sequential designs, you often plan to return to participants for additional data gathering. This can cause some problems, because you may need to get permission to collect private contact information. Moreover, if an IRB reviewer, who may possibly be outside of your field, can understand your procedures, then it is likely that your potential research participants will understand what you intend for them to do in your study. Likewise, if the IRB reviewer does not understand your procedures, chances are that your potential participants will have a difficult time as well. In short, take great care when crafting your IRB application.

Given the importance of the IRB process, it is necessary that you spend time learning about it. Here are a couple of suggestions: First, ask other people for copies of proposals that have already received IRB approval. This will give you a road map of how you should approach your particular IRB approval. Second, it may be useful for you to speak with someone at the IRB before submitting your application. After you have a draft of your proposal and your IRB documents, set up an appointment with someone in the IRB office so that you have a contact person and can get help with the specifics from someone in that office. Bottom line is that this process takes time, and you need to plan for it.

Publishing Mixed Methods Research

Your mixed methods study should not be considered to be just one study. It should be seen as a part of your overall research agenda or program of research. A program of research is the development of a particular theme or line of research that is significant to your field, builds from the research literature, is relevant to your discipline, and is a reflection of your commitment, passion, and interests (Holzemer, 2009). If you are a doctoral student, your mixed methods proposal (for your dissertation) is probably the first real step in firmly developing your program of research. Although you may enjoy conducting mixed methods research studies, it does not necessarily mean that all of your research will be mixed methods studies. It is quite possible that you may have a mixture of mixed methods, quantitative, and qualitative studies.

While you are writing your proposal, you should begin to think about potential publication outlets for your work. We know that it is a bit early, especially since you do not have any data yet; however, it is never too soon to consider the many ways you can potentially publish your work. After you have conducted the research that you intend to propose, you will need to have a plan for publishing. You should ask yourself the following questions: Will you attempt to publish your work as a mixed methods study? Will you publish the quantitative and qualitative components separately? Will you be able to publish in your academic field? Thinking about these questions ahead of time will help streamline the process once you are actually ready to begin publishing.

Determining where to publish is not always an easy decision. Unfortunately, there are only a few journals that cater to publishing mixed methods research, including the *Journal of Mixed Methods Research* and the *International Journal of Multiple Research Approaches*. However, many journals within disciplines are receptive to publishing mixed methods articles. There are even special mixed methods issues in discipline-based journals. We recommend that you take time to investigate the various journals in your field by reading what the journals say they will publish (aims and scope of the journal) and what they actually publish (published articles). Take note of how often you see mixed methods articles. If you see mixed methods articles published frequently, this means that particular journal is potentially a good target for your work. If you see mixed methods articles infrequently or not at all, this suggests that journal may not be the best option for your mixed methods study. However, some journals are not receptive to mixed methods work because they have rigid page limit requirements or do not have reviewers with expertise in mixed methods research. In such cases, you may have to publish the quantitative and qualitative components separately. You may even have to consider publishing outside of your academic discipline. This practice is becoming more accepted with the increase in interdisciplinary work. Whatever choice you make for publishing your work, make sure that you choose outlets that best showcase the quality of your work and that will be accepted by your discipline.

Procuring Grants Using Mixed Methods Approaches

If you are in any way affiliated with a university, you have heard about the importance of procuring grants, not only to fund your line of research, but in some cases, to fund your position and/or your students and other employees. Because of this, understanding the importance of the grant-writing process is a necessity. As such, we highly recommend that you become familiar with the governmental and private grant-funding agencies that are relevant to your field. Also, we recommend that you read previously awarded proposals. Reading previously awarded proposals is the best way to understand the types of research that the foundations are interested in funding. In addition, it shows you the best way to craft your argument so that you can create a successful proposal. Mixed methods studies are complicated to explain. You will need to learn to write succinctly because of the limited number of pages that are often allowed by grant proposal guidelines.

Granting agencies support, if not highly recommend, mixed methods approaches in order to be granted funding. This is supported by the steady increase in the number of mixed methods proposals that have been funded in recent years (Plano Clark, 2010). Also, increasing numbers of granting agencies are directly promoting mixed methods approaches. For instance, the National Institute of Health's Office of Behavioral and Social Sciences Research published a report to provide researchers with the best practices in mixed methods research (see Creswell, Klassen, Clark, & Smith, 2011). Also, the W.T. Grant Foundation provides access to mixed methods resources and consultants on its website (see http://wtgrantmixedmethods.com/).

Likewise, if you are affiliated with a university, you have also heard that granting agencies, especially federal agencies, are awarding fewer grants, because less money is being allocated to grant programs. Because of this, granting agencies want to get more bang for the buck, making this the perfect time for mixed methods grant proposals. It is very useful if not necessary to procure grants to fund your research, because mixed methods studies tend to be more complicated and more expensive than single method studies. (See Chapter 1 for a refresher on this.) Grant funding will also help to further move along your program of research. You can always conduct your research without a grant, but having a grant will allow your research to move along a lot more quickly.

PRACTICE SESSION

Guided Questions

These questions will help you to think about your writing style and your approach to writing as you begin to craft your first draft of your mixed methods research proposal.

1. What is your timeline to write your mixed methods proposal?
2. How much time will you dedicate to writing daily and weekly?
3. Where will you write your mixed methods proposal?

Activity for Mixed Methods Proposal Additions

Although this book focused on the main components of the mixed methods proposal, there are several supporting components that are necessary to include. This activity will allow you to create drafts of those components, including the title, abstract, references, and appendix.

1. What is your working title for your mixed methods proposal? It may be helpful to craft three to four different alternatives.

2. Write a draft of your abstract for your mixed methods proposal. Aim for 150–200 words.

3. What items will you need to include in your appendix? Create a list of the items that you will include in your appendix section.

4. Combine the references you used in the introduction, literature review outline, and the research methods summary activities to create a working list of references for your mixed methods proposal.

Additional Resources on Writing and Writing Styles

American Psychological Association. (2009). *Publication manual of the American Psychological Association* (6th ed.). Washington, DC: American Psychological Association.

Bolker, J. (1998). *Writing your dissertation in fifteen minutes a day: A guide to starting, revising, and finishing your doctoral thesis.* New York, NY: Owl Books.

Modern Language Association. (2008). *MLA style manual and guide to scholarly publishing* (3rd ed.). New York, NY: Modern Language Association.

Rocco, T. S., & Hatcher, T. (2011). *Handbook of scholarly writing and publishing.* New York, NY: Jossey-Bass.

Rossman, M. H. (2002). *Negotiating graduate school: A guide for graduate students.* Thousand Oaks, CA: Sage.

Silvia, P. J. (2007). *How to write a lot: A practical guide to productive academic writing.* Washington, DC: American Psychological Association.

University of Chicago Press Staff. (2010). *Chicago manual of style* (16th ed.). Chicago, IL: University of Chicago Press.

Sample Session—Mixed Methods Proposal Additions

Below are our responses to the questions that we posed in the practice session activity.

Working Title

1. African American College Students' Experiences With Racial Microaggressions: A Mixed Methods Study

2. A Mixed Methods Exploration of African American College Students' Experiences With Racial Microaggressions

3. The Impact of Experiencing Racial Microaggressions on African American Students in the College Context: An Explanatory Sequential Mixed Methods Study

Working Abstract

African American students often experience racial microaggressions in the college context, particularly at predominately white institutions (PWIs). Within an explanatory sequential mixed methods design, using Likert surveys and interviews, we will examine how African American students are impacted socially, culturally, emotionally, and motivationally by experiencing racial microaggressions. In doing so, we will explore how racial microaggressions impact African American students' sense of racial identity, as well as their ability to cope with and regulate the unpleasant emotions that are associated with those experiences. Further, we will focus on how experiencing racial microaggressions can impact how their basic psychological needs are being met at college, particularly their needs for autonomy, competence, and relatedness. Suggestions will be made to help PWIs create environments that are more receptive to the needs of African American students. In addition, we will discuss how African American students can better manage the emotional labor that is associated with experiencing racial microaggressions.

Working List of Items for Appendices

1. Racial and Ethnic Microaggressions Scale (Nadal, 2011)
2. Coping With Discrimination Scale (Wei, Alvarez, Ku, Russell, & Bonett, 2010)
3. Emotional Regulation Questionnaire (Gross & John, 2003)
4. Multidimensional Inventory of Black Identity (Sellers, Smith, Shelton, Rowley, & Chavous, 1998)
5. Basic Psychological Needs at College Scale (Deci & Ryan, 2000)
6. A semistructured interview schedule
7. Participant recruitment script and informed consent form/documentation
8. Proposed procedural diagram for the study

● WORKING REFERENCES FOR MIXED METHODS PROPOSAL

Allen, Q. (2010). Racial microaggresssions: The schooling experiences of Black middle-class males in Arizona's secondary schools. *Journal of African American Males in Education, 1*(2), 125–142.

Baber, L. D. (2012). A qualitative inquiry on the multidimensional racial development among first-year African American college students attending a predominately White institution. *The Journal of Negro Education, 81*(1), 67–81.

Bell, D. A. (1980). *Brown v. Board of Education* and the interest-convergence dilemma. *Harvard Law Review, 93*(3), 518–533.

Bell, D. (1992). Racial realism. *Connecticut Law Review, 24*(2), 363–379.

Bell, D. (1993). *Faces at the bottom of the well: The permanence of racism.* New York, NY: Basic Books.

Brondolo, E., ver Halen, N., Pencille, M., Beatty, D., & Contrada, R. (2009). Coping with racism: A selective review of the literature and a theoretical and methodological critique. *Journal of Behavioral Medicine, 32*, 64–88.

Brown, T. L., Phillips, C. M., Abdullah, T., Vinson, E., & Robertson, J. (2010). Dispositional versus situational coping: Are the coping strategies African Americans use different for general versus racism-related stressors? *Journal of Black Psychology, 37*(3), 311–335.

Cabrera, N. L. (2014). Exposing Whiteness in higher education: White male college students minimizing racism, claiming victimization, and recreating White supremacy. *Race Ethnicity and Education, 17*(1), 30–55.

Coffey, A., & Atkinson, P. (1996). *Making sense of qualitative data: Complementary research designs.* Thousand Oaks, CA: Sage.

Constantine, M. G. (2007). Racial microaggressions against African American clients in cross-racial counseling relationships. *Journal of Counseling Psychology, 54*, 1–16.

Corbin, J. M., & Strauss, A. L. (2015). *Basics of qualitative research: Techniques and procedures for developing grounded theory* (4th ed.). Thousand Oaks, CA: Sage.

Crenshaw, K. (1989). Demarginalizing the intersection of race and sex: A Black feminist critique of antidiscrimination doctrine, feminist theory and anti-racist politics. *University of Chicago Legal Forum*, pp. 139–167.

Deci, E. L., & Ryan, R. M. (2000). The "what" and "why" of goal pursuits: Human needs and the self-determination of behavior. *Psychological Inquiry, 11*, 227–268.

DeCuir, J. T., & Dixson, A. (2004). "So when it comes out, they aren't that surprised that it is there": Using critical race theory as a tool of analysis of race and racism in education. *Educational Researcher, 33*(5), 26–31.

Delgado, R. (1989). Storytelling for oppositionists and others: A plea for narrative. *Michigan Law Review, 87*, 2411–2441.

Delgado, R., & Stefancic, J. (2012). *Critical race theory: An introduction* (2nd ed.). New York: New York University Press.

Folkman, S., & Moskowitz, J. T. (2004). Coping: Pitfalls and promise. *Annual Review of Psychology, 55*, 745–774.

Forsyth, J., & Carter, R. (2012). The relationship between racial identity status attitudes, racism-related coping, and mental health among Black Americans. *Cultural Diversity and Ethnic Minority Psychology, 18*(2), 128–140.

Gomez, M. L., Khurshid, A., Freitag, M. B., & Lachuk, A. J. (2011). Microaggressions in graduate students' lives: How they are encountered and their consequences. *Teaching and Teacher Education, 27*, 1189–1199.

Gotanda, N. (1991). A critique of "Our constitution is color-blind." *Stanford Law Review, 44*, 1–68.

Gross, J. J., & John, O. P. (2003). Individual differences in two emotion regulation processes: Implications for affect, relationships, and well-being. *Journal of Personality and Social Psychology, 85*, 348–362.

Harper, B. E. (2007). The relationship between Black racial identity and academic achievement in urban settings. *Theory Into Practice, 46*(3), 230–238.

Harper, S. R. (2012). *Black male student success in higher education: A report from the national Black male college achievement study.* Philadelphia: University of Pennsylvania, Center for the Study of Race and Equity in Education.

Harrell, S. P. (2000). A multidimensional conceptualization of racism-related stress: Implications for the well-being of people of color. *American Journal of Orthopsychiatry, 70*, 42–57.

Harris, C. (1993). Whiteness as property. *Harvard Law Review, 106*(8), 1707–1791.

Harwood, S. A., Huntt, M. B., Mendenhall, R., & Lewis, J. A. (2012). Racial microaggressions in the residence halls: Experiences of students of color at a predominantly White university. *Journal of Diversity in Higher Education, 5*(3), 159.

Helms, J. (Ed.). (1990). *Black and White racial identity: Theory, research, and practice.* New York, NY: Greenwood Press.

Helms, J., Jernigan, M., & Mascher, J. (2005). The meaning of race in psychology and how to change it: A methodological perspective. *American Psychologist, 60*(1), 27–36.

Kohli, R., & Solórzano, D. 2012. Teachers, please learn our names!: Racial microaggressions and the K–12 classroom. *Race Ethnicity and Education, 15*(4), 441–462.

Ladson-Billings, G., & Tate, W. F. (1995). Towards a critical race theory of education. *Teachers College Record, 97*(1), 47–68.

Lazarus, R. S., & Folkman, S. (1984). *Stress, appraisal, and coping.* New York, NY: Springer.

Lewis, J. A., Mendenhall, R., Harwood, S., & Huntt, M. B. (2013). Coping with racial microaggressions among Black women. *Journal of African American Studies, 17*, 51–73.

McGee, M. C. (2013). *James Meredith: Warrior and the America that created him.* New York, NY: Praeger.

McWhorter, J. (2014, March 21). Microaggression is the new racism on campus. *Time.* Retrieved from http://time.com/32618/microaggression-is-the-new-racism-on-campus/

Melor, D. (2004). Responses to racism: A taxonomy of coping styles used by Aboriginal Australians. *American Journal of Orthopsychiatry, 74*(1), 56–71.

Merriam, S. B. (2009). *Qualitative research: A guide to design and implementation.* San Francisco, CA: Jossey-Bass.

Moustakas, C. E. (1994). *Phenomenological research methods.* Thousand Oaks, CA: Sage.

Nadal, K. (2011). The racial and ethnic microaggressions scale (REMS): Construction, reliability, and validity. *Journal of Counseling Psychology, 58*(4), 470–480.

Paradies, Y. (2006). A systematic review of empirical research on self-reported racism and health. *International Journal of Epidemiology, 35*(4), 888–901.

Pieterse, A. L., Todd, N. R., Neville, H. A., & Carter, R. T. (2012). Perceived racism and mental health among Black American adults: A meta-analytic review. *Journal of Counseling Psychology, 59*(1), 1–9.

Polkinghorne, D. E. (1995). Narrative configuration in qualitative analysis. *Qualitative Studies in Education, 8*(1), 5–23.

Ryan, R. M., Huta, V., & Deci, E. L. (2008). Living well: A self-determination theory perspective on eudaimonia. *Journal of Happiness Studies, 9,* 139–170.

Scottham, K. M., Sellers, R. M., & Nguyen, H. X. (2008). A measure of racial identity in African American adolescents: The development of the multidimensional inventory of Black identity–Teen. *Cultural Diversity and Ethnic Minority Psychology, 14*(4), 297–306.

Sellers, R. M., Rowley S. A. J., Chavous, T. M., Shelton J. N., & Smith M. A. (1997). Multidimensional Inventory of Black Identity: A preliminary investigation of reliability and construct validity. *Journal of Personality and Social Psychology, 73,* 805–815.

Sellers, R. M., Smith, M. A., Shelton, J. N., Rowley, S. A. J., & Chavous, T. M. (1998). Multidimensional Model of Racial Identity: A reconceptualization of African American racial identity. *Personality and Social Psychology Review, 2(1),* 18–39.

Smith, W. A., Hung, M., & Franklin, J. D. (2011). Racial battle fatigue and the miseducation of Black men: Racial microaggressions, societal problems, and environmental stress. *Journal of Negro Education, 80*(1), 63–82.

Solórzano, D. G., & Yosso, T. J. (2002). Critical race methodology: Counterstorytelling as an analytical framework for education research. *Qualitative Inquiry, 8*(1), 23–44.

Sue, D., Capodilupo, C., Torino, G., Bucceri, J., Holder, A., Nadal, K., & Esquilin, M. (2007). Racial microaggressions in everyday life: Implications for clinical practice. *American Psychologist, 62*(4), 271–286.

Suls, J., & Fletcher, B. (1985). The relative efficacy of avoidant and nonavoidant coping strategies: A meta-analysis. *Health Psychology, 4,* 249–288.

Thomas, O. N., Caldwell, C. H., Faison, N., & Jackson, J. S. (2009). Promoting academic achievement: The role of racial identity in buffering perceptions of teacher discrimination on academic achievement among African American and Caribbean Black adolescents. *Journal of Educational Psychology, 101*(2), 420–431.

Torres, L., Driscoll, M. W., & Burrow, A. L. (2010). Racial microaggressions and psychological functioning among highly achieving African-Americans: A mixed-methods approach. *Journal of Social and Clinical Psychology, 29* (10), 1074–1099.

Utsey, S. O., Giesbrecht, N., Hook, J., & Stanard, P. M. (2008). Cultural, sociofamilial, and psychological resources that inhibit psychological distress in African Americans exposed to stressful life events and race-related stress. *Journal of Counseling Psychology, 55*(1), 49–62.

Vega, T. (2014, March 21). Students see many slights as racial microaggressions. *New York Times.* Retrieved from http://www.nytimes.com/2014/03/22/us/as-diversity-increases-slights-get-subtler-but-still-sting.html

Wang, J., Leu, J., & Shoda, Y. (2011). When the seemingly innocuous "stings": Racial microaggressions and their emotional consequences. *Personality and Social Psychology Bulletin, 37*(12), 1666–1678.

Wei, M., Alvarez, A., Ku, T., Russell, D., & Bonett, D. (2010). Development and validation of a coping with discrimination scale: Factor structure, reliability, and validity. *Journal of Counseling Psychology, 57*(3), 328–344.

Yosso, T. J., Smith, W. A., Ceja, M., & Solórzano, D. G. (2009). Critical race theory, racial microaggressions, and campus racial climate for Latina/o undergraduates. *Harvard Educational Review, 79*(4), 659–691.

9

An Example of a Real-World Mixed Methods Study

The Racial Microaggressions Study Proposal

Objectives

1. To review the components of a mixed methods research proposal.

2. To examine a real-world mixed methods research proposal.

hroughout this book we have discussed the development of our research study on African American college students' experiences with racial microaggressions. We are now going to unveil the full proposal. Before we begin, it is important for you to review all of the components of a mixed methods proposal. Table 9.1 features a list of all of the components that we discussed in this book. In addition, the table highlights the chapters in which the components were discussed as well as reminds you of the activities that accompanied the discussion of each component. We encourage you to use this as a checklist while you are crafting your own proposal as well as reviewing the example mixed methods proposal.

Table 9.1 Components of a Mixed Methods Proposal

Chapter in Book	Mixed Methods Proposal Section	Mixed Methods Proposal Components	Mixed Methods Proposal Subcomponents	Book Activity/ Discussion
8	Title			Mixed Methods Proposal Additions Activity (Ch. 8)
8	Abstract			Mixed Methods Proposal Additions Activity (Ch. 8)
4	Introduction			Introduction Writing Activity (Ch. 4)
4		Background of the Study		
2, 4		Theoretical Framework		Inquiry Worldview Activity (Ch. 2)
2, 4			*Inquiry Worldview*	
2, 4			*Subjectivity Statement*	
2, 4			*Substantive Content Theories*	
4		Purpose Statement		
4			*Statement of the Problem*	
4			*Goal of the Research*	
1, 4, 7			*Mixed Methods Definition*	
1, 4, 7			*Mixed Methods Rationale*	
4		Significance of the Study		
5	Literature Review			Literature Review Outline (Ch. 5)
4, 5		Statement of the Problem		
5		Synthesis of the Research Literature		

				Research Methods Summary (Ch. 7)
3, 5		Research Question/Purpose Summary		
6, 7	Methods			
3, 7		Research Questions/Hypotheses		
1, 7		Mixed Methods Definition		
6		Mixed Methods Design		
7		Sample/Participants		
7			*Context*	
7			*Sampling*	
7		Data Collection		
7			*Instrumentation*	
7			*Procedures*	
7		Data Analysis		
7			*Procedures*	
7			*Data Integration*	
7			*Role of Theoretical Framework*	
7			*Reliability/Credibility*	
7			*Validity/Trustworthiness*	
8	References			**Mixed Methods Proposal Additions Activity (Ch. 8)**
8	Appendix			**Mixed Methods Proposal Additions Activity (Ch. 8)**

In addition to providing a full proposal in this chapter, we also include snapshots of sample research methods in this book's appendices. The snapshots focus on the methods section, the central component of the research proposal. Using the previously described designs, the snapshots provide a variety of methods from the perspectives of different disciplines. Take time to review the various snapshots, thinking of them as potential templates for crafting and organizing your own methods section. Use the questions in Table 9.2 as a guide to help you review the snapshots. Thinking through these questions and reviewing the examples will help you to solidify your methodological choices. You want to make sure that you have considered all of your options before making a commitment. Doing so will ensure that you create the best proposal possible.

Without further ado, here is a complete example of a mixed methods research proposal as well as the research methods snapshots.

Table 9.2 Reviewing Your Methodological Choices

Proposal Component	Questions to Consider	Answers
Research Questions/ Hypotheses	What are some additional research questions/hypotheses that you can consider for your study?	
Mixed Methods Definition	What are some alternative definitions of mixed methods research?	
Mixed Methods Design	Are you using the best design to answer your research question? What other designs could you potentially use?	
Data Collection		
	What are some other data source options for your design? What other instruments can you use?	
	What are potential variations to the data collection procedures?	
Data Analysis		
	What are some other data analysis techniques you can potentially use with your data?	
	What other ways can you integrate your data?	

Proposal Component	Questions to Consider	Answers
	Are there other theories or inquiry worldviews that could be added to your theoretical framework?	
	What other ways can you address reliability/credibility? How will ensure that you are making quality inferences from your data?	
	What other ways can you address validity/trustworthiness? How will ensure that you are making quality inferences from your data?	
References	Do you have a working list of references? Do you have a plan to obtain hard-to-get references?	
Appendices	Are there other items that you will consider adding to the appendices?	

A Mixed Methods Exploration of African American College Students'

Experiences with Racial Microaggressions

Jessica T. DeCuir-Gunby

NC State University

and

Paul A. Schutz

University of Texas at San Antonio

AFRICAN AMERICAN COLLEGE STUDENTS' EXPERIENCES   2

Abstract

African American students often experience racial microaggressions in the college context, particularly at predominately White institutions (PWIs). Within an explanatory sequential mixed methods design, using Likert surveys and interviews, we will examine how African American students are impacted socially, culturally, emotionally, and motivationally by experiencing racial microaggressions. In doing so, we will explore how racial microaggressions impact African American students' sense of racial identity, as well as their ability to cope with and regulate the unpleasant emotions that are associated with those experiences. Further, we will focus on how experiencing racial microaggressions can impact whether and how students' basic psychological needs are being met at college, particularly their needs for autonomy, competence, and relatedness. Suggestions will be made to help PWIs create environments that are more receptive to the needs of African American students. In addition, we will discuss how African American students can better manage the emotional labor that is associated with experiencing racial microaggressions.

Introduction

Background of the Study

On October 1, 1962, President John F. Kennedy federalized the Mississippi National Guard to help escort James Meredith, an African American, onto the University of Mississippi campus. Upon Meredith's arrival, he found an angry mob shouting a series of racial slurs. He continued to receive this type of treatment until he graduated in 1963 (McGee, 2013). Because of Meredith's sacrifice, as well as the sacrifices of many others, African Americans and other racial/ethnic minority groups can now enroll and matriculate in predominately White universities without the fear of being accosted by racist angry mobs. However, students of color can still be subjected to more subtle forms of racism. Recently, expressions of racism on college campuses, and in society in general, have become more sophis-ticated, morphing from overt expressions that are relatively easy to detect to more muted forms of racism that are subtle and often overlooked. One aspect of this contemporary form of racism is known as racial microaggressions.

Racial microaggressions can be defined as "brief, everyday exchanges that send denigrating messages to people of color because they belong to a racial minority group" (Sue, Capodilupo, Torino, Bucceri, Holder, Nadal, & Esquilin, 2007, p. 273). Racial microaggressions are further described as being frequently and automatically expressed by majority group members and manifested as "subtle snubs or dismissive looks, gestures, and tones" (Sue et al., p. 273). They are present in all contexts, including schools. Studies have examined racial microaggressions in a variety of educational contexts, including high school (Allen, 2010) and college (Yosso, Smith, Ceja, & Solórzano, 2009). Racial microaggressions have been negatively associated with the emotional well-being of students of color (Wang, Leu, & Shoda, 2011), often causing extreme stress (Smith, Hung, & Franklin, 2011). A growing area of research has focused on racial microaggressions within the college environment, particularly among college students. The experiences of students of color on college campuses are even receiving national attention. Recently, *Time* magazine featured an article by John McWhorter (2014) entitled "Microaggression Is the New Racism on Campus." Similarly, the *New York Times* featured an article by Tanzina Vega (2014) called "Students See Many Slights as Racial Microaggressions." Because microaggressions are pervasive on college campuses, it is important to better understand how African Americans experience and are being impacted by racial microaggressions.

Theoretical Framework

The following theories and experiences have shaped our perspective and help guide our approach to this research study. These theories and experiences will be used to assist us in better understanding African American college students' experiencing of racial microaggressions within the PWI context.

Inquiry Worldview. Our work is situated within a critical framework. Specifically, we are guided by critical race theory (CRT), which places race as the center of focus and explores the transformations of the relationships

AFRICAN AMERICAN COLLEGE STUDENTS' EXPERIENCES 5

among race, racism, and power (Bell, 1992, 1993; Delgado & Stefancic, 2012). CRT is composed of six tenets:

- *Counterstorytelling* is the use of narratives that challenge majority perspective by focusing on the experiences of marginalized groups (Delgado, 1989).

- The *permanence of racism* investigates the pervasiveness of racism (Bell, 1992, 1993).

- The *critique of liberalism* challenges liberal discourses regarding colorblindness (not seeing race), meritocracy (beliefs of equal access and opportunity), and incremental change (the need to make small changes rather than systematic changes) (Gotanda, 1991).

- *Interest convergence* explores how racial progress occurs only when it is beneficial to Whites (Bell, 1980).

- *Intersectionality* examines the intersection of identities, specifically race and gender (Crenshaw, 1989).

- *Whiteness as property* explores White privilege (Harris, 1993).

Within the educational system, CRT is frequently used to expose African Americans' experiences of racism in the educational context, both blatant and subtle, as well as to make change and bring about equity (DeCuir & Dixson, 2004; Ladson-Billings & Tate, 1995). We will use a CRT lens to help guide our research process, including the data collection and analysis processes.

Subjectivity Statement. I (Jessica DeCuir-Gunby) attended predominately White universities in the South where it was common for African

AFRICAN AMERICAN COLLEGE STUDENTS' EXPERIENCES   6

American students to experience racial microaggressions from both their peers and professors. As an African American, I too experienced racial microaggressions in those contexts. Because of my personal experience, I am very sensitive to issues of race and racism with the college context. As such, I am interested in learning how African American students on predominately White college campuses experience and deal with racial microaggressions in this supposed postracial context. I am a trained social scientist with research and methodological interests in racial identity development and mixed methods research. In addition, the CRT perspective informs my approach to research.

As a White, heterosexual male, who is progressively getting older, I (Paul Schutz) have tried to unpack the "gifts" that I have received due to my birth in this particular social historical context. Thus, for the most part, my life is one where I have played the role of being the "norm" while also attempting to problematize that "norm-ness" or White privilege wherever possible. To that end, I am also informed by CRT, which for me brings important understanding to the racial microaggressions experienced by college students. In addition, I am a trained social scientist with interests in learning, motivation, and emotion. As such, I bring to this research project an interest in research as problem solving within a social historical context with a focus on social justice.

Substantive Content Theories. In addition to being guided by CRT and our personal experiences, we are also guided by theories and their associated assumptions. One such theory is the multidimensional model of racial identity (MMRI) (Sellers, Smith, Shelton, Rowley, & Chavous,

1998). The MMRI conceptualizes Black racial identity as a multidimensional construct. It assumes that racial identity is situationally influenced yet somewhat stable. One assumption of this theory is that every individual has multiple identities within some type of hierarchical structure, and that some identities are more important than others. Another assumption is that personal perception of racial identity is the most valid indicator of identity. The MMRI focuses on the current status of an individual's racial identity rather than on the development of identity over time.

A theorist with an MMRI perspective attempts to explain the variety of ways in which Black racial identity is manifested. In order to empirically test the theory, the MMRI has been operationalized through the creation of several inventories including the *Multidimensional Inventory of Black Identity* (MIBI) (Sellers, Rowley, Chavous, Shelton, & Smith, 1997) and the *Multidimensional Inventory of Black Identity–teen* (MIBI-t) (Scottham, Sellers, & Nguyen, 2008). We intend to utilize the MMRI in the creation of our research study focusing on African American college students' experiences of racial microaggressions.

A second theory that informs our work is self-determination theory (SDT). Researchers, who are informed by SDT, tend to assume that the roots of human motivation and well-being are tied to innate psychological needs for autonomy, competence, and relatedness (Deci & Ryan, 2000; Ryan, Huta, & Deci, 2008). Specifically, *autonomy* refers to the human need to determine, control, and organize your own behavior and goals or to see yourself as having control in your world. *Competence* refers to the human need to learn and master challenging tasks or to be good at some activities. Finally, *relatedness* refers to the human need to feel attached to others or to be meaningfully involved in relationships with other humans.

From this perspective, having these needs met within the college context is a necessary condition for psychological growth, integrity, and well-being. This would suggest that within social historical contexts, activities and individuals who provide support to college students in meeting those basic needs will help natural growth processes, whereas contexts and individuals who constrain or inhibit the meeting of those needs (e.g., through the use of racial microaggressions) tend to be associated with lower motivation, performance, and psychological well-being (Deci & Ryan, 2000; Ryan et al., 2008).

Purpose Statement

The following discussion describes what we intend to do in our study as well as why our study is relevant relevant:

Statement of the Problem. African American students frequently experience racial microaggressions within predominately White university settings. These experiences can impact their emerging racial identity as well as require them to develop appropriate coping and emotional regulation skills for dealing with racism. Ultimately, experiencing racial microaggressions can impact their ability to meet their psychological needs for autonomy, competence, and relatedness within the college context (Deci & Ryan, 2000; Ryan et al., 2008).

Goals of the Research. The purpose of this research project is four-fold. The first goal is to better understand how African American students experience racial microaggressions within the college context. The second goal is to explore how students' racial identity influences their experiencing of racial microaggressions. The third goal is to explore how students cope with and regulate the emotions associated with experiencing racial microaggressions within the college context. The final goal is to investigate the relationships among racial microaggressions, racial identity, coping and emotional regulation, and innate psychological needs for autonomy, competence, and relatedness during their college experience. We will draw implications to help students to better recognize and more positively address racial microaggressions within the college context.

Mixed Methods Definition and Rationale. In order to engage in this study, we will be taking a mixed methods approach. We will be guided by Tashakkori and Creswell's (2007) definition of mixed methods as "research in which the investigator collects and analyzes data, integrates the findings, and draws inferences using both qualitative and quantitative approaches or methods in a single study or program of inquiry" (p. 4). A mixed methods approach will be used for our study because we will explore both the breadth and depth of African American college students' experiences with racial microaggressions. Mixed methods research allows us to access a large number of participants through surveys and engage in in-depth interviews with a smaller number of participants. The integrated findings will provide for a more nuanced interpretation of the participants' experiences.

Significance of the Study

The proposed study is significant in the field of educational psychology in various ways. First, little research examines how issues of racism, or racial microaggressions specifically, impact the coping skills, emotional regulation, and basic psychological needs of African American students at college. Second, there is a paucity of race-focused research (i.e., research focused on racial constructs) in the larger area of motivation in education; this study would be able to make a significant contribution to the motivation literature (DeCuir-Gunby & Schutz, 2014). Last, there are a limited number of research studies within the area of racial microaggressions and psychological needs at college that have been conducted using mixed methods approaches; this study will make a significant methodological contribution.

Literature Review

African American students are increasingly enrolling in institutions of higher learning. In 2013, nearly 2.5 million African Americans were enrolled in institutions of higher learning, twice as many as were enrolled in 1990, with the majority of them attending PWIs (Kena et al., 2015). As the presence of African Americans at PWIs has increased, there has also been an increase in racial incidents on college campuses. An African American student can be one of few people of color in classes and other campus community contexts at PWIs, if not the only such person. In such contexts, African American students often feel alienated, as though they do not belong (Harper, 2012). African American students frequently experience both overt racist and covert racist acts, or racial microaggressions. It is not uncommon for African American students to experience racial microaggressions from administrators, professors, and peers as well as the curriculum, which can have a negative psychological and emotional impact (Baber, 2012; Cabrera, 2014; Johnson-Ahorlu, 2012).

The purpose of this study is to explore African American college students' experiences with racial microaggressions within the predominately White college context. Before we begin to discuss our study, it is necessary to situate our research problem within the theoretical context. Thus we will begin by examining the relevant literature. Specifically, we will discuss the racial microaggressions research literature, providing an emphasis on racial microaggressions within the PWI context. Then we will examine the coping and emotional regulation literature, focusing on the ways in which African Americans cope with and regulate emotions associated with racism. Next we will discuss racial identity, particularly as it relates to experiencing racial microaggressions. Then we will discuss self-determination theory; its focus on the psychological needs of autonomy, competence, and relatedness; and how the psychological needs of African Americans are being met within PWIs. We will end the review with a discussion of the relationships among racial microaggressions, coping, racial identity, and psychological needs.

Racial Microggressions in the Predominately White Context

As previously described, racial microaggressions are negative, race-based verbal and nonverbal messages that people of color receive from the members of the dominant culture (Sue et al., 2007). There are three categories of microaggressions, including microassaults, microinsults, and microinvalidations. Microassaults are explicit verbal or nonverbal attacks that are purposely used to hurt, offend, or discriminate against someone. Examples include using racial slurs or displaying racially charged symbols such as the swastika or confederate flag. The use of microassaults can be considered the "traditional" form of expressing racist beliefs. They are easy to detect and difficult to defend. Microinsults and microinvalidations, on the other hand, are the more contemporary ways of communicating racist beliefs. Microinsults are subtle snubs that indirectly insult a person's racial heritage or racial identity. In many cases the comment is intended to be a compliment. An example of a microinsult is telling an African American student, "I can't believe that you are so good in mathematics." The comment is intended to compliment the student's ability, but at the same time it reinforces racist stereotypes that African Americans are not good at mathematics. Similarly, microinvalidations are statements that tend to "exclude, negate, or nullify the psychological thoughts, or feelings or experiential reality of a person of color" (Sue et al., p. 274). For example, telling an African American that "I don't think of you as Black" suggests that you are denying this person's racialized experience as an African American.

Racial microaggressions are pervasive in all aspects of society, including education, which means that African American students often experience racial microaggressions at PWIs. Although the number of African American students has increased at PWIs, they continue to encounter psychologically damaging racism on campuses. There have been numerous studies that have documented African American college students' experiences with racial microaggressions, particularly at PWIs (Gomez, Khurshid, Freitag, & Lachuk, 2011; Harwood, Huntt, Mendenhall, & Lewis, 2012; Yosso, Smith, Ceja, & Solórzano, 2009). Such studies have found that experiencing racial microaggressions can have an impact on African American students' academic involvements and campus experiences as well as their health (emotional and physical).

Experiencing racial microaggressions in the college context can place a strain on African American students' academic involvements, interactions, and feelings of belonging. Particularly, experiencing racial microaggressions can have an impact on academic achievement or competency, including negatively impacting motivation in the classroom as well as academic choices or autonomy (Reynolds, Sneva, & Beehler, 2010). Racial microaggressions also impact the quality of academic experiences. Often within PWIs, African American students experience a lack of relatedness and perceive that they are not receiving as much academic support from their professors as their White peers (Gildersleeve, Croom, & Vasquez, 2011). Also, African American students often perceive bias (overt or subtle, or being ignored) from their White professors in the classroom (Boysen, Vogel, Cope, & Hubbard, 2009; Kohli & Solórzano, 2012). The perceptions of bias can lead students to disconnect from their courses or even from college in general.

In addition to academic issues, campus climate issues are associated with racial microaggressions. African American students often describe PWIs as not being culturally affirming. African American students frequently view the racial climate at PWIs as negative (Pieterse, Carter, Evans, & Walter, 2010). Specifically, African American students discuss having negative encounters with White peers (Torres, Driscoll, & Burrow, 2010). Similar to African American students, African American faculty, themselves, even encounter racial microaggressions within PWIs and find the climates nonsupportive (Constantine, Smith, Redington, & Owens, 2008; Pittman, 2012).

Experiencing racial microaggressions can also have a negative impact on African American students' health (Paradies, 2006). Experiencing racial microaggressions can cause social/emotional issues such as racism-related stress, which can lead to psychological issues such as anxiety and depression (Constantine, 2007; Franklin, Boyd-Franklin, & Kelly, 2006; Pieterse, Todd, Neville, & Carter, 2012; Wang, Leu, & Shoda, 2011). Experiencing racism has also been shown to have an impact on the physical health of African Americans (Harrell, 2000; Utsey, 1998). For instance, racism has been associated with negative health outcomes such as hypertension and obesity (Brondolo, ver Halen, Pencille, Beatty, & Contrada, 2009; Paradies, 2006). Race-related stress can also be linked to other health issues such as preterm births and low birth weights (Giscombé & Lobel, 2005).

Specifically, the pervasive experiencing of racial microaggressions and its associated emotional stress can lead to a chronic mental health condition. Racial Battle Fatigue Syndrome is "the result of constant physiological, psychological, cultural, and emotional coping with racial microaggressions in less-than-ideal and racially hostile or unsupportive environments" (Smith, Allen, & Danley, 2007, p. 555). Associated with Racial Battle Fatigue

Syndrome are a variety of psychological and physiological symptoms, including headaches, stomach problems, depression, and difficulty thinking, among other serious issues (see Clark, Anderson, Clark, & Williams, 1999). African Americans must learn to cope with these symptoms while negotiating and challenging their environments. Doing so can be particularly difficult in PWI contexts (see Mitchell, Fasching-Varner, Albert, & Allen, 2015).

Coping and Emotional Regulation

Enduring racism, particularly racial microaggressions, within the college context requires African American students to engage in specific coping and emotional regulation strategies (Brondolo et al., 2009; Brown, Phillips, Abdullah, Vinson, & Robertson, 2011). Coping, in particular, involves the effort used to solve or minimize stress or conflict (Thomas, Witherspoon, & Speight, 2008). There are two traditional approaches to understanding coping: approach and avoidance coping (Suls & Fletcher, 1985) and problem-focused and emotion-focused (Lazarus & Folkman, 1984). Approach coping is a type of active coping where a person directly attempts to address a problem, while avoidance coping is a form of passive or maladaptive coping strategy in which a person attempts to address a situation by avoiding the issue. On the other hand, problem-focused approaches concern reducing a stressor by focusing on the behaviors that could be used to address the problem. Emotion-focused approaches involve focusing on one's emotional reactions to the situation. The problem-focused and emotion-focused approaches are often used in conjunction. However, research suggests that racism requires approaches that differ from traditional coping models.

Coping with racism requires additional coping skills (Forsyth & Carter, 2012; Lewis, Mendenhall, Harwood, & Huntt, 2012; Melor, 2004). Specifically, Melor recommends that in order to cope with racism, individuals must be able to protect the self, engage in self-control, and confront the racism. In protecting the self, individuals have to make sure that their safety is the number one priority and that they have a psychologically and physically safe space to regroup after experiencing racism in a particular context (e.g., talking with a friend off campus after a racist event). Next, by engaging in self-control, individuals have to make sure that they do not react in a manner that could put them in danger or at a loss. For instance, if someone experiences a racist event on the job, it is imperative to not react in a way that breaks company policy and is punishable by firing. The last skill, confronting the racism, involves educating the perpetrator about what was said/done. It also requires that the victim actively confront the perpetrator about the behavior, shortly after it occurs. For example, an African American student confronts a peer after he makes a joke stating that most Jamaicans are undocumented. Using such coping strategies allows African Americans to better cope with racism.

In addition to coping, African American students also have to regulate their emotions when experiencing racial microaggressions (Utsey, Giesbrect, Hook, & Stanard, 2008). Emotional regulation can be described as the process of initiating, controlling, or modulating both pleasant and unpleasant emotional reactions/episodes (Folkman & Moskowitz, 2004). Emotional regulation can include affective (focusing on the emotions),

AFRICAN AMERICAN COLLEGE STUDENTS' EXPERIENCES   17

cognitive (focusing on appraisals and meaning making), and/or social approaches (focusing on interactions with others).

Among the potential effects of experiencing racial microaggressions are the unpleasant emotions that are often associated with such experiences. Research on emotions and emotional regulation has identified that individuals tend to regulate or deal with their emotions in at least a couple of ways, such as cognitive reappraisal and expressive suppression (Gross & John, 2003). In essence, cognitive reappraisals tend to occur early in the emotional episode and have the potential to change the emotional experience. (For example, changing the way you judge or look at the situation has the potential to reduce unpleasant emotional experiences or enhance pleasant emotional experiences.) On the other hand, the focus during expressive suppression, which tends to occur later in the emotional episode, involves attempts to control the expression of the unpleasant or pleasant emotions after they have already emerged (Gross & John, 2003).

It is important to note that these differing emotional regulation strategies also have implications for affect, well-being, and social relationships. For example, cognitive reappraisal involves appraising or making attributions about an event that changes the emotions associated with the event. Reappraisal is also considered an antecedent-focused strategy, which means that it can be used early in the process and therefore may help to avoid unpleasant emotions in the first place. Expressive suppression, on the other hand, involves attempting to suppress or hide the felt emotion; as such it is referred to as an affective or response-focused strategy. For instance, with expressive suppression, you actively work to not show or

AFRICAN AMERICAN COLLEGE STUDENTS' EXPERIENCES   18

acknowledge your emotions. Researchers have demonstrated that reappraisal has been shown to be more effective in regulating unpleasant and pleasant emotions, whereas students who attempt to suppress their unpleasant emotions may suffer additional psychological burdens (Gross & John, 2003; Sheldon, Ryan, Rawsthorne, & Ilardi, 1997).

Racial Identity and Racial Microaggressions

Although the aforementioned coping strategies are essential to addressing the experiencing of racial microaggressions, one of the most important ways to cope and regulate the emotions that are associated with experiencing racism within the college context is to have a strong sense of racial identity. Attending a PWI and experiencing racial microaggressions impacts African American students' sense of self, particularly their racial identity (Smith, Hung, & Franklin, 2011). Racial identity is defined as the attitudes and beliefs that one has about belonging to a racial group, about the racial group collectively, and about other racial groups (Helms, 1990).

Racial identity, according to Sellers et al. (1998), consists of four basic dimensions: racial salience, racial centrality, racial regard (public and private), and racial ideology (nationalist, oppressed minority, assimilationist, and humanist). The first dimension, racial salience, examines the manner in which race is an important component of one's self-concept. Racial centrality, the second dimension, explores the extent to which persons view themselves in racial terms. The third dimension, racial regard, refers to how one feels about being Black. This dimension involves two components—public and private regard. Public regard refers to one's perceptions of how others view African Americans, while private regard examines how one personally feels about being Black. The final dimension, ideology, examines one's attitudes, beliefs, and opinions on how Black people should act. This dimension consists of four components: nationalist (stresses the uniqueness of being Black and connection to African American communities), oppressed minority (focuses on the similarities of oppressed groups), assimilationist (focuses on the similarities between African Americans and American society), and humanist (focuses on the similarities of all humans).

These four components provide a sense of support for individuals experiencing racial microaggressions. However, racial regard is particularly essential for understanding the experiencing of racial microaggressions within the PWI context. Racial regard examines racial identity in terms of private beliefs (one's personal feelings about being Black) and public beliefs (one's perceptions of how others view African Americans). Within the PWI context, African American students have to continuously negotiate not only how they feel about themselves but also how they think others feel about them. Public regard, specifically, enables a focus on how experiencing racial microaggressions impacts racial identity.

Exploring the link between racial identity and racial microaggressions is important, because there is a relationship between racial identity and healthy outcomes (Helms, Jernigan, & Mascher, 2005). Research demonstrates that positive racial identity can be used as a strategy or means of coping with racism (Brondolo et al., 2009). Racial pride, in particular, has been found to serve as a protective factor against racism and racial microaggressions

AFRICAN AMERICAN COLLEGE STUDENTS' EXPERIENCES   20

(Forsyth & Carter, 2012). That is to say, if you have a positive or strong sense of racial identity and you experience racial microaggressions, you will be less likely to engage in negative or unhealthy coping strategies such as suppression and internalization. Your racial pride itself will enable you to more positively navigate the negative racial experience. In addition, positive racial identity has been associated with positive academic outcomes. Particularly within the educational context, there is a relationship between racial identity and academic achievement (Harper, 2007; Thomas, Caldwell, Faison, & Jackson, 2009). Thus since racial identity is related to both coping and academic outcomes, it is important to understand how racial identity assists in coping with racial microaggressions within the college context.

Psychological Needs and Racial Microaggressions

Ultimately, African American college students' experiencing of racial microaggressions within the college context, their means of coping with racism, and their racial identity beliefs impact their motivation, particularly their psychological needs while at college. According to self-determination theory, all humans have three basic psychological needs that must be met in order to be motivated to achieve or thrive. These psychological needs are autonomy, competence, and relatedness (Deci & Ryan, 2000; Ryan, Huta, & Deci, 2008).

The psychological need of autonomy is related to one's ability to determine, control, and organize one's own behavior. Within the college context, students have substantial autonomy in terms of what courses they select, when they take courses, if and when they attend class, what clubs they join, et cetera. The college context provides students with an abundant amount of freedom. When African American students experience racial microaggressions within PWIs, their autonomy can be perceived as being taken away. They feel as though they no longer have control over situations and sometimes their behaviors (e.g., emotional reactions). This lack of autonomy can result in the lack of motivation to succeed in school.

The second psychological need, competence, concerns being successful or a good student. Within the college context, students have to feel confident in themselves in order to be academically successful. When African American students experience racial microaggressions on a regular basis, they are more likely to become disconnected from their classes and school in general. When this happens, they are more likely to feel less competent, which can lead to a decrease in motivation and ultimately in failing courses or even dropping out of college. In some cases, African American students begin to doubt their ability, which may lead to a decrease in self-efficacy and can result in lower performance that can even further erode their beliefs about their competency as students.

The last psychological need is relatedness, which involves the establishment of meaningful connections with the environment, and in this case students and faculty (Deci & Ryan, 2000). This need is particularly important for African American college students, because they want to feel as though they belong on campus. In addition, they need to feel connected to the campus community, particularly through the establishment of meaningful relationships. The constant experiencing of racial microaggressions only serves to diminish African American college students' ability to satisfy this need. They are not able to make as many meaningful relationships within PWIs as they could make elsewhere. Not feeling related to the campus community will eventually undermine their motivation.

Summary

As demonstrated throughout our discussion, racial microaggressions are pervasive in education, particular within PWIs. Continuously experiencing racial microaggressions within the college context can have a negative impact on African American students' psychological needs of autonomy, competence, and relatedness while they are at college. However, the ability to engage in appropriate coping as well as to effectively regulate emotions may have the potential to lessen the impact of racial microaggressions. In addition, having a positive racial identity can potentially buffer any negative experiences associated with racial microaggressions. Thus, being able to engage in appropriate coping and emotional regulations strategies, and having a positive sense of racial identity, can help to meet their autonomy, competence, and relatedness needs while at college.

Methods

As demonstrated in the literature review, understanding African American college students' experiences with racial microaggressions is a complicated process. As an attempt to do so, we will utilize the following research questions to guide our study:

RQ #1:   What are African American college students' experiences with racial microaggressions?

RQ #1A: How do African American college students cope with and regulate the emotions associated with the experience of racial microaggressions?

RQ #1B: How is their experience of racial microaggressions related to African American college students' sense of racial identity?

RQ #1C: Where do African American college students see the boundary between microaggressions and nonmicroaggressions?

RQ #2:   What are the psychological need profiles of African American college students?

RQ #2A: How do African American college students who score high on the measure of psychological needs scale address racial microaggressions?

RQ #3:   What is the relationship among racial microaggressions, racial identity, coping and emotional regulation strategies, and psychological needs for African American college students?

Mixed Methods Definition and Design

In order to answer the aforementioned research questions, we will take a mixed methods approach. Mixed methods research can be defined as "research in which the investigator collects and analyzes data, integrates the findings, and draws inferences using both qualitative and quantitative approaches or methods in a single study or program of inquiry" (Tashakkori & Creswell, 2007, p. 4). According to Greene (2007), mixed methods research also includes taking into consideration the roles of philosophical lenses in order to address social inquiry. As such, we are taking a critical race mixed methods approach, in that we are using critical race theory as our inquiry worldview (DeCuir-Gunby & Walker-DeVose, 2013). A mixed methods approach is essential for our study, because it will allow us to capture the breadth of students' experiences as well as provide in-depth descriptions of students' experiences with racial microaggressions. Specifically, we will use an explanatory sequential mixed methods design (QUAN → qual). In this type of design, the quantitative data will be collected first and will inform the collection of the qualitative data. The qualitative data helps to explain findings from the quantitative data (Creswell & Plano Clark, 2011). See Proposal Appendix A for a diagram of the research design for this study.

Sample/Participants

Context. This study will take place in the context of predominately White institutions (PWIs). PWIs are defined as universities that are over 50% White. It must be added that the majority of these schools are also historically White and practiced the exclusion of African Americans as well as other people of color (Brown & Dancy, 2010). This specific context is necessary for our study because African American students will most likely be underrepresented, making the experiencing of racial microaggressions more plausible. We will recruit students from both public and private universities across the United States.

Participants. A total of 400 African American undergraduate students who are currently enrolled in predominately White colleges and universities will be recruited to complete an online survey. This number was chosen in order to meet the requirements needed to conduct our statistical analyses. We will recruit participants from a variety of PWIs throughout the United States. We will recruit as diverse a sample as possible (e.g., age, gender, type of school, major, etc.). After the quantitative data has been analyzed, a subset of participants ($n = 20$) will be selected to participate in the qualitative portion of the study. Participants will be chosen based upon their scores on various instruments used in the study.

Data Collection

Instrumentation. Several instruments will be used in this study. For the quantitative component, participants will be asked to respond to six different instruments, including a demographics questionnaire, the Racial and Ethnic Microaggressions Scale (i.e., two subscales) (Nadal, 2011), the Coping With Discrimination Scale (i.e., two subscales) (Wei, Alvarez, Ku, Russell, & Bonett, 2010), the Emotional Regulation Questionnaire (i.e., two subscales) (Gross & John, 2003), the Multidimensional Inventory of Black Identity (i.e., two subscales) (Sellers et al., 1998), and the Basic Need Satisfaction in General Scale (i.e., three subscales) (Deci & Ryan, 2000). To best address our research questions and because we want to keep the overall number of survey questions manageable for the participants, we have selected particular subscales from the aforementioned scales and will be using 59 items. For the qualitative component, we will use a semistructured interview schedule/ guide. See Proposal Appendix B for copies of the study instruments.

Demographics Questionnaire. The demographics questionnaire includes questions regarding personal characteristics and issues such as age, gender, academic classification, and academic major. Additional questions will address the university context. Such questions include the type of university, the location of the university, and the racial composition of the university, among others.

Racial and Ethnic Microaggressions Scale. The Racial and Ethnic Microaggressions Scale (Nadal, 2011) was designed to examine experiences of various types of racial microaggressions in multiple contexts. The scale consists of 131 items that are divided into six subscales. Nadal (2011) provides a variety of construct validity evidence via exploratory principal components analysis and correlations with other measures measuring similar constructs, such as experiences with racism. Using a five-point Likert format, the scale focuses on how many times racial microaggressions have been experienced within the last six months (0 to 10 times). We will focus on two of the subscales and a small subset of the items based upon previous research (DeCuir-Gunby & Gunby, Jr, 2016): Assumptions of Inferiority (8 items; α = .943) and Microinvalidations (5 items; α = .910). This scale will be used to assess the African American college students' experiences with racial microaggressions.

Coping With Discrimination Scale. The Coping With Discrimination Scale (Wei et al., 2010) uses a six–point Likert scale (*never like me* to *always like me*) and consists of 25 items with five subscales. Wei et al. (2010) provide a variety of construct validity evidence via exploratory and confirmatory factor analysis and correlations with other measures measuring similar constructs, such as experiences with racism. The scale explores numerous ways in which people of color cope with racial discrimination. The items and subscales to be used in this study consist of Education/Advocacy (5 items; $\alpha = .885$), whose items reflect efforts to deal with discrimination through educational or advocacy efforts at individual and societal levels; and Internalization (4 items; $\alpha = .877$), which involves the tendency to attribute the cause or responsibility of a discriminatory incident to oneself (DeCuir-Gunby & Gunby, Jr., 2016). This scale will be used to assess how African American college students cope with racial microaggressions.

Emotional Regulation Questionnaire. The Emotional Regulation Questionnaire (ERQ) was designed to examine the many ways in which individuals regulate their emotions (Gross & John, 2003). The scale focuses on how individuals engage in the reappraisal and suppression of both pleasant and unpleasant emotions. The ERQ is a 10-item scale using a seven-point Likert format (strongly disagree to strongly agree). It has two subscales: Reappraisal (6 items; $\alpha = .80$) and Suppression (6 items; $\alpha = .75$). Gross and John (2003) provide a variety of construct validity evidence via exploratory and confirmatory factor analysis and correlations with other measures measuring similar constructs, such as mood management. This scale will be used to examine how African American college students regulate their emotions.

Multidimensional Inventory of Black Identity. The Multidimensional Inventory of Black Identity (MIBI) was developed to explore the multidimensionality of Black identity (Sellers et al., 1997, 1998). The scale consists of seven subscales with 54 items and uses a seven-point Likert format (*strongly disagree* to *strongly agree*). However, only two subscales will be used for this study, Private Regard (6 items; $\alpha = .81$) and Public Regard (6 items, $\alpha = .82$). Sellers et al. (1997) provide a variety of construct validity evidence via exploratory and confirmatory factor analysis and correlations with other instruments measuring similar constructs, such as interracial contact. This scale will be used to explore African American students' sense of Black racial identity within the PWI context.

Basic Psychological Needs at College Scale. The Basic Psychological Needs at College Scale was adapted from the Basic Psychological Needs at Work Scale (Brien, Forest, Mageau, Boudrias, Desrumaux, Brunet, & Morin, 2012; Deci & Ryan, 2000; Deci, Ryan, Gagné, Leone, Usunov, & Kornazheva, 2001), which is based on an extension of self-determination theory that explores the basic psychological needs at work. The scale consists of three subscales with 21 items and uses a seven-point Likert format (*not at all true* to *very true*). The subscales are Autonomy (7 items; $\alpha = .86$), Competence (6 items; $\alpha = .89$), and Relatedness (8 items; $\alpha = .88$) (Brien et al., 2012). Brien et al. (2012) also provide a variety of construct validity evidence via exploratory and confirmatory factor analysis and correlations with the other instruments that measure similar constructs, such as optimism and intrinsic motivation. We have adapted this scale to focus on the college context and as opposed to the work context. This scale will be used to examine the African American students' basic psychological needs at college within the PWI context.

Semistructured Interview Schedule. In order to conduct individual interviews, we will use a semistructured interview schedule (Moustakas, 1994) featuring broad, open-ended questions. This approach will allow us to ask each participant the same questions but remain flexible in order to cater to their individual experiences. The interview schedule will be used to help capture the participants' experiences with racial microaggressions, coping, and emotional regulation as well as their psychological needs and sense of racial identity.

Procedures. The study will be conducted in two phases. In the first phase, the quantitative phase, potential participants will be recruited using e-mail, Facebook, and discussion lists. In the recruitment letter, participants will be provided a direct hyperlink to an Internet-based survey using the Qualtrics software. (See Proposal Appendix C for the recruitment letter.) Once participants click on the survey hyperlink, they will be redirected to a consent form and explicitly asked if they are interested in participating in the survey. If they choose "yes," they will be confirming that they do consent to participate in the study and will be directed to the survey questions. (See Proposal Appendix D for the consent form.) If they choose "no," they will be directed to a page that thanks participants for their interest in the survey. After consenting, the participants will be asked to complete the surveys enumerated in the previous section, which include a demographics survey as well as surveys concerning racial microaggressions, coping, emotional regulation, racial identity, and needs. Once the surveys have been completed, participants will be asked if they are willing to participate in an interview. If they are willing, they will be asked to give their contact information (name and email address). If not, their participation in the survey will be completed and the survey will end. The data collected will be confidential; IP addresses will not be collected.

The second phase of the study will not begin until after the results from the first phase have been analyzed. The results of our quantitative analyses will help dictate our initial selection of the participants for the interviews that will be conducted later. We will use the qualitative data to further explore the quantitative findings. We will use the results of the quantitative data to identify participants who scored high on the psychological needs subscales. A high score on these subscales indicates these participants are being successful at meeting their psychological needs within their college contexts. Once the interviewees have been chosen, we will send each potential participant an invitation to participate in the study. (See Proposal Appendix C for recruitment letter.) Before the interviews are conducted, participants will be asked to complete a consent form. (See Proposal Appendix D for the consent form.) The interviews will be conducted using a semistructured interview guide over the telephone, via Skype videoconference, or in person at an agreed upon, neutral location. (The interview protocol is included in Proposal Appendix B.) All interviews will be audio-recorded using a digital recording device. If the interview is a videoconference, only the audio portion will be recorded. Although we are planning to interview 20 participants, it is possible that we will stop conducting interviews once we have reached saturation, or when the interviews no longer produce any new information

(Guest, Bunce, & Johnson, 2006). All interview participants will be informed that they may be contacted for follow-up interviews if necessary.

Data Analysis

In order to adhere to our sequential explanatory mixed methods design, our data analysis will occur in two phases. We will first analyze the quantitative data and then we will analyze the qualitative data. Once all of the data has been analyzed, we will then integrate the findings and make relevant conclusions.

Procedures. Once the survey information has been collected, we will take time to ensure that we have a complete data set. This will require that we examine the data for inconsistences as well as make decisions about incomplete data and data cleaning. After we have a complete and cleaned data set, we will analyze the data using SPSS. We will begin by calculating descriptive statistics (means, standard deviations, etc.). We will also perform exploratory factor analyses per scale; confirmatory factor analyses may also be conducted using other software packages, such as LISREL. Next we will calculate inferential statistics such as correlations, multiple regressions, cluster analyses, and ANOVAs in order to address our research questions. We will also engage in structural equation modeling (SEM).

After the interviews have been conducted, they will be transcribed verbatim. We will then use Atlas.ti, a qualitative software package, to help analyze and sort the data. We will code the data, organize the data into themes, and connect the data to the larger research literature. Specifically, the interviews will be analyzed using thematic content analysis (Coffey & Atkinson, 1996) through the implementation of grounded theory techniques (Corbin & Strauss, 2015). We will develop a codebook using both a priori and emergent codes (see DeCuir-Gunby, Marshall, & McCulloch, 2011). In using the codebook, we will begin with open coding at the sentence/paragraph level. Next, we will list all of the codes and organize them into categories. We will then utilize the statements that best illustrate these categories to construct each participant's counterstory (Solórzano & Yosso, 2002). In order to explore their counterstories, we will use the analysis of narratives approach (see Polkinghorne, 1995). In the analysis of narratives approach, the goal is to find common themes across participants' stories (Polkinghorne, 1995). Critical race theory will serve as the lens of analysis (DeCuir & Dixson, 2004).

To address RQ #1, "What are African American college students' experiences with racial microaggressions," we will use both quantitative and qualitative data. For the quantitative data we will utilize descriptive statistics from the Racial and Ethnic Microaggressions Scale. We will also use the data from Interview Questions 3 and 4 to allow the participants to tell us about their experiences with racial microaggressions. As such, we will use the interview data along with the survey data to elaborate on the types of microaggressions that African American college students experience in PWIs.

For RQ #1A, "How do African American college students cope with and regulate the emotions associated with the experience of racial microaggressions," we will again use both quantitative and qualitative data. For the quantitative data, we will conduct descriptive and inferential statistical analyses using the Coping With Discrimination Scale and the Emotional Regulation Questionnaire, and we will also conduct a correlation

AFRICAN AMERICAN COLLEGE STUDENTS' EXPERIENCES   33

analysis to investigate the relationships among the subscales. In addition, Interview Questions 7, 8, and 9 will allow the participants to tell us about how they attempt to handle the racial microaggressions that they experience as college students. We will use the interview data along with the survey data to elaborate on the ways that African American college students attempt to deal with their racial microaggressions experiences.

For RQ #1B, "How is their experience of racial microaggressions related to African American college students' sense of racial identity," we will again use both quantitative and qualitative data. For the quantitative data, we will conduct descriptive and inferential statistical analyses using the Racial and Ethnic Microaggressions Scale and the Multidimensional Inventory of Black Identity. We will also use a correlation analysis to investigate the relationships among students' scores on the subscales of the Racial and Ethnic Microaggressions Scale and their scores on the Multidimensional Inventory of Black Identity. In addition, Interview Questions 2–5 will allow the participants to tell us about how they see and identify themselves as African American, and how that sense of identity influences the way they attempt to handle the racial microaggressions that they experience as college students. We will use the interview data along with the survey data to elaborate on the ways that African American college students see their racial identity and how they think those identity beliefs influence their attempts to deal with their racial microaggression experiences.

For RQ #1C, "Where do African American college students see the boundary between microaggressions and non-microaggressions," we will be using qualitative data collected via Interview Question 5. Here we would like our participants to talk about how they determine whether a transaction—such as a subtle snub, a dismissive look, or a gesture—is a microaggression. It would seem that some transactions are clearly microaggressions, whereas others might be more ambiguous and harder to identify. We would like to begin to examine how African American college students develop an understanding of where their "border" or "boundary line" is between a microaggression and something that is offensive but not considered a microaggression.

For RQ #2, "What are the psychological need profiles of African American college students," we want to identify groups or clusters of African American college students. We plan to use the three subscales of the Basic Need Satisfaction at College Scale and conduct a cluster analysis to identify those profiles. Our goal is to identify one or more profiles of African American college students who are successfully meeting their needs in the PWI context.

For RQ #2A, "How do African American college students who score high on the measure of psychological needs scale address racial microaggressions," we want to use the profile(s) developed in RQ #2 to identify 20 participants to interview. Our overall goal is to tell the (counter) stories of the students who are meeting their needs within this college context. This will help us to identify strategies that other African American college students can use to be successful in their contexts.

For RQ #3, "What is the relationship among racial microaggressions, racial identity, coping and emotional regulation strategies, and psychological needs for African American college students," we will use SEM to develop an understanding of the relationship among all of the quantitative scales we collected data with. See Proposal Appendix E for our preliminary model.

Data Integration. After we have analyzed both the quantitative and qualitative data, we will engage in data integration, particularly the *explaining* form of data integration (Creswell, 2015). Consistent with our explanatory sequential design, the quantitative and qualitative findings will be discussed separately as well as together. The qualitative data will be used to support, contradict, or expand the quantitative findings. In integrating the data, will use the *narrative* approach in that we will discuss our findings through text as well as create *joint displays* where we will use tables and charts to illustrate what we have found.

Role of Theoretical Framework. As described by Greene (2007), philosophical lenses play a critical role in the implementation of mixed methods studies. As such, our theoretical framework, including our inquiry worldview of critical race theory (counterstorytelling, permanence of racism, critique of liberalism, interest convergence, and Whiteness as property) and our substantive content theories (multidimensional model of racial identity, coping with racism, emotional regulation, and self-determination theory), will be used in all stages of the study. The theoretical framework has already been used in the creation of the research questions and the literature review. In addition, the theoretical framework will be used in both the data collection and analysis processes. The theoretical framework was used in selecting project instruments and will be drawn upon while collecting data, particularly the interviews. For the data analysis process, the theoretical framework will be used to help make decisions for both the quantitative and qualitative data reductions as well as during the data integration process. Most important, the theoretical framework will be of center focus while writing up the research findings.

Reliability/Credibility. Establishing reliability/credibility is essential when engaging in mixed methods research. In our study, we will utilize a variety of techniques in order to demonstrate the consistency of our research findings. In order to address reliability for the quantitative component, reliability analyses (Cronbach's alpha) will be calculated on the survey results. Measuring internal consistency helps to demonstrate how well the items on each scale correlate with each other or measure the same construct. Addressing credibility for the qualitative component, however, requires more involvement. We will develop a codebook featuring theory-driven, data-driven, and *in vivo* codes (see DeCuir-Gunby, Marshall, & McCulloch, 2011). The codebook will help to ensure that the coding process is systematic. Next, the interviews will be coded at least twice to ensure that we do not miss any significant findings. This is necessary to check our interpretations. Also, peer reviewers will be used to code a subset of the interviews. Cohen's kappa, an index for measuring interrater agreement, will be calculated as a means of demonstrating credibility (Hruschka, Schwartz, St. John, Picone-Decaro, Jenkins, & Carey, 2004).

Validity/Trustworthiness. In addition to establishing reliability/credibility, it is also imperative to demonstrate validity/trustworthiness. For the quantitative component, we will focus on helping to establish construct validity. Specifically, we will examine the underlying structures of the instruments used in the study through the use of exploratory and confirmatory factor analyses (Benson, 1998). Also, we will examine the nomological network (Cronbach & Meehl, 1955) of the racial microaggressions construct by exploring its relationships with coping, emotional regulation, racial identity, and basic needs satisfaction (autonomy, competence, and relatedness). Trustworthiness, on the other hand, will be addressed using two approaches—thick, rich descriptions, and member checking (Merriam, 2009). Thick, rich descriptions will be used to allow readers to see the participants' actual language and words, helping to support the interpretations that we make. Also, member checking will be used in order for participants themselves to check the accuracy of the interpretations that we make from their own words.

In mixed methods research, it is also important to discuss the quality of the metainferences that we will make from combining the quantitative and qualitative data (Teddlie & Tashakkori, 2009). This will be done in a variety of ways, including examination of multiple validities as previously described as well as sequential collection and analysis of data (Onwuegbuzie & Johnson, 2006). In addition, we will attend to consequences that could potentially arise from the conducting of our study (Dellinger & Leech, 2007). We will examine how our participants will be impacted from participating in this study, because examination of racial incidents can potentially be emotional. Also, we will consider the impact such a study can have on changing the racial climates of PWIs.

References

Allen, Q. (2010). Racial microaggressions: The schooling experiences of Black middle-class males in Arizona's secondary schools. *Journal of African American Males in Education, 1*(2), 125–142.

Baber, L. D. (2012). A qualitative inquiry on the multidimensional racial development among first-year African American college students attending a predominately White institution. *The Journal of Negro Education, 81*(1), 67–81.

Bell, D. (1980). *Brown v. Board of Education* and the interest–convergence dilemma. *Harvard Law Review, 93*(3), 518–533.

Bell, D. (1992). Racial realism. *Connecticut Law Review, 24*(2), 363–379.

Bell, D. (1993). *Faces at the bottom of the well: The permanence of racism.* New York, NY: Basic Books.

Benson, J. (1998). Developing a strong program of construct validation: A test anxiety example. *Educational Measurement: Issues and Practice, 17*(1), 10–17.

Boysen, G. A., Vogel, D. L., Cope, M. A., & Hubbard, A. (2009). Incidents of bias in college classrooms: Instructor and student perceptions. *Journal of Diversity in Higher Education, 2*(4), 219–231.

Brien, M., Forest, J., Mageau, G. A., Boudrias, J. S., Desrumaux, P., Brunet, L., & Morin, E. M. (2012). The basic psychological needs at work scale: Measurement invariance between Canada and France. *Applied Psychology: Health and Well-Being, 4*(2), 167–187.

Brondolo, E., ver Halen, N., Pencille, M., Beatty, D., & Contrada, R. (2009). Coping with racism: A selective review of the literature and a theoretical and methodological critique. *Journal of Behavioral Medicine, 32*, 64–88.

Brown, M. C., II, & Dancy, T. E., II. (2010). Predominantly White institutions. In K. Lomotey (Ed.), *Encyclopedia of African American education* (pp. 524–527). Thousand Oaks, CA: Sage.

Brown, T. L., Phillips, C. M., Abdullah, T., Vinson, E., & Robertson, J. (2011). Dispositional versus situational coping: Are the coping strategies African Americans use different for general versus racism-related stressors? *Journal of Black Psychology, 37*(3), 311–335.

Cabrera, N. L. (2014). Exposing Whiteness in higher education: White male college students minimizing racism, claiming victimization, and recreating White supremacy. *Race Ethnicity and Education, 17*(1), 30–55.

Clark, R., Anderson, N. B., Clark, V. R., & Williams, D. R. (1999). Racism as a stressor for African Americans: A biopsychosocial model. *American Psychologist, 54*(10), 805–816.

Coffey, A., & Atkinson, P. (1996). *Making sense of qualitative data: Complementary research designs.* Thousand Oaks, CA: Sage.

Constantine, M. G. (2007). Racial microaggressions against African American clients in cross–racial counseling relationships. *Journal of Counseling Psychology, 54*, 1–16

AFRICAN AMERICAN COLLEGE STUDENTS' EXPERIENCES   40

Constantine, M. G., Smith, L., Redington, R. M., & Owens, D. (2008). Racial microaggressions against Black counseling and psychology faculty: A central challenge in the multicultural counseling movement. *Journal of Counseling and Development, 86*(3), 348–355.

Corbin, J. M., & Strauss, A. L. (2015). *Basics of qualitative research: Techniques and procedures for developing grounded theory* (4th ed.). Thousand Oaks, CA: Sage.

Crenshaw, K. (1989). Demarginalizing the intersection of race and sex: A Black feminist critique of antidiscrimination doctrine, feminist theory and antiracist politics. *University of Chicago Legal Forum,* 139–167.

Creswell, J. W. (2015). *A concise introduction to mixed methods research.* Thousand Oaks, CA: Sage.

Creswell, J., & Plano Clark, V. (2011). *Designing and conducting mixed methods research* (2nd ed.). Thousand Oaks, CA: Sage.

Cronbach, L. J., & Meehl, P. E. (1955). Construct validity in psychological tests. *Psychological Bulletin, 52,* 281–302.

Deci, E. L., & Ryan, R. M. (2000). The "what" and "why" of goal pursuits: Human needs and the self–determination of behavior. *Psychological Inquiry, 11,* 227–268.

Deci, E. L., Ryan, R. M., Gagné, M., Leone, D. R., Usunov, J., & Kornazheva, B. P. (2001). Need satisfaction, motivation, and well-being in the work organizations of former Eastern Bloc country: A cross-cultural study of self-determination. *Personality and Psychology Bulletin, 27,* 930–942.

DeCuir, J. T., & Dixson, A. D. (2004). "So when it comes out, they aren't that surprised that it is there": Using critical race theory as a tool of analysis of race and racism in education. *Educational Researcher*, 26–31.

DeCuir-Gunby, J. T., & Gunby, N. W., Jr., (2016). Racial microaggressions in the workplace: A critical race analysis of the experiences of African American educators. *Urban Education, 51(4),* 390-414.

DeCuir-Gunby, J. T., Marshall, P., & McCulloch, A. (2011). Developing and using a codebook for the analysis of interview data: An example from a professional development research project. *Field Methods, 23*(2), 136–155.

DeCuir-Gunby, J. T., & Schutz, P. A. (2014). *Researching race within educational psychology contexts. Educational Psychologist, 49*(4), 244–260.

DeCuir-Gunby, J. T., & Walker-DeVose, D. C. (2013). Expanding the counterstory: The potential for critical race mixed methods studies in education. In M. Lynn & A.D. Dixson (Eds.), *Handbook of critical race theory in education* (pp. 248–259). New York, NY: Routledge.

Delgado, R. (1989). Storytelling for oppositionists and others: A plea for narrative. *Michigan Law Review, 87,* 2411–2441.

Delgado, R., & Stefancic, J. (2012). *Critical race theory: An introduction* (2nd ed.). New York: New York University Press.

Dellinger, A. B., & Leech, N. L. (2007). Towards a unified validation framework in mixed methods research. *Journal of Mixed Methods Research, 1*(4), 309–332.

AFRICAN AMERICAN COLLEGE STUDENTS' EXPERIENCES   42

Folkman, S., & Moskowitz, J. T. (2004). Coping: Pitfalls and promise. *Annual Review of Psychology, 55*, 745–774.

Forsyth, J., & Carter, R. (2012). The relationship between racial identity status attitudes, racism-related coping, and mental health among Black Americans. *Cultural Diversity and Ethnic Minority Psychology, 18*(2), 128–140.

Franklin, A. J., Boyd-Franklin, N., & Kelly, S. (2006). Racism and invisibility: Race-related stress, emotional abuse and psychological trauma for people of color. *Journal of Emotional Abuse, 6*(2–3), 9–30.

Gildersleeve, R. E., Croom, N. N., & Vasquez, P. L. (2011). "Am I going crazy?!": A critical race analysis of doctoral education. *Equity & Excellence in Education, 44*(1), 93–114.

Giscombé, C. L., & Lobel, L. (2005). Explaining disproportionately high rates of adverse birth outcomes among African Americans: The impact of stress, racism, and related factors in pregnancy. *Psychological Bulletin, 131*, 662–683.

Gomez, M. L., Khurshid, A., Freitag, M. B., & Lachuk, A. J. (2011). Microaggressions in graduate students' lives: How they are encountered and their consequences. *Teaching and Teacher Education, 27,* 1189–1199.

Gotanda, N. (1991). A critique of "Our constitution is color-blind." *Stanford Law Review, 44*, 1–68.

Greene, J. C. (2007). *Mixed methods in social inquiry.* San Francisco, CA: Jossey-Bass.

Gross, J. J., & John, O. P. (2003). Individual differences in two emotion regulation processes: Implications for affect, relationships, and well-being. *Journal of Personality and Social Psychology, 85,* 348–362.

Guest, G., Bunce, A., & Johnson, L. (2006). How many interviews are enough? An experiment with data saturation and variability. *Field Methods, 18*(1), 59–82.

Harper, B. E. (2007). The relationship between Black racial identity and academic achievement in urban settings. *Theory Into Practice, 46*(3), 230–238.

Harper, S. R. (2012). *Black male student success in higher education: A report from the national Black male college achievement study.* Philadelphia: University of Pennsylvania, Center for the Study of Race and Equity in Education.

Harrell, S. P. (2000). A multidimensional conceptualization of racism-related stress: Implications for the well-being of people of color. *American Journal of Orthopsychiatry, 70,* 42–57.

Harris, C. (1993). Whiteness as property. *Harvard Law Review, 106*(8), 1707–1791.

Harwood, S. A., Huntt, M. B., Mendenhall, R., & Lewis, J. A. (2012). Racial microaggressions in the residence halls: Experiences of students of color at a predominantly White university. *Journal of Diversity in Higher Education, 5*(3), 159.

AFRICAN AMERICAN COLLEGE STUDENTS' EXPERIENCES 44

Helms, J. (Ed.). (1990). *Black and White racial identity: Theory, research, and practice.* New York, NY: Greenwood Press.

Helms, J., Jernigan, M., & Mascher, J. (2005). The meaning of race in psychology and how to change it: A methodological perspective. *American Psychologist, 60*(1), 27–36.

Hruschka, D. J., Schwartz, D., St. John, D. C., Picone-Decaro, E., Jenkins, R. A., & Carey, J. W. (2004). Reliability in coding open-ended data: Lessons learned from coding HIV behavioral research. *Field Methods, 16*(3), 307–331.

Johnson-Ahorlu, N. R. (2012). The academic opportunity gap: How racism and stereotypes disrupt the education of African American undergraduates. *Race, Ethnicity, and Education, 15*(5), 633–652.

Kena, G., Musu-Gillette, L., Robinson, J., Wang, X., Rathbun, A., Zhang, J., Wilkinson-Flicker, S., . . . & Dunlop Velez, E. (2015). *The Condition of Education 2015* (NCES 2015-144). Washington, DC: U.S. Department of Education, National Center for Education Statistics. Retrieved from http://nces.ed.gov/pubsearch

Kohli, R., & Solórzano, D. 2012. Teachers, please learn our names!: Racial microaggressions and the K–12 classroom. *Race Ethnicity and Education, 15*(4), 441–462.

Ladson-Billings, G., & Tate, W. F. (1995). Towards a critical race theory of education. *Teachers College Record, 97*(1), 47–68.

Lazarus, R. S., & Folkman, S. (1984). *Stress, appraisal, and coping.* New York, NY: Springer.

Lewis, J. A., Mendenhall, R., Harwood, S., & Huntt, M.B. (2013). Coping with racial microaggressions among Black women. *Journal of African American Studies, 17,* 51–73.

McGee, M. C. (2013). *James Meredith: Warrior and the America that created him.* New York, NY: Praeger.

McWhorter, J. (2014, March 21). Microaggression is the new racism on campus. *Time.* Retrieved from http://time.com/32618/microaggression-is-the-new-racism-on-campus/

Melor, D. (2004). Responses to racism: A taxonomy of coping styles used by Aboriginal Australians. *American Journal of Orthopsychiatry, 74*(1), 56–71.

Merriam, S. B. (2009). *Qualitative research: A guide to design and implementation.* San Francisco, CA: Jossey-Bass.

Mitchell, R., Fasching-Varner, K. J., Albert, K., & Allen, C. (Eds.). (2015). *Racial battle fatigue in higher education: Exposing the myth of post-racial America.* Lanham, MD: Rowan & Littlefield.

Moustakas, C. E. (1994). *Phenomenological research methods.* Thousand Oaks, CA: Sage.

Nadal, K. (2011). The racial and ethnic microaggressions scale (REMS): Construction, reliability, and validity. *Journal of Counseling Psychology, 58*(4), 470–480.

AFRICAN AMERICAN COLLEGE STUDENTS' EXPERIENCES   46

Onwuegbuzie, A. J., & Johnson, R. B. (2006). The validity issue in mixed research. *Research in the Schools, 13*(1), 48–63.

Paradies, Y. (2006). A systematic review of empirical research on self-reported racism and health. *International Journal of Epidemiology, 35*(4), 888–901.

Pieterse, A. L., Carter, R. T., Evans, S. A., & Walter, R. A. (2010). An exploratory examination of the associations among racial and ethnic discrimination, racial climate, and trauma-related symptoms in a college student population. *Journal of Counseling Psychology, 57,* 255–263.

Pieterse, A. L., Todd, N. R., Neville, H. A., & Carter, R. T. (2012). Perceived racism and mental health among Black American adults: A meta-analytic review. *Journal of Counseling Psychology, 59*(1), 1–9.

Pittman, C. T. (2012). Racial microaggressions: The narratives of African American faculty at a predominately White university. *Journal of Negro Education, 81*(1), 82–92.

Polkinghorne, D. E. (1995). Narrative configuration in qualitative analysis. *Qualitative Studies in Education, 8*(1), 5–23.

Reynolds, A. L., Sneva, J. N., & Beehler, G. P. (2010). The influence of racism-related stress on the academic motivation of Black and Latino/a students. *Journal of College Student Development, 51*(2), 135–149.

Ryan, R. M., Huta, V., & Deci, E. L. (2008). Living well: A self-determination theory perspective on eudaimonia. *Journal of Happiness Studies, 9,* 139–170.

AFRICAN AMERICAN COLLEGE STUDENTS' EXPERIENCES   47

Scottham, K. M., Sellers, R. M., & Nguyen, H. X. (2008). A measure of racial identity in African American adolescents: The development of the multidimensional inventory of Black identity–teen. *Cultural Diversity and Ethnic Minority Psychology, 14*(4), 297–306.

Sellers, R. M., Rowley S. A. J., Chavous, T. M., Shelton, J. N., & Smith, M.A. (1997). Multidimensional Inventory of Black Identity: A preliminary investigation of reliability and construct validity. *Journal of Personality and Social Psychology, 73,* 805–815.

Sellers, R. M., Smith, M. A., Shelton , J. N., Rowley, S. A. J., & Chavous, T. M. (1998). Multidimensional Model of Racial Identity: A reconceptualization of African American racial identity. *Personality and Social Psychology Review, 2 (1),* 18–39.

Sheldon, K. M., Ryan, R. M., Rawsthorne, L., & Ilardi, B. (1997). "True" self and "trait" self: Cross role variation in the big five traits and its relations with authenticity and well being. *Journal of Personality and Social Psychology, 73*(6), 1380–1393.

Smith, W. A., Allen, W. R., & Danley, L. L. (December 2007). "Assume the position . . . You fit the description": Campus racial climate and the psychoeducational experiences and racial battle fatigue among African American male college students. *American Behavioral Scientist, 51*(4), 551–578.

Smith, W. A., Hung, M., & Franklin, J. D. (2011). Racial battle fatigue and the miseducation of Black men: Racial microaggressions, societal problems, and environmental stress. *Journal of Negro Education, 80*(1), 63–82.

AFRICAN AMERICAN COLLEGE STUDENTS' EXPERIENCES   48

Solórzano, D. G., & Yosso, T. J. (2002). Critical race methodology: Counter-storytelling as an analytical framework for education research. *Qualitative Inquiry, 8*(1), 23–44.

Sue, D., Capodilupo, C., Torino, G., Bucceri, J., Holder, A., Nadal, K., & Esquilin, M. (2007). Racial microaggressions in everyday life: Implications for clinical practice. *American Psychologist, 62*(4), 271–286.

Suls, J., & Fletcher, B. (1985). The relative efficacy of avoidant and nonavoidant coping strategies: A meta-analysis. *Health Psychology, 4,* 249–288.

Tashakkori, A., & Creswell, J. W. (2007). The new era of mixed methods. *Journal of Mixed Methods Research, 1,* 3–7.

Teddlie, C., & Tashakkori, A. (2009). *Foundations of mixed methods research: Integrating quantitative and qualitative approaches in the social and behavioral sciences.* Thousand Oaks, CA: Sage.

Thomas, A. J., Witherspoon, K. M., & Speight, S. L. (2008). Gendered racism, psychological distress, and coping styles of African American women. *Cultural Diversity and Ethnic Minority Psychology, 14*(4), 307–314.

Thomas, O. N., Caldwell, C. H., Faison, N., & Jackson, J. S. (2009). Promoting academic achievement: The role of racial identity in buffering perceptions of teacher discrimination on academic achievement among African American and Caribbean Black adolescents. *Journal of Educational Psychology, 101*(2), 420–431.

AFRICAN AMERICAN COLLEGE STUDENTS' EXPERIENCES   49

Torres, L., Driscoll, M. W., & Burrow, A. L. (2010). Racial microaggressions and psychological functioning among highly achieving African-Americans: A mixed-methods approach. *Journal of Social and Clinical Psychology, 29*(10), 1074–1099.

Utsey, S. O. (1998). Assessing the stressful effects of racism: A review of instrumentation. *Journal of Black Psychology, 24*(3), 269–288.

Utsey, S. O., Giesbrecht, N., Hook, J., & Stanard, P. M. (2008). Cultural, sociofamilial, and psychological resources that inhibit psychological distress in African Americans exposed to stressful life events and race-related stress. *Journal of Counseling Psychology, 55*(1), 49–62.

Vega, T. (2014, March 21). Students see many slights as racial microaggressions. *New York Times*. Retrieved from http://www.nytimes.com/2014/03/22/us/as-diversity-increases-slights-get-subtler-but-still-sting.html

Wang, J., Leu, J., & Shoda, Y. (2011). When the seemingly innocuous "stings": Racial microaggressions and their emotional consequences. *Personality and Social Psychology Bulletin, 37*(12), 1666–1678.

Wei, M., Alvarez, A., Ku, T., Russell, D., & Bonett, D. (2010). Development and validation of a coping with discrimination scale: Factor structure, reliability, and validity. *Journal of Counseling Psychology, 57*(3), 328–344.

Yosso, T. J., Smith, W. A., Ceja, M., & Solórzano, D. G. (2009). Critical race theory, racial microaggressions, and campus racial climate for Latina/o undergraduates. *Harvard Educational Review, 79*(4), 659–691.

PROPOSAL APPENDIX A: MIXED METHODS DIAGRAM

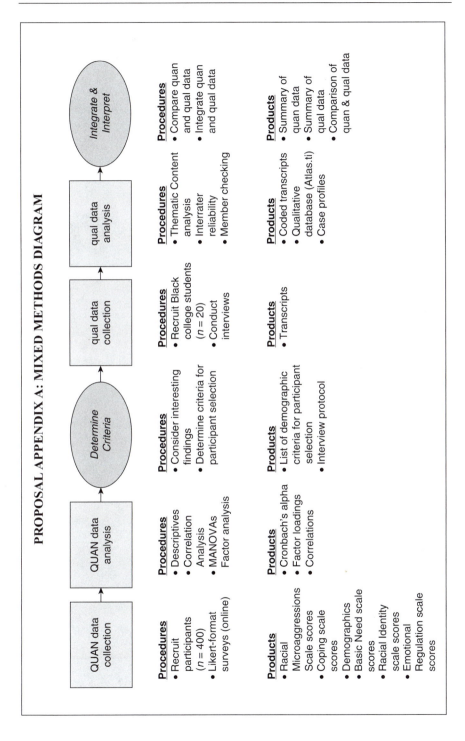

PROPOSAL APPENDIX B: STUDY INSTRUMENTS

Demographics Questionnaire

1. What is your race/ethnicity?
   a. African American/Black
   b. Hispanic/Latino
   c. Asian/Pacific Islander
   d. Native American
   e. Other_____

2. What is your gender?
   a. Male
   b. Female

3. What is your age?_____

4. What is your religious affiliation?
   a. Christianity
   b. Islam
   c. Hinduism
   d. Buddhism
   e. Sikhism
   f. Judaism
   g. Bahaism
   h. Confucianism
   i. Jainism
   j. Shintoism
   k. Other

5. Are you a member of an African American Greek organization?
   a. Yes
   b. No

6. What is your household income?
   a. $0–9,999
   b. $10,000–29,999
   c. $30,000–59,999
   d. $60,000–99,999
   e. $100,000–$199,999
   f. $200,000–$499,999
   g. $500,000+

7. What is your current academic standing?
   a. Freshman
   b. Sophomore
   c. Junior
   d. Senior
   e. Graduate student
   f. Professional student

8. What is your major area of study (e.g., psychology, business)?
   _____

9. What is your current enrollment status?
   a. Full time
   b. Part time

10. What type of university do you attend?
    a. Public
    b. Private

11. How long have you attended your current university?_____

12. What is the zip code of your university?_____

13. How large is your university?
    a. Fewer than 5,000 students
    b. 5,000 to 15,000 students
    c. More than 15,000 students

14. What best characterizes the racial distribution of your university?
    a. Less than 5% people of color
    b. 5% people of color
    c. 10% people of color
    d. 15% people of color
    e. 20% people of color
    f. 25% people of color
    g. 30% people of color
    h. 35% people of color
    i. 40% people of color
    j. 45% people of color
    k. 50% people of color

LIKERT SURVEYS

Racial and Ethnic Microaggressions Scale (Nadal, 2011)

Directions: Racial microaggressions are "brief, everyday exchanges that send denigrating messages to people of color because they belong to a racial minority group." Further, racial microaggressions are often automatic, manifested in the form of "subtle snubs or dismissive looks, gestures, and tones." On the scales to follow, indicate how often you have experienced racial microaggression at school during the past three months. There are no right or wrong answers. Respond to these items using a 5-point scale: (1) *never*, (2) *rarely*, (3) *occasionally/sometimes*, (4) *often*, (5) *always*.

Assumptions of Inferiority

1. Someone assumed that I would have less education because of my race.
2. Someone assumed that I was poor because of my race.
3. Someone assumed that I would not be educated because of my race.
4. Someone acted surprised at my scholastic or professional success because of my race.
5. Someone assumed that I would not be intelligent because of my race.
6. Someone assumed that I held a lower-paying job because of my race.
7. Someone assumed that I grew up in a particular neighborhood because of my race.
8. Someone told me that I was "articulate" after assuming I wouldn't be.

Microinvalidations

1. Someone told me that they "don't see color."
2. Someone told me that they do not see race.
3. Someone told me that people should not think about race anymore.
4. Someone told me that she or he was color-blind.
5. I was told that people of all racial groups experience the same obstacles.

Coping With Discrimination Scale
(Wei, Alvarez, Ku, Russell, & Bonett, 2010)

Directions: This is a list of strategies that some people have used to deal with their experience of discrimination. Please respond to the following items as honestly as possible to reflect how much each strategy describes the ways you cope with discrimination at school. There are no right or wrong answers.

Respond to these items using six response options: (1) *never like me*, (2) *a little like me*, (3) *sometimes like me*, (4) *often like me*, (5) *usually like me*, and (6) *always like me*.

Education/Advocacy

1. I educate others about the negative impact of discrimination.
2. I help people to be better prepared to deal with discrimination.
3. I try to stop discrimination at the societal level.
4. I try to educate people so that they are aware of discrimination.
5. I educate myself to be better prepared to deal with discrimination.

Internalization

1. I wonder if I did something to provoke this incident.
2. I wonder if I did something to offend others.
3. I wonder if I did something wrong.
4. I believe I may have triggered the incident.

Emotional Regulation Questionnaire (Gross & John, 2003)

Directions: We would like to ask you some questions about your emotional life, in particular, how you control (that is, regulate and manage) your emotions. The questions below involve two distinct aspects of your emotional life. One is your emotional experience, or what you feel like inside. The other is your emotional expression, or how you show your emotions in the way you talk, gesture, or behave. Although some of the following questions may seem similar to one another, they differ in important ways. For each item, please respond to these items using the five response options: (1) *never like me*, (2) *a little like me*, (3) *somewhat like me*, (4) *often like me*, and (5) *always like me*.

Reappraisal Factor

1. I control my emotions by changing the way I think about the situation I'm in.
2. When I want to feel less negative emotion, I change the way I'm thinking about the situation.
3. When I want to feel more positive emotion, I change the way I'm thinking about the situation.
4. When I want to feel more positive emotion (such as joy or amusement), I change what I'm thinking about.
5. When I want to feel less negative emotion (such as sadness or anger), I change what I'm thinking about.
6. When I'm faced with a stressful situation, I make myself think about it in a way that helps me stay calm.

Suppression Factor

1. I control my emotions by not expressing them.
2. When I am feeling negative emotions, I make sure not to express them.

3. I keep my emotions to myself.

4. When I am feeling positive emotions, I am careful not to express them.

Multidimensional Inventory of Black Identity (MIBI) (Sellers, Smith, Shelton, Rowley, & Chavous, 1998)

Private Regard Subscale

1. I feel good about Black people.

2. I am happy that I am Black.

3. I feel that Blacks have made major accomplishments and advancements.

4. I often regret that I am Black. (R)[1]

5. I am proud to be Black.

6. I feel that the Black community has made valuable contributions to this society.

Public Regard Subscale

1. Overall, Blacks are considered good by others.

2. In general, others respect Black people.

3. Most people consider Blacks, on the average, to be more ineffective than other racial groups. (R)

4. Blacks are not respected by the broader society. (R)

5. In general, other groups view Blacks in a positive manner.

6. Society views Black people as an asset.

Basic Psychological Needs at College Scale (adapted from Deci, Ryan, Gagné, Leone, Usunov, & Kornazheva, 2001)

Instructions: The following questions concern your feelings about your college during the PAST three months. Please indicate how much you agree with each of the following statements given your experiences at college. Remember that no one from your college will ever know how you responded to the questions. Please use the following scale in responding to the items: (1) *never like me*, (2) *a little like me*, (3) *somewhat like me*, (4) *often like me*, and (5) *always like me*.

Need for Autonomy at College

1. At college, I feel a sense of choice and freedom in the things I undertake.

2. I feel that my decisions at college reflect what I really want.

---

[1] (R) indicates that an item is to be reverse-scored.

3. I feel my choices college express who I really am.

4. My daily activities at college feel like a chain of obligations. (R)

5. I feel I have been doing what really interests me at my college.

Need for Competency at College

1. I feel confident that I can do things well at my college.

2. I feel disappointed with my performance at college. (R)

3. When I am at college, I feel competent to achieve my goals.

4. I feel insecure about my abilities at my college. (R)

5. At my college, I feel I can successfully complete difficult tasks.

Need for Relatedness at College

1. I feel excluded from the group I want to belong to at college. (R)

2. I feel that the people I care about at college also care about me.

3. I feel that people who are important to me at college are cold and distant toward me. (R)

4. I feel the relationships I have at college are just superficial. (R)

5. I experience a warm feeling with the people I spend time with at college.

Microaggression Interview Protocol

Introduction: On predominately White college campuses, African Americans often feel discredited, disrespected, or discriminated against because of their race. In answering the questions, think about your daily experiences at your university.

1. Tell me a little bit about your university.

2. Talk to me about what it is like to be an African American student at your university.

3. Tell me about a time in which you felt discredited, disrespected, or discriminated against because of your race at your university.

   Probe for faculty—Instances with professors and administrators?

   Probe for students—Instances with colleagues, peers, et cetera?

4. Describe a time in which you witnessed invalidation, disrespect, or discrimination because of race at your university.

   Probe for faculty—Instances with professors and administrators?

   Probe for students—Instances with colleagues, peers, et cetera?

5. How do you determine if you are being disrespected or discredited because of race?

   a. Was there a time recently where you had trouble discerning whether you were being disrespected because of race or because of some other issue?

6. How did you address these experiences of invalidation, disrespect, or discrimination?

   Probe—speak out, formal complaint, talk to others, ignore, et cetera.

7. How did these experiences make you feel? How did you handle your emotions?

8. How have these experiences affected your physical or mental well-being?

9. How did you cope with these experiences of invalidation, disrespect, or discrimination?

10. How have these experiences influenced your perceptions of your university?

11. Is there anything else you would like to add?

PROPOSAL APPENDIX C: RECRUITMENT LETTERS

Recruitment Letter for Survey

   A research team is conducting an examination of an extremely relevant phenomenon. The study will assess the impact of racial microaggressions on African American students in the predominately White college context. Racial microaggressions are characterized as negative, race-based messages that people of color experience in everyday conversations and interactions. This study is important because it will inform research into the understanding of how African American college students are psychologically impacted by racial microaggressions.

   The research team invites you to participate in our research project. As a participant, you will be asked to complete a short online survey about your experiences at your university. The questions will ask you about your experiences with racial microaggressions, as well as questions about racial identity, coping, emotional regulation, and psychological needs (autonomy, competence, and relatedness). Additionally, you will be asked to provide basic demographic information, such as your age, and information about your university. It should take approximately 20 minutes to complete the entire survey, which can be accessed via the following hyperlink: [Insert hyperlink].

   We greatly appreciate your assistance in making this research study possible and would also ask that you electronically forward this solicitation to anyone that you feel would also like to participate. Consider your Facebook friends, discussion list members, fraternity and sorority brothers and sisters, and professional organization members. Please be mindful of the policies of your individual institution regarding solicitations and the use of institutional e-mail systems.

   If you have any questions related to the study, please feel free to contact [insert contact information for primary investigator].

Sincerely,

The Research Team

Recruitment Letter for Interview

   A research team is conducting an examination of an extremely relevant phenomenon. The study will assess the impact of racial microaggressions on African American students in the predominately White college context. Racial microaggressions are characterized as negative, race-based messages that people of color experience in everyday conversations and interactions. This study is important because it will inform research into the understanding of how African American college students are psychologically impacted by racial microaggressions.

   The research team would like to invite you to participate in our research project. You will be asked to participate in a short interview about your experiences at your university. The interview is expected to take 45 minutes to an hour. The interviews will be conducted over the telephone or in person, at an agreed upon, neutral location.

We would really appreciate your assistance in making this research study possible. If you have any questions related to the study, please feel free to contact [insert contact information for primary investigator].

Sincerely,

The Research Team

PROPOSAL APPENDIX D: CONSENT FORMS

INFORMED CONSENT FORM for RESEARCH—SURVEY

Title of Study: A Mixed Methods Exploration of African American College Students' Experiences With Racial Microaggressions

What are some general things you should know about research studies?—You are being asked to take part in a research study. Your participation in this study is voluntary. You have the right to be a part of this study or to choose not to participate, or to stop participating at any time without penalty. The purpose of research studies is to gain a better understanding of a certain topic or issue. You are not guaranteed any personal benefits from being in a study. Research studies also may pose risks to those that participate. In this consent form you will find specific details about the research in which you are being asked to participate. If you do not understand something in this form, it is your right to ask the researcher for clarification or more information. A copy of this consent form will be provided to you. If at any time you have questions about your participation, do not hesitate to contact the researcher(s) named below.

What is the purpose of this study?—The purpose of this study is to examine the impact of racial microaggressions on African American college students in predominately White college contexts. Racial microaggressions are negative, race-based messages that people of color experience in everyday conversations and interactions. This study is important because it helps to better understand how African American college students experience racial microaggressions as well as their psychological impact.

Who should participate in the study?—African American college students, 18 and over, and currently enrolled at a predominately White college/university.

What will happen if you take part in the study?—You will be asked to complete a short survey about your experiences at your university, including aspects regarding racial microaggressions, racial identity, coping, emotional regulation, and psychological needs (autonomy, competence, and relatedness). In addition, you will be asked to provide demographic information, such as your age and race, and information about your university, among other questions. It will take *no more than* 20 minutes to complete the entire survey.

What are the risks?—There is little expected risk. However, discussing race and racial issues can be potentially unpleasant for some individuals. You do not need to answer any questions that you do not feel comfortable with. It is recommended that you complete the survey in a private location and clear and close your browser when the survey is complete.

What are the benefits?—As a participant you will gain insight into your own feelings and beliefs because of the opportunity to discuss your experiences.

How will your confidentiality be maintained?—The survey is confidential. The web survey uses data encryption technology to encode responses. There is also firewall technology to further protect data from unauthorized access. There is always a risk of intrusion into the database, loss of data, unauthorized identification of participants, or other misuse of data by outside agents. Although these risks have been minimized by the researcher, it is essential to understand that they exist. However, steps have been taken with the use of this online survey site to protect your privacy.

The information in the study records will be kept strictly confidential and accessed only by the research team. All information concerning you will be kept private. If information about you is published, it will be published in aggregate. No reference will be made in oral or written reports that could link you to the study. Neither your university nor your professors will have access to the data.

How will you be compensated?—There will be no compensation for participating in this study.

What if you have questions about this study?—If you have questions at any time about the study or the procedures, you may contact the researcher at [insert contact information for primary investigator].

What if you have questions about your rights as a research participant?—If you feel you have not been treated as described in this form, or your rights as a participant in research have been violated during the course of this project, you may contact the regulatory compliance administrator at [insert contact information for institution regulatory compliance administrator].

Participant's Agreement (via electronic survey):

Please remember: No identifying information connecting you to your survey responses will be collected.

❑ Yes I have read this consent form, I am over the age of 18, and I agree to take part in this survey.

❑ No I do not wish to participate in the survey at this time.

This is a common template used at NC State University.

INFORMED CONSENT FORM for RESEARCH—INTERVIEW

Title of Study: A Mixed Methods Exploration of African American College Students' Experiences With Racial Microaggressions

What are some general things you should know about research studies?—You are being asked to take part in a research study. Your participation in this study is voluntary. You have the right to be a part of this study or to choose not to participate, or to stop participating at any time without penalty. The purpose of research studies is to gain a better understanding of a certain topic or issue. You are not guaranteed any personal benefits from being in a study. Research studies also may pose risks to those that participate. In this consent form you will find specific details about the research in which you are being asked to participate. If you do not understand something in this form it is your right to ask the researcher for clarification or more information. A copy of this consent form will be provided to you. If at any time you have questions about your participation, do not hesitate to contact the researcher(s) named below.

What is the purpose of this study?—The purpose of this study is to examine the impact of racial microaggressions on African American college students in predominately White college contexts. Racial microaggressions are negative, race-based messages that people of color experience in everyday conversations and interactions. This study is important because it helps to better understand how African American college students experience racial microaggressions as well as their psychological impact.

What will happen if you take part in the study?—You may be asked to participate in a personal interview regarding your experiences with racial microaggressions at your university, as well as aspects of your university experience regarding racial identity, coping, emotional regulation, and psychological needs (autonomy, competence, and relatedness). The interviews will be audio-taped and transcribed. The amount of time required for the interview is 45 minutes to 1 hour. The interviews will be conducted over the telephone or in person, at an agreed upon, neutral location.

Risks—There is little expected risk. However, discussing race and racial issues can be potentially unpleasant for some individuals. If you report feeling distress, you will be referred to a community counselor or social worker.

Benefits—As a participant you will gain insight into your own feelings and beliefs because of the opportunity to discuss your experiences.

Confidentiality—The information in the study records will be kept strictly confidential and utilized only by the research team. Data will be stored securely in a locked cabinet in the principal investigator's office. The audiotapes and copies of transcripts will be kept for up to 7 years by the researcher for research and educational purposes. No reference will be made in oral or written reports that could link you to the study. Direct quotes may be used in reports about the research, with identities protected by a fake name. Neither your university nor your professors will have access to information that associates you with your responses.

Compensation—There will be no compensation for participating.

What if you have questions about this study?—If you have questions at any time about the study, you may contact the researcher at [insert contact information for primary investigator].

What if you have questions about your rights as a research participant?—If you feel you have not been treated as described in this form, or your rights as a participant in research have been violated during the course of this project, you may contact the regulatory compliance administrator at [insert contact information for institution regulatory compliance administrator].

Consent to Participate

"I have read and understand the above information. I have received a copy of this form. I agree to participate in this study with the understanding that I may choose not to participate or to stop participating at any time without penalty or loss of benefits to which I am otherwise entitled."

Participant's signature_____ **Date** _____

Investigator's signature_____ **Date** _____

This is a common template used at NC State University.

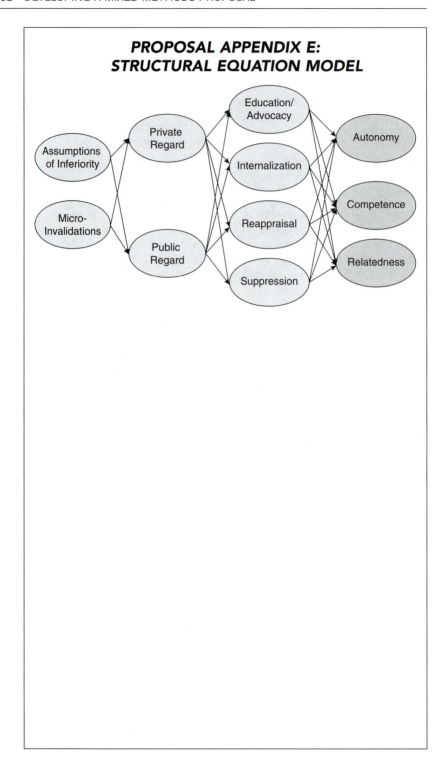

PROPOSAL APPENDIX E:
STRUCTURAL EQUATION MODEL

Appendixes

Appendix A

Explanatory Sequential Design

Becoming a Civilian Again: A Mixed Methods Explanation of the Experiences of Veterans' Reintegration to Civilian Life		
Components	Subcomponents	Examples
Research Questions/ Hypotheses		• What are the health profiles of veterans reintegrating into civilian life? (quantitative) • How are veterans with various health profiles reintegrating into civilian life? (qualitative)
Mixed Methods Definition		• "Qualitative data—'words, pictures, and narrative'—can be combined with quantitative, numerical data from a larger-scale study on the same issue, allowing our research results to be generalized for future studies and examinations" (Hesse-Biber, 2010a, p. 3).
Mixed Methods Design & Rationale		• An explanatory sequential design (quan→ QUAL) is being used, where the qualitative data is used to extend or expand upon the quantitative data. In this study, the qualitative data will be the dominant approach (Hesse-Biber, 2010b). • A mixed methods approach is being used in order to provide a broader understanding of participants' experiences.

(Continued)

(Continued)

Components	Subcomponents	Examples
Sample/Participants		
	Context	• Participants will be recruited from local Department of Veterans Affairs medical centers as well as agencies that cater to the needs of veterans. Data collection will occur at a local health clinic.
	Sampling	• Male veterans who have actively served in the military within the last 3 years (120 participants for the quantitative component and 18 participants for the qualitative component). • Receiving treatment or services from a veterans' organization.
Data Collection		
	Instrumentation	• **Demographics Survey**—Used to capture basic information about the participants, including their age, race/ethnicity, years in the military, etc. • **Health Indicators**—Used to provide a snapshot of the participants' physical health, including potential substance abuse. o Blood pressure, BMI, blood sample (comprehensive metabolic panel), and urine sample (10 panel drug test and alcohol test) • **PTSD Checklist Military Version** 17 Likert items (*not at all* to *extremely* ([α = 0.92]) (Weathers, Litz, Herman, Huska, & Keane, 1993)—Used to diagnose PTSD and to identify PTSD symptoms. A total symptom severity score is determined by summing the scores from each item. The scores are then compared to the prevalence of PTSD in the population (35 or lower—low; 36–44—medium; 45 or above—high) (Yeager, Magruder, Knapp, Nicholas, & Frueh, 2007).

Components	Subcomponents	Examples
		• **Focus Group Interviews**—Weekly interviews will be used to better understand the veterans' experiences with adjusting to civilian life. Topics will include dealing with stress, food choices, alcohol, drug usage, relationships, and work. The interview guides will be semistructured to allow for the veterans to suggest topics that are relevant to their lives.
	Procedures	• Potential participants will be solicited from various veterans' organizations to participate in the study. • Participants will be asked to fast at least 8 hours before completing the health portion. • Participants will be first asked to sign a consent form and then complete the demographics survey and the PTSD Checklist. Next they will provide urine and blood samples. • Participants will receive $50 gift cards for participating. • The quantitative data will then be analyzed and used to create risk profiles (i.e., low, medium, and high). • 18 participants (6 per group) who are considered to be low, medium, and high risk in terms of a combination of their PTSD score and health indicators will be randomly selected and asked to participate in a series of focus group interviews. • There will be three weekly focus group interviews, lasting 1–2 hours each, that will be organized according to risk level. Each group will have three interviews (Umana-Taylor & Bamaca, 2004). • All focus group interviews will be both video- and audio-recorded. The audio recordings will be transcribed for analysis. • Participants will receive $50 gift cards for participating in the interviews.

(Continued)

(Continued)

Components	Subcomponents	Examples
Data Analysis		
	Procedures	• Urine and blood samples will be sent to a lab for analysis, while the demographic and PTSD data will be analyzed using descriptive statistics. • Findings from urine and blood analyses, demographic surveys, and the PTSD Checklist will be used in a cluster analysis to create risk profiles—low, medium, and high. The profiles will be used to choose the participants for the focus groups. • After the interviews are transcribed, they will be coded using both first cycle coding (initial) and second cycle coding (classifying, integrating, and theory building) (Saldaña, 2015).Themes will be organized according to risk profile.
	Data Integration	• The quantitative and qualitative data will be analyzed separately and then later combined for discussion. • The quantitative data will be used to help select participants for the qualitative component. • Risk profile descriptions will be combined with findings from the respective focus group interviews using joint displays.
	Role of Theoretical Framework	• Posttraumatic stress, resiliency, and thriving will be the main substantive theories that will guide this study. • A transformative inquiry worldview (Mertens, 2007) will be used, in that the ultimate goal is to help empower the veterans and help make their transitions to civilian life easier.
	Reliability/ Credibility	• Reliability will be addressed by measuring internal consistency (Cronbach's alpha) of the PTSD Checklist. • Credibility will be addressed using random sampling of participants and negative case analysis (Guba, 1981).

Components	Subcomponents	Examples

	Validity/ Trustworthiness	• Will use the integrative framework for inference quality (Teddlie & Tashakkori, 2009) to address the following:
		  ○ Design suitability (consistency between research questions and study)
		  ○ Design fidelity (implementation of study components)
		  ○ Within-design consistency (fit between components)
		  ○ Analytic adequacy (fit of data analysis techniques)
		  ○ Interpretive consistency (study inferences consistent with findings)
		  ○ Theoretical consistency (inferences consistent with theory)
		  ○ Interpretive agreement (researchers' interpretations consist with participants')
		  ○ Interpretive distinctiveness (study inferences are credible)
		  ○ Integrative efficacy (quan and qual inferences create metainferences)
		  ○ Correspondence (metainferences reflect study purpose)

Appendix B

Exploratory Sequential Design

Understanding What It Is Like to Be a Child Suffering From Food Insecurity: A Mixed Methods Scale Development Study		
Components	Subcomponents	Examples
Research Questions/ Hypotheses		• How do rural and urban children experience food insecurity? (qualitative) • What is the structure of the Food Insecurity Diagnostic Inventory? (quantitative) • Are there differences between rural and urban children's experiences with food insecurity? (quantitative)
Mixed Methods Definition		• "Mixed methods research is an intellectual and practical synthesis based on qualitative and quantitative research" (Johnson, Onwuegbuzie, & Turner, 2007, p. 129).
Mixed Methods Design		• An exploratory sequential design (qual→ QUAN) is being used, where the quantitative data expands or builds upon what is found in the qualitative data (Creswell & Plano Clark, 2011). A mixed methods perspective is being used in order to engage in scale development (DeCuir-Gunby, 2008; Onwuegbuzie, Bustamante, & Nelson, 2010).

(Continued)

(Continued)

Components	Subcomponents	Examples
Sample/Participants		

	Context	• Areas that have high rates of food insecurity:
		  ○ Low-SES urban neighborhoods
		  ○ Low-SES rural areas
		  ○ Rural and urban areas considered to be food deserts

	Sampling	• Experts in the area of food insecurity ($n = 5$). • Children of families who live in low-SES urban or rural areas, who participate in food bank/pantry services or in WIC, SNAP, or other social services that are used to acquire food ($n = 300$ for quantitative; $n = 25$ for qualitative).
Data Collection		
	Instrumentation	**Phase 1** • **Observation Tool:** An observation tool will be used in order to capture and describe the environments in which children suffering from food insecurity reside. The tool will consist of open-ended descriptions and field notes. • **Semistructured Interviews:** (1) The first set of interviews is designed to increase understanding of children's experiences as being food insecure. (2) The second set of interviews is constructed to obtain experts' opinions in the field of food insecurity regarding their understandings and observations. **Phase 2** • **Food Insecurity Diagnostic Inventory**—A ten-item inventory will be created to identify children suffering from food insecurity. The inventory will be created based upon the findings from Phase 1. • **Household Food Security Scale (short form)** (Blumberg, Bialostosky, Hamilton, & Briefel, 1999)—This is a six-item scale ($\alpha = 0.87$) used to assess food security and insecurity. It focuses on how frequently a person has eaten as well as what the person has eaten.

Components	Subcomponents	Examples
	Procedures	**Phase 1** • Researchers will observe low-SES rural and urban environments with high levels of food insecurity using the observation tool and take field notes. • Five experts in the field of food insecurity will be interviewed regarding their knowledge of children's experiences with food insecurity as well as the type of environments in which the children live. **Phase 2** • The Food Insecurity Diagnostic Inventory will be created based upon the findings of the qualitative analysis. • Families with children under the age of 18 who participate in food programs will be invited to participate. • With parental consent, the children will be asked to complete the Food Insecurity Diagnostic Inventory. • Children will receive $5 gift cards for their participation. • The Food Insecurity Diagnostic Inventory will be piloted to a sample of 150 children. • After the piloted data has been analyzed, the survey items will be reviewed and possibly revised. • The revised Food Insecurity Diagnostic Inventory and the Household Food Security Scale will be given to an additional sample of 150 children.
Data Analysis		
	Procedures	• RQ #1: The observations and interviews will be coded using thematic content analysis. • RQ #2: This question will be answered using descriptive statistics, correlations, Cronbach's alpha, and confirmatory factor analysis (CFA). • RQ #3: This question will be answered using ANOVAs.

(Continued)

(Continued)

Components	Subcomponents	Examples
	Data Integration	• The themes from the qualitative data will be used to create the items in the survey. Also the findings from the quantitative data will be compared to the findings from the qualitative data.
	Role of Theoretical Framework	• Theories of hunger, including food insecurity, will be used as substantive theories. • A pragmatic inquiry worldview will influence the study. • A theoretical framework will guide all aspects of the study.
	Reliability/ Credibility	• Reliability will be addressed by measuring the internal consistency (Cronbach's alpha) of the Food Insecurity Diagnostic Inventory. • For the interviews, credibility will be addressed through the use of multiple coders to code interview transcriptions. Interrater reliability will be calculated using Cohen's kappa.
	Validity/ Trustworthiness	• Content validity will be addressed by examining the structure of the Food Insecurity Diagnostic Inventory using CFA. • Construct validity will be addressed by comparing the scores from the Food Insecurity Diagnostic Inventory to scores from the Household Food Security Scale. • Trustworthiness will be addressed using thick, rich descriptions; member checks; and data triangulation (Golafshani, 2003).

Appendix C

Convergent Parallel Design

Women Executives as Organizational Leaders and Change Agents: Integrating Qualitative and Quantitative Methods		
Components	Subcomponents	Examples
Research Questions/ Hypotheses		1. Are there differences among women executives' approaches to leadership? (quantitative) 2. How do women executives experience leadership? (qualitative) 3. To what extent do the quantitative results on leadership agree with the interview data on leadership by women executives? (mixed methods)
Mixed Methods Definition & Rationale		• Mixed methods research is the process of using quantitative and qualitative methods in order to provide "multiple ways of making sense of the social world" (Greene, 2007, p. 20). • A mixed methods approach is being used in order to provide a better understanding of women in leadership, particularly in terms of the complexity of leadership practices of women executives.
Mixed Methods Design		• A convergent parallel design (QUAN + qual) will be used, where the quantitative and qualitative data are collected simultaneously (Creswell & Plano Clark, 2011).

(Continued)

(Continued)

Components	Subcomponents	Examples
Sample/Participants		
	Context	• A mixture of firms will be used (e.g., education organizations, industrial organizations, accounting firms), ranging from mom-and-pop organizations that have small numbers of employees to Fortune 500 companies that have thousands of employees.
	Sampling	• Women executives will be recruited from leadership related organizations (e.g., American Business Women's Association, the National Organization for Women) in order to obtain women executives from different types (e.g., education, industrial, accounting) and sizes (small, medium, and large) of firms. • An executive is defined as anyone with senior managerial responsibility. • 300 participants will be targeted for the quantitative portion of the study, and 30 participants for the qualitative component.
Data Collection		

	Instrumentation	• **Demographics Survey**—Used to ascertain background information regarding the participants, including race/ethnicity, age, education, type of firm, size of firm, years in leadership, years in current position, number of employees in firm, number of employees under direct supervision, et cetera.
		• The **Multifactor Leadership Questionnaire** (MLQ- 5x)—Designed to identify basic leadership styles: transformational, transactional, and laissez-faire (Bass & Avolio, 1995). The MLQ has 45 items using a 5-point Likert scale (0 = *not at all* to 5 = *frequently, if not always*). It is theorized to have nine subscales:
		  1. idealized influence attributed (6 items; $\alpha = .88$)
		  2. idealized influenced behavior (6 items; $\alpha = .86$)

Components	Subcomponents	Examples
		3. inspirational motivation (6 items; $\alpha = .90$) 4. individual consideration (6 items; $\alpha = .91$) 5. intellectual stimulation (6 items; $\alpha = .86$) 6. contingent reward (6 items; $\alpha = .87$) 7. management-by-exception-active (6 items; $\alpha = .71$) 8. management-by-exception-passive (6 items; $\alpha = .82$) 9. laissez-faire (6 items; $\alpha = .82$) (Tejeda, Scandura, & Pillai, 2001). The scale has been evaluated in terms of structural validity and has been compared to other leadership scales (Muenjohn & Armstrong, 2008). • **A Semistructured Interview**—Designed in order to improve understanding of the participants' experiences as women leaders in their respective organizations. Questions will be designed to elicit responses regarding their unique positions as leaders in male-oriented and male-dominated fields.
	Procedures	• Participants will be recruited using e-mail and discussion lists. In the recruitment letter, participants will be provided a direct hyperlink to a web-based survey featuring a consent form, the demographics survey, and the MLQ. • The qualitative and quantitative portions of the study will be conducted at the same time. • Potential interviewees will be recruited using e-mail. • The interviews will be conducted using a semistructured interview guide, over the telephone, using videoconferencing, or in person at an agreed upon, neutral location. • All interviews will be audio-recorded using a digital recording device. • The interviews will be transcribed for analysis.

(Continued)

(Continued)

Components	Subcomponents	Examples
Data Analysis		
	Procedures	• RQ #1 will be addressed by ANOVAs and MANOVAs, focusing on the responses from the MLQ and the demographics questionnaires. • RQ #2 will be answered using grounded theory techniques (Charmaz, 2014). With open coding, the data is read, chunked, and labeled. Then, with the process of axial coding, relationships are found among the open codes. Last, the codes are connected to the larger research literature. • RQ #3 will be answered by comparing and contrasting the findings from RQ #1 and RQ #2.
	Data Integration	• Quantitative and qualitative data will be collected and analyzed separately, and the results will be compared and contrasted, with the goal of triangulation (Denzin, 2012). • The reports will use joint displays.
	Role of Theoretical Framework	• The study is guided by feminist theory (Hesse-Biber, 2007). • Feminist theory will be used during data collection and analysis (Hesse-Biber, 2007). • Triangulation is a means of promoting social change (Hesse-Biber, 2012).
	Reliability/ Credibility	• Internal consistency will be calculated for all of the scales (Cronbach's alpha). • Credibility will be addressed through the use of multiple coders. They will be used to code the interview data. Interrater reliability will be calculated using Cohen's kappa.

Components	Subcomponents	Examples

	Validity/ Trustworthiness	• Content validity will be addressed by examining the structure of the MLQ using confirmatory factor analysis.
		• Trustworthiness will be addressed using thick, rich descriptions; member checks; and data triangulation (Shenton, 2004).
		• A mixed methods approach to validity will examine
		  ○ the consistency of inferences made throughout the study,
		  ○ the history of the instruments, specifically their use with women, and
		  ○ the potential consequences of the research (Leech, Dellinger, Brannagan, & Tanaka, 2010).

Appendix D

Embedded Design

Using Electronic Tablets to Help Modify Behavior in Special Education Classrooms: A Mixed Methods Experiment		
Components	**Subcomponents**	**Examples**
Research Questions/ Hypotheses		• Do comprehension monitoring prompts delivered via electronic tablets increase student reading comprehension scores in a fourth-grade special education classroom? (quantitative) • What are the postintervention perceptions of students and teachers regarding the intervention? (qualitative)
Mixed Methods Definition		• Mixed methods research involves data collection and analysis, and inference development, via the use of both qualitative and quantitative approaches in a particular study (Tashakkori & Creswell, 2007).
Mixed Methods Design		• An embedded design [QUAN (qual)] will be used, where the qualitative data is embedded within the quantitative data (Creswell & Plano Clark, 2011).
Sample/Participants		
	Context	• The study will be conducted in six fourth-grade special classrooms.

(Continued)

(Continued)

Components	Subcomponents	Examples
	Sampling	• Elementary schools will be contacted, and arrangements will be made with interested schools. Classrooms will be randomly assigned to either the control group or intervention group.
Data Collection		
	Instrumentation	• **Demographics Survey**—Used to collect background information regarding the students' home reading environments as well as teachers' race/ethnicity, age, and number of years as a teacher. • **Reading Pre/Post Test**—Used to assess students' reading comprehension levels. • **A Semistructured Interview**— Designed to increase understanding of the participants' experiences during the intervention. Questions will be designed to elicit responses from students and teachers regarding their perceptions of their motivations and emotions associated with the intervention. In addition, teachers will be asked about the level of implementation of the intervention.
	Procedures	• Intact classes will be randomly assigned to either the traditional instruction group or the electronic tablet comprehension monitoring intervention group. • Students and teachers will fill out the demographics survey. • Students will take the reading comprehension pretest to assess baseline information. • Next, for four weeks, students will be taught strategies for comprehension monitoring via the two different teaching methods. • Then the posttesting for reading comprehension will be conducted. • The interviews will be conducted during and after the intervention using a semistructured interview guide.

Components	Subcomponents	Examples
		• All interviews will be audio-recorded using a digital recording device. • The interviews will be transcribed for analysis.
Data Analysis		
	Procedures	• RQ #1 will be addressed using a mixed-design ANOVA to measure the difference between the control group and the treatment group (between groups test) in change from the pretest to the posttest (within group test). • RQ #2 will be answered using grounded theory techniques (Charmaz, 2014). With open coding, the data is read, chunked, and labeled. Then, with the process of axial coding, relationships are found between the open codes. Last, the codes are connected to the larger research literature.
	Data Integration	• Interview data regarding level of implementation will be quantified, and the data will be used as a covariate in the mixed-design ANOVA. • The remaining interview data will be used to better understand the quantitative findings.
	Role of Theoretical Framework	• Metacognitive strategies for reading comprehension will be the main substantive theory that will guide this study (Brown, 1987; Schunk, 2004). • A transformative inquiry worldview (Mertens, 2007) will be used, in that the ultimate goal is to help struggling readers improve their reading skills.
	Reliability/ Credibility	• Internal consistency will be calculated on all of the scales (Cronbach's alpha). • Credibility will be addressed through the use of multiple coders to code the interview data. Interrater reliability will be calculated using Cohen's kappa.

(Continued)

(Continued)

Components	Subcomponents	Examples

	Validity/ Trustworthiness	• The integrative framework for inference quality (Teddlie & Tashakkori, 2009) will be used to address the following:
		   ○ Design suitability (consistency between research questions and study)
		   ○ Design fidelity (implementation of study components)
		   ○ Within-design consistency (fit among components)
		   ○ Interpretive consistency (study inferences consistent with findings)
		   ○ Interpretive agreement (researchers' interpretations consist with participants')
		   ○ Interpretive distinctiveness (study inferences are credible)
		   ○ Integrative efficacy (quan and qual inferences create metainferences)
		   ○ Correspondence (metainferences reflect study purpose)

Appendix E

Multiphase Design

The Mixed Methods Development and Evaluation of a Training Program to Teach Nurses How to Care for Patients With Ebola		
Components	**Subcomponents**	**Examples**
Research Questions/ Hypotheses		• Does the Care for Patients with Ebola Training (CPET) program increase patient care and protect caregivers? • Does the CPET program increase caregivers' self-efficacy regarding safety and effectiveness?
Mixed Methods Definition		• Mixed methods research is the process of using quantitative and qualitative methods in order to provide "multiple ways of making sense of the social world" (Greene, 2007, p. 20).
Mixed Methods Design		• A multiphase design will be used, in that data collection at Time 1 will inform data collection and analyses at subsequent times (Creswell & Plano Clark, 2011). • Also, a mixed methods evaluation approach will be used (Greene, Caracelli, & Graham, 1989).
Sample/Participants		
	Context	• Nurses and staff at a hospital that has been designated as an Ebola treatment center.
	Sampling	• Nurses and staff at the treatment center will be recruited to participate in the study.

(Continued)

(Continued)

Components	Subcomponents	Examples
Data Collection		
	Instrumentation	• **Care for Patients with Ebola Training (CPET) program**— A program to be developed in order to help train caregivers to care for patients with Ebola. • **Self-Efficacy Scale**—Used to measure effectiveness in treating Ebola patients and to measure self-efficacy for perceived safety in the Ebola treatment center. • **Focus Group Interviews**—Used to focus on perceived strengths and weaknesses of the program, and to identify potential actions to improve the program.
	Procedures	• **Phase 1** involves assessing self-efficacy of participants as well as conducting focus group interviews regarding current safety and care protocols within the treatment facility. • **Phase 2** will use the findings from Phase 1 to develop the CPET program. • During **Phase 3**, the CPET program will be implemented at the treatment facility. • **Phase 4** involves the evaluation of the CPET program. Self-efficacy measures as well as focus group interviews regarding changes in the safety and care protocols within the treatment facility will be assessed.
Data Analysis		
	Procedures	• RQ #1 will be answered using grounded theory techniques (Charmaz, 2014). With open coding, the data is read, chunked, and labeled. Then, with the process of axial coding, relationships are found among the open codes. Last, the codes are connected to the larger research literature. • RQ #2 will be addressed by repeated measure ANOVAs focusing on the responses from self-efficacy measures.

Components	Subcomponents	Examples
	Data Integration	• The quantitative self-efficacy data will be combined with the qualitative focus group data to identify where care protocols can be improved as well as to assess the confidence of the nurses in the facility.
	Role of Theoretical Framework	• A transformative inquiry worldview (Mertens, 2007) will be used, in that the ultimate goal is to help empower the caregivers and help make them feel safer and more effective in their jobs.
	Reliability/ Credibility	• Internal consistency will be calculated on all of the scales (Cronbach's alpha). • Credibility will be addressed through the use of multiple coders to code the interview data. Interrater reliability will be calculated using Cohen's kappa.
	Validity/ Trustworthiness	• Will use the integrative framework for inference quality (Teddlie & Tashakkori, 2009) to address the following: ○ Design suitability (consistency between research questions and study) ○ Design fidelity (implementation of study components) ○ Within-design consistency (fit between components) ○ Interpretive consistency (study inferences consistent with findings) ○ Interpretive agreement (researchers' interpretations consist with participants') ○ Interpretive distinctiveness (study inferences are credible) ○ Integrative efficacy (quan and qual inferences create metainferences) ○ Correspondence (metainferences reflect study purpose)

References

Agee, J. (2009). Developing qualitative research questions: A reflective process. *International Journal of Qualitative Studies in Education*, 22(4), 431–447.

Allen, Q. (2010). Racial microaggressions: The schooling experiences of Black middle-class males in Arizona's secondary schools. *Journal of African American Males in Education*, 1(2), 125–142.

American Psychological Association. (2009). *Publication manual of the American Psychological Association* (6th ed.). Washington, DC: American Psychological Association.

Angen, M. J. (2000). Evaluating interpretive inquiry: Reviewing the validity debate and opening the dialogue. *Qualitative Health Research*, 10(3), 378–395.

Bass, B. M., & Avolio, B. J. (1995). *The Multifactor Leadership Questionnaire*. Palo Alto, CA: Mind Garden.

Bell, D. (1992). Racial realism. *Connecticut Law Review*, 24(2), 363–379.

Bell, D. (1993). *Faces at the bottom of the well: The permanence of racism*. New York, NY: Basic Books.

Bell, D. A. (1980). *Brown v. Board of Education* and the interest-convergence dilemma. *Harvard Law Review*, 93(3), 518–533.

Benson, J., & Nasser, F. (1998). On the use of factor analysis as a research tool. *Journal of Vocational Education Research*, 23(1), 13–33.

Bergman, M. (Ed.). (2008). *Advances in mixed methods research*. Thousand Oaks, CA: Sage.

Berry, J. W., Poortinga, Y. H., Segall, M. H., & Dasen, P. R. (2002). Acculturation and intercultural relations. In J. W. Berry, Y. Poortinga, M. H. Segall, & P. R. Dasen (Eds.), *Cross-cultural psychology: Research and applications* (2nd ed., pp. 345–383). Cambridge, UK: Cambridge University Press.

Blumberg, S. J., Bialostosky, K., Hamilton, W. L., & Briefel, R. R. (1999). The effectiveness of a short form of the household food security scale. *American Journal of Public Health*, 89, 1231–1234.

Boote, D. N., & Beile, P. (2005). Scholars before researchers: On the centrality of the dissertation literature review in research preparation. *Educational Researcher*, 34(6), 3–15.

Brady, B., & O'Regan, C. (2009). Meeting the challenge of doing an RCT evaluation of youth mentoring in Ireland: A journey in mixed methods. *Journal of Mixed Methods Research*, 3(3), 265–280.

Brondolo, E., ver Halen, N., Pencille, M., Beatty, D., & Contrada, R. (2009). Coping with racism: A selective review of the literature and a theoretical and methodological critique. *Journal of Behavioral Medicine, 32*, 64–88.

Brown, A. (1987). Metacognition, executive control, self-regulation, and other more mysterious mechanisms. In F. Weinert & R. Kluwe (Eds.), *Metacognition, motivation, and understanding* (pp. 65–116). Hillside, NJ: Lawrence Erlbaum.

Buck, G., Cook, K., Quigley, C., Eastwood, J., & Lucas, Y. (2009). Profiles of urban, low SES, African American girls' attitudes toward science: A sequential explanatory mixed methods study. *Journal of Mixed Methods Research*, 386–410.

Bui, Y. N. (2009). *How to write a master's thesis*. Thousand Oaks, CA: Sage.

Charmaz, K. (2014). *Constructing grounded theory* (2nd ed.). Thousand Oaks, CA: Sage.

Chilisa, B., & Tsheko, G. N. (2014). Mixed methods in indigenous research: Building relationships for sustainable intervention outcomes. *Journal of Mixed Methods Research, 8*(3), 222–233.

Coffey, A., & Atkinson, P. (1996). *Making sense of qualitative data: Complementary research designs*. Thousand Oaks, CA: Sage.

Collins, K. M., Onwuegbuzie, A. J., & Jiao, Q. G. (2007). A mixed methods investigation of mixed methods sampling designs in social and health science research. *Journal of Mixed Methods Research, 1*(3), 267–294.

Crenshaw, K. (1989). Demarginalizing the intersection of race and sex: A Black feminist critique of antidiscrimination doctrine, feminist theory and anti-racist politics. *University of Chicago Legal Forum*, 139–167.

Creswell, J. W. (2010). Mapping the developing landscape of mixed methods research. In A. Tashakkori & C. Teddlie (Eds.), *Sage handbook of mixed methods in social & behavioral research* (2nd ed., pp. 45–68). Thousand Oaks, CA: Sage.

Creswell, J. W. (2015). *A concise introduction to mixed methods research*. Thousand Oaks, CA: Sage.

Creswell, J. W., Klassen, A. C., Plano Clark, V. L., & Smith, K. C., for the Office of Behavioral and Social Sciences Research. (2011, August). *Best practices for mixed methods research in the health sciences*. Washington, DC: National Institutes of Health. Retrieved from http://obssr.od.nih.gov/mixed_methods_research

Creswell, J., & Plano Clark, V. (2011). *Designing and conducting mixed methods research* (2nd ed.). Thousand Oaks, CA: Sage.

Crotty, M. (1998). *The foundations of social research: Meaning and perspective in the research process*. Thousand Oaks, CA: Sage.

Deci, E. L., & Ryan, R. M. (2000). The "what" and "why" of goal pursuits: Human needs and the self-determination of behavior. *Psychological Inquiry, 11*, 227–268.

DeCuir, J. T., & Dixson, A. D. (2004). "So when it comes out, they aren't that surprised that it is there": Using critical race theory as a tool of analysis of race and racism in education. *Educational Researcher, 33*(5), 26–31.

DeCuir-Gunby, J. T. (2008). Designing mixed methods research in the social sciences: A racial identity scale development example. In J. Osborne (Ed.), *Best practices in quantitative methods* (pp. 125–136). Thousand Oaks, CA: Sage.

DeCuir-Gunby, J. T., Marshall, P., & McCulloch, A. (2011). Developing and using a codebook for the analysis of interview data: An example from a professional development research project. *Field Methods, 23*(2), 136–155.

DeCuir-Gunby, J. T., & Schutz, P. A. (2014). Researching race within educational psychology contexts. *Educational Psychologist, 49*(4), 244–260.

Delgado, R. (1989). Storytelling for oppositionists and others: A plea for narrative. *Michigan Law Review, 87*, 2411–2441.

Delgado, R., & Stefancic, J. (2012). *Critical race theory: An introduction* (2nd ed.). New York: New York University Press.

Dellinger, A. B., & Leech, N. L. (2007). Towards a unified validation framework in mixed methods research. *Journal of Mixed Methods Research, 1*(4), 309–332.

Denzin, N. (2012). Triangulation 2.0. *Journal of Mixed Methods Research, 6*(2), 80–88.

Dewey, J. (1910). *How we think*. Lexington, MA: D. C. Heath.

Durham, J., Tan, B. K., & White, R. (2011). Utilizing mixed research methods to develop a quantitative assessment tool: An example from explosive remnants of a war clearance program. *Journal of Mixed Methods Research, 5*(3), 212–226.

Enfield, K. B., & Truwit, J. D. (2008). The purpose, composition, and function of an institutional review board: Balancing priorities. *Respiratory Care, 53*(10), 1330–1336.

Ercikan, K., & Roth, W. (2006). What good is polarizing research into qualitative and quantitative? *Educational Researcher, 35*(5), 14–23.

Fetters, M. D., Curry, L. A., & Creswell, J. W. (2013). Achieving integration in mixed methods designs—Principals and practices. *Health Services Research, 48*(6), 2134–2156.

Fetters, M. D., Yoshioka, T., Greenberg, G. M., Gorenflo, D. W., & Yeo, S. (2007). Advance consent in Japanese during prenatal care for epidural anesthesia during childbirth. *Journal of Mixed Methods Research, 1*(4), 333–365.

Forsyth, J., & Carter, R. (2012). The relationship between racial identity status attitudes, racism-related coping, and mental health among Black Americans. *Cultural Diversity and Ethnic Minority Psychology, 18*(2), 128–140.

Fowler, J. W. (1981). *Stages of faith*. New York, NY: Harper & Row.

Gall, M. D., Gall, J. P., & Borg, W. R. (2007). *Educational research: An introduction* (8th ed.). New York, NY: Pearson.

Gilmour, R., & Cobus-Kuo, L. (2011). Reference management software: A comparative analysis of four products. *Issues in Science and Librarianship*. Retrieved from http://www.istl.org/11-summer/refereed2.html

Giroux, H. (1988). Critical theory and the politics of culture and voice: Rethinking the discourse of educational research. In R. Sherman & R. Webb (Eds.),

Qualitative research in education: Focus and methods (pp. 190–210). New York, NY: Falmer.

Glaser, B. S., & Strauss, A. A. (1967). *The discovery of grounded theory*. New York, NY: Transaction.

Glasersfeld, E. (1995). *Radical constructivism: A way of knowing and learning*. London, UK: Routledge Falmer.

Glass, G. V., MacGaw, B., & Smith, M. L. (1984). *Meta-analysis in social research*. Beverly Hills, CA: Sage.

Golafshani, N. (2003). Understanding reliability and validity in qualitative research. *The Qualitative Report, 8*(4), 597–607.

Gotanda, N. (1991). A critique of "Our constitution is color-blind." *Stanford Law Review, 44*, 1–68.

Greene, J. C. (2007). *Mixed methods in social inquiry*. San Francisco, CA: Jossey-Bass.

Greene, J. C., Caracelli, V. J., & Graham, W. D. (1989). Toward a conceptual framework for mixed-method evaluation designs. *Educational Evaluation and Policy Analysis, 11*(3), 255–274.

Greene, J. C., & Hall, J. N. (2010). Dialectics and pragmatism: Being of consequence. In A. Tashakkori & C. Teddlie (Eds.), *SAGE handbook of mixed methods in social and behavioral research* (2nd ed., pp. 119–143). Thousand Oaks, CA: Sage.

Guba, E. G. (1981). Criteria for assessing the trustworthiness of naturalistic inquiries. *Educational Communication and Technology Journal, 29*, 75–91.

Guba, E. G., & Lincoln, Y. S. (1994). Competing paradigms in qualitative research. In N. K. Denzin & Y. S. Lincoln (Eds.), *Handbook of qualitative research* (pp. 105–117). London, UK: Sage.

Guest, G., Bunce, A., & Johnson, L. (2006). How many interviews are enough? An experiment with data saturation and variability. *Field Methods, 18*(1), 59–82.

Habermas, J. (1971). *Knowledge and human interests* (J. Shapiro, Trans.). Boston, MA: Beacon.

Harper, B. E. (2007). The relationship between Black racial identity and academic achievement in urban settings. *Theory Into Practice, 46*(3), 230–238.

Harris, C. (1993). Whiteness as property. *Harvard Law Review, 106*(8), 1707–1791.

Hart, C. (2001). *Doing a literature search: A comprehensive guide for the social sciences*. Thousand Oaks, CA: Sage.

Hayden, H. E., & Chiu, M. M. (2015). Reflective teaching via a problem exploration–teaching adaptations–resolution cycle: A mixed methods study of preservice teachers' reflective notes. *Journal of Mixed Methods Research, 9*(2), 133–153.

Helms, J. (Ed.). (1990). *Black and White racial identity: Theory, research, and practice*. New York, NY: Greenwood Press.

Henwood, B. F., Rhoades, H., Hsu, H. T., Couture, J., Rice, E., & Wenzel, S. L. (in press). Changes in social networks and HIV risk behaviors among homeless adults transitioning into permanent supportive housing: A mixed methods pilot study. *Journal of Mixed Methods Research.*

Hesse-Biber, S. N. (2007). *Handbook of feminist research: Theory and praxis.* Thousand Oaks, CA: Sage.

Hesse-Biber, S. N. (2010a). *Mixed methods research: Merging theory with practice.* New York, NY: Guilford.

Hesse-Biber, S. (2010b). Qualitative approaches to mixed methods practice. *Qualitative Inquiry, 16*(6), 455–468.

Hesse-Biber, S. N. (2012). Feminist approaches to triangulation: Uncovering subjugated knowledge and fostering social change in mixed methods research. *Journal of Mixed Methods Research, 6*(2), 137–146.

Holzemer, W. L. (2009). Building a program of research. *Japanese Journal of Nursing Science, 6*(1), 1–5.

Ivankova, N. V. (2015). *Mixed methods applications in action research: From methods to community action.* Thousand Oaks, CA: Sage.

Ivankova, N. V., Creswell, J. W., & Stick, S. L. (2006). Using mixed-methods sequential explanatory design: From theory to practice. *Field Methods, 18*(1), 3–20.

Ivankova, N., & Kawamura, Y. (2010). Emerging trends in the utilization of integrated designs in social, behavioral, and health sciences. In A. Tashakkori & C. Teddlie (Eds.), *SAGE handbook of mixed methods in social and behavioral research* (2nd ed., pp. 581–611). Thousand Oaks, CA: Sage.

James, W. (1907). *Pragmatism, a new name for some old ways of thinking.* New York, NY: Longmans, Green.

Jick, T. D. (1979). Mixing qualitative and quantitative methods: Triangulation in action. *Administrative Science Quarterly, 24*, 602–611.

Johnson, B., & Turner, L. A. (2003). Data collection strategies in mixed methods research. In A. Tashakkori & C. Teddlie (Eds.), *Handbook of mixed methods in social and behavioral research* (pp. 297–320). Thousand Oaks, CA: Sage.

Johnson, R., Onwuegbuzie, A., & Turner, L. (2007). Toward a definition of mixed methods research. *Journal of Mixed Methods Research, 1*, 112–133.

Kerrigan, M. R. (2014). A framework for understanding community colleges' organizational capacity for data use: A convergent parallel mixed methods study. *Journal of Mixed Methods Research, 8*(4), 341–362.

Koro-Ljungberg, M., Yendol-Hoppey, D., Smith, J. J., & Hayes, S. B. (2009). (E)pistemological awareness, instantiation of methods, and uniformed methodological ambiguity in qualitative research projects. *Educational Researcher, 38*(9), 687–699.

Krosch, A. R., & Amodio, D. M. (2014). Economic scarcity alters the perception of race. *Proceedings of the National Academy of Sciences, 111*(25), 9079–9084.

Ladson-Billings, G., & Tate, W. F. (1995). Towards a critical race theory of education. *Teachers College Record, 97*(1), 47–68.

Lather, P. (1991). *Getting smart.* New York, NY: Routledge.

Lazarus, R. S., & Folkman, S. (1984). *Stress, appraisal, and coping.* New York, NY: Springer.

LeCompte, M. D. (2000). Analyzing qualitative research. *Theory Into Practice,* *39*(3), 146–154.

Leech, N. L., Dellinger, A. B., Brannagan, K. B., & Tanaka, H. (2010). Evaluating mixed research studies: A mixed methods approach. *Journal of Mixed Methods Research,* *4*(1), 17–31.

Leech, N. L., & Onwuegbuzie, A. J. (2009). A typology of mixed methods research designs. *Quality & Quantity,* *43,* 265–275.

Lincoln, Y., & Guba, E. G. (1985). *Naturalistic inquiry.* Newbury Park, CA: Sage.

Lincoln, Y., & Guba, E. (2000). Paradigmatic controversies, contradictions, and emerging confluences. In N. Denzin & Y. Lincoln (Eds.), *Handbook of qualitative research* (2nd ed., pp. 163–188). Thousand Oaks, CA: Sage.

Lipsey, M. W., & Wilson, D. B. (2001). *Practical meta-analysis.* Thousand Oaks, CA: Sage.

Locke, L. F., Spirduso, W. W., & Silverman, S. J. (2013). *Proposals that work: A guide for planning dissertations and grant proposals* (6th ed.). Thousand Oaks, CA: Sage.

Machi, L. A., & McEvoy, B. T. (2009). *The literature review: Six steps to success.* Thousand Oaks, CA: Corwin.

Mack, N., Woodsong, C., MacQueen, K. M., Guest, G., & Namey, E. (2005). *Qualitative research methods: A data collector's field guide.* Durham, NC: Family Health International.

Marshall, P. L., DeCuir-Gunby, J. T., & McCulloch, A. W. (2015). *When critical multiculturalism meets mathematics: A mixed methods study of professional development and teacher identity.* New York, NY: Rowman & Littlefield.

Maxwell, J. A. (1996). Research questions: What do you want to understand? In J. A. Maxwell, *Qualitative research design: An interactive approach* (pp. 73–83). Thousand Oaks, CA: Sage.

Maxwell, J. A. (2013). Research questions: What do you want to understand? In J. A. Maxwell, *Qualitative research design: An interactive approach* (3rd ed., pp. 73–76). Thousand Oaks, CA: Sage.

Maykut, P. S., & Morehouse, R. E. (1994). *Beginning qualitative research: A philosophic and practical guide* (vol. 6). Oxford, UK: Falmer Press/Taylor & Francis.

McGee, M. C. (2013). *James Meredith: Warrior and the America that created him.* New York, NY: Praeger.

McWhorter, J. (2014, March 21). Microaggression is the new racism on campus. *Time.* Retrieved from http://time.com/32618/microaggression-is-the-new-racism-on-campus/

Melor, D. (2004). Responses to racism: A taxonomy of coping styles used by aboriginal Australians. *American Journal of Orthopsychiatry,* *74*(1), 56–71.

Merriam, S. B. (2007). *Qualitative research and case study applications in education* (2nd ed.). San Francisco CA: Jossey-Bass.

Merriam, S. B. (2009). *Qualitative research: A guide to design and implementation.* San Francisco, CA: Jossey-Bass.

Mertens, D. M. (2003). Mixed methods and the politics of human research: The transformative-emancipatory perspective. In A. Tashakkori & C. Teddlie (Eds.), *Handbook of mixed methods in social and behavioral research* (pp. 135–164). Thousand Oaks, CA: Sage.

Mertens, D. M. (2007). Transformative paradigm: Mixed methods and social justice. *Journal of Mixed Methods Research, 1*(3), 212–225.

Mertens, D. M. (2014). *Research and evaluation in education and psychology: Integrating diversity with quantitative, qualitative, and mixed methods* (4th ed.). Thousand Oaks, CA: Sage.

Messick, S. (1995). Validity of psychological assessment: Validation of inferences from persons' responses and performances as scientific inquiry into score meaning. *American Psychologist, 50*(9), 741–749.

Miles, M. B., Huberman, A. M., & Saldaña, J. (2013). *Qualitative data analysis: A methods sourcebook.* Thousand Oaks, CA: Sage.

Morgan, D. L. (2014). *Integrating qualitative and quantitative methods: A pragmatic approach.* Thousand Oaks, CA: Sage.

Morse, J. (2003). Principles of mixed methods and multi methods research design. In A. Tashakkori & C. Teddlie (Eds.), *Handbook of mixed methods in social and behavioral research* (pp. 189–208). Thousand Oaks, CA: Sage.

Morse, J. (2010). Procedures and practice of mixed method design: Maintaining control, rigor, and complexity. In A. Tashakkori & C. Teddlie (Eds.), *SAGE handbook of mixed methods in social and behavioral research* (2nd ed., pp. 339–352). Thousand Oaks, CA: Sage.

Moustakas, C. E. (1994). *Phenomenological research methods.* Thousand Oaks, CA: Sage.

Muenjohn, N., & Armstrong, A. (2008). Evaluating the structural validity of the multifactor leadership questionnaire (MLQ), capturing the leadership factors of transformational-transactional leadership. *Contemporary Management Research, 4*(1), 3–14.

Newman, I., Ridenour, C. S., Newman, C., & DeMarco G. M. P., Jr., (2003). A typology of research purposes and its relationship to mixed methods. In A. Tashakkori & C. Teddlie (Eds.), *Handbook of mixed methods in social and behavioral research* (pp. 167–188). Thousand Oaks, CA: Sage.

Ogden, T. E., & Goldberg, I. A. (2002). *Research proposals: A guide to success* (3rd ed.). Waltham, MA: Academic Press.

Onwuegbuzie, A. J., Bustamante, R. M., & Nelson, J. A. (2010). Mixed research as a tool for developing quantitative instruments. *Journal of Mixed Methods Research, 4*, 56–78.

Preissle, J. (2008). Subjectivity statement. In L. M. Given (Ed.), *The SAGE encyclopedia of qualitative research methods* (Vol. 2, pp. 844–845). Thousand Oaks, CA: Sage.

Onwuegbuzie, A. J., & Johnson, R. B. (2006). The validity issue in mixed research. *Research in the Schools, 13*(1), 48–63.

Rosenberg, B. D., Lewandowski, J. A., & Siegel, J. T. (2013). Goal disruption theory, military personnel, and the creation of merged profiles: A mixed methods investigation. *Journal of Mixed Methods Research, 9*(1), 51–69.

Rossman, M. H. (2002). *Negotiating graduate school: A guide for graduate students.* Thousand Oaks, CA: Sage.

Rowe, M. (1990). Barriers to equality: The power of subtle discrimination. *Employee Responsibilities and Rights Journal, 3*(2), 153–163.

Ryan, R. M., Huta, V., & Deci, E. L. (2008). Living well: A self-determination theory perspective on eudaimonia. *Journal of Happiness Studies, 9,* 139–170.

Saldaña, J. (2015). *The coding manual for qualitative researchers* (3rd ed.). Thousand Oaks, CA: Sage.

Sandelowski, M., & Barroso, J. (2006). *Handbook for synthesizing qualitative research.* New York, NY: Springer.

Schunk, D. H. (2004). *Learning theories: An educational perspective* (4th ed.). Columbus, OH: Merrill/Prentice-Hall.

Schutz, P. A. (2014). Inquiry on teachers' emotions. *Educational Psychologist, 49*(1), 1–12.

Schutz, P. A., Chambless, C. B., & DeCuir, J. T. (2004). Multimethods research. In K. B. de Marrais & S. D. Lapan (Eds.), *Research methods in the social sciences: Frameworks for knowing and doing* (pp. 267–281). Hillsdale, NJ: Erlbaum.

Schutz. P. A., Nichols, S. L., & Rodgers, K. (2009). Using multimethod approaches. In S. D. Lapan & M. T. Quartaroli, *Research essentials: An introduction to design and practices* (pp. 243–258). San Francisco, CA: Jossey-Bass.

Scottham, K. M., Sellers, R. M., & Nguyen, H. X. (2008). A measure of racial identity in African American adolescents: The development of the Multidimensional Inventory of Black Identity–Teen. *Cultural Diversity and Ethnic Minority Psychology, 14*(4), 297–306.

Sellers, R. M., Rowley, S. A. J., Chavous, T. M., Shelton. J. N., & Smith, M. A. (1997). Multidimensional inventory of Black identity: A preliminary investigation of reliability and construct validity. *Journal of Personality and Social psychology, 73,* 805–815.

Sellers, R. M., Smith, M. A., Shelton, J. N., Rowley, S. A. J., & Chavous, T. M. (1998). Multidimensional Model of Racial Identity: A reconceptualization of African American racial identity. *Personality and Social Psychology Review, 2(1),* 18–39.

Shenton, A. K. (2004). Strategies for ensuring trustworthiness in qualitative research projects. *Education for Information, 22,* 63–75.

Shepard, L. A. (1993). Evaluating test validity. *Review of Research in Education, 19,* 405–450.

Smith, W. A., Hung, M., & Franklin, J. D. (2011). Racial battle fatigue and the miseducation of Black men: Racial microaggressions, societal problems, and environmental stress. *Journal of Negro Education, 80*(1), 63–82.

Stoller, E. P., Webster, N. J., Blixen, C. E., McCormick, R. A., Hund, A. J., Perzynski, A. T., . . . Dawson, N. V. (2009). Alcohol consumption decisions among nonabusing drinkers diagnosed with hepatitis C: An exploratory sequential mixed methods study. *Journal of Mixed Methods Research, 3*(1), 65–86.

Strauss, A., & Corbin, J. M. (1990). *Basics of qualitative research: Grounded theory procedures and techniques* (2nd ed.). Newbury Park, CA: Sage.

Strauss, A., & Corbin, J. M. (Eds.). (1997). *Grounded theory in practice.* Thousand Oaks, CA: Sage.

Sue, D., Capodilupo, C., Torino, G., Bucceri, J., Holder, A., Nadal, K., & Esquilin, M. (2007). Racial microaggressions in everyday life: Implications for clinical practice. *American Psychologist, 62*(4), 271–286.

Suls, J., & Fletcher, B. (1985). The relative efficacy of avoidant and nonavoidant coping strategies: A meta-analysis. *Health Psychology, 4,* 249–288.

Tashakkori, A., & Creswell, J. W. (2007). The new era of mixed methods [editorial]. *Journal of Mixed Methods Research, 1*(1), 3–7.

Tashakkori, A., & Teddlie, C. (1998). *Mixed methodology: Combining qualitative and quantitative approaches* (Applied Social Research Methods Series, vol. 46). Thousand Oaks, CA: Sage.

Tashakkori, A., & Teddlie, C. (Eds.). (2010). *Sage handbook of mixed methods in social and behavioral research* (2nd ed.). Thousand Oaks, CA: Sage.

Teddlie, C., & Tashakkori, A. (2009). *Foundations of mixed methods research: Integrating quantitative and qualitative approaches in the social and behavioral sciences.* Thousand Oaks, CA: Sage.

Tejeda, M. J., Scandura, T. A., & Pillai, R. (2001). The MLQ revisited: Psychometric properties and recommendations. *Leadership Quarterly, 12,* 31–52.

Thomas, O. N., Caldwell, C. H., Faison, N., & Jackson, J. S. (2009). Promoting academic achievement: The role of racial identity in buffering perceptions of teacher discrimination on academic achievement among African American and Caribbean Black adolescents. *Journal of Educational Psychology, 101*(2), 420–431.

Timulak, L. (2014). Qualitative meta-analysis. In U. Flick (Ed.), *The SAGE handbook of qualitative data analysis* (pp. 481–496). Thousand Oaks, CA: Sage.

Torraco, R. J. (2005). Writing integrative literature reviews: Guidelines and examples. *Human Resource Development Review, 4*(3), 356–367.

Umana-Taylor, A. J., & Bamaca, M. Y. (2004). Conducting focus groups with Latino populations: Lessons from the field. *Family Relations, 53*(3), 261–272.

Vega, T. (2014, March 21). Students see many slights as racial microaggressions. *New York Times.* Retrieved from http://www.nytimes.com/2014/03/22/us/as-diversity-increases-slights-get-subtler-but-still-sting.html

Vrkljan, B. H. (2009). Constructing a mixed methods design to explore the older driver copilot relationship. *Journal of Mixed Methods Research, 3*(4), 371–385.

Wang, J., Leu, J., & Shoda, Y. (2011). When the seemingly innocuous "stings": Racial microaggressions and their emotional consequences. *Personality and Social Psychology Bulletin, 37*(12), 1666–1678.

Weathers, F. W., Litz, B. T., Herman, D., Huska, J. A., & Keane, T. M. (1993, October). *The PTSD checklist: Reliability, validity, and diagnostic utility.* Paper presented at the Annual Meeting of the International Society for Traumatic Stress Studies, San Antonio, TX.

Weaver-Hightower, M. B. (2014). A mixed methods approach for identifying influence on public policy. *Journal of Mixed Methods Research, 8*(2), 115–138.

Williams, B., Brown, T., & Onsman, A. (2010). Exploratory factor analysis: A five-step guide for novices. *Australasian Journal of Paramedicine, 8*(3).

Yeager, D. E., Magruder, K. M., Knapp, R. G., Nicholas, J. S., & Frueh, B. C. (2007). Performance characteristics of the Posttraumatic Stress Disorder Checklist and SPAN in Veterans Affairs primary care settings. *General Hospital Psychiatry, 29*, 294–301.

Yosso, T. J., Smith, W. A., Ceja, M., & Solórzano, D. G. (2009). Critical race theory, racial microaggressions, and campus racial climate for Latina/o undergraduates. *Harvard Educational Review, 79*(4), 659–691.

Youngs, H., & Piggot-Irvine, E. (2012). The application of a multiphase triangulation approach to mixed methods: The research of an aspiring school principal development program. *Journal of Mixed Methods Research, 6*(3), 184–198.

Zusho, A., & Clayton, K. (2011). Culturalizing achievement goal theory and research. *Educational Psychologist, 46*(4), 239–260.

Index

Figures, boxes, and tables are indicated by f, b, or t following the page number.